ILLUSION AND DISILLUSIONMENT

ILLUSION AND DISILLUSIONMENT

Core Issues in Psychotherapy

Stanley H. Teitelbaum, Ph.D.

JASON ARONSON INC.
Northvale, New Jersey
London

Production Editor: Elaine Lindenblatt

This book was set in 11 pt. New Baskerville and printed and bound by Book-mart Press, Inc. of North Bergen, NJ.

Library of Congress Cataloging-in-Publication Data

Teitelbaum, Stanley H.
    Illusion and disillusionment: core issues in psychotherapy / by Stanley H. Teitelbaum.
        p. cm.
    Includes bibliographical references and index.
    ISBN 0-7657-0219-3
    1. Hallucinations and illusions. 2. Delusions. 3. Psychodynamic psychotherapy. 4. Mental illness—Treatment. I. Title.
    RC553.H3T45 1999
    616.89'14—dc21   99-11056

Printed in the United States of America on acid-free paper. For information and catalog write to Jason Aronson Inc., 230 Livingston Street, Northvale, NJ 07647 1726, or visit our website: www.aronson.com

To Rose, Reuben, Lawrence, and Leighsa,
and to Sylvia, my best friend and beacon

Contents

Preface

This book discusses the themes of illusion and disillusionment, and the role they play in human functioning, from a developmental, theoretical, and clinical perspective. I use the term *disillusionment* to connote the dynamic *process* involved in dealing with the loss and/or disruption of core illusions. The systematic exploration of these themes is necessary as an integral part of psychodynamic psychotherapy in a large number of cases. Although these themes have been acknowledged as important dimensions, they are generally not dealt with in any comprehensive way. Issues related to illusion and disillusionment as they apply to the conflicts presented by our patients, as well as to the psychotherapeutic relationship, are sometimes conscious and sometimes unconscious. In the course of treatment they may emerge on a manifest level, or, as is often the case, through a deeper exploration of unconscious derivatives.

I focus on the importance of these dimensions and the implications for treatment, especially with patients whose core conflicts are rooted around the polarities of expectation and disappointment, as well as idealization and devaluation. When the conditions are ripe for idealization and devaluation, the opportunities for illusion and disillusionment proliferate.

With the expanding range of diagnostic categories amenable to psychoanalytic psychotherapy, we encounter a wider range of individuals with primitive issues of early development whose ego functions are compromised. Experiences early in life in which basic emotional needs were either frustrated or excessively gratified is the soil from which subsequent illusions and disillusionments are formed. Although relatively well-structured individuals may have issues that center around illusion and disillusionment, these themes tend to be less central, less damaging, and less challenging to the treatment process.

Mental health professionals are increasingly faced with the challenge of creating more effective treatment strategies to deal with patients whose problems are fueled by and organized around powerful illusions about themselves and their world. Acquiring a fuller appreciation of the centrality of issues around illusion and disillusionment will enable therapists to solidify more durable working alliances, and can forestall many premature terminations.

Acknowledgments

I gratefully acknowledge the many patients, colleagues, supervisors, teachers, mentors, supervisees, and students who have substantially shaped and influenced the thinking presented in this book. I am grateful to Don Marion Wolfe, who taught me how to write, to Edrita Fried, for her contribution to the inchoate phase of this project, and to Celia Mitchell, for her encouragement in moving this work from inside my head to the written page.

I wish to thank Verne Dawson, Lee Mackler, and Edward Osokowich at the Postgraduate Center for Mental Health Library for their unflagging efforts in providing me with an ongoing source of reference material, and Connie Stroboulis and Maxine Mindling for their typing and secretarial assistance in the preparation of the manuscript.

Most of all, I have endless gratitude toward Sylvia Teitelbaum for her suggestions and elaboration of the ideas formulated in this book. Her wisdom and support have been essential in bringing this work to fruition.

Introduction

The themes of illusion and disillusionment play a central role in many people's lives. Throughout life individuals maintain illusions about themselves and their world that sustain them and serve as organizing principles, and the loss of these illusions in the harsh light of reality requires a psychological negotiation with the impact of disillusionment. The question of how individuals address and manage their issues in illusion and disillusionment warrants considerable examination. Chapter 1 focuses on this process at different stages in the life cycle.

The importance of these themes as they are encompassed from different vantage points in the major psychoanalytic theories is the subject of Chapter 2. Illusions about oneself and one's world are part of normal development and are necessary for emotional survival. For example, young children need to believe in Santa Claus; they also need to maintain the illusion that their parents are omnipotent and omniscient. Gradually, these illusions are dismantled in the course of emotional development. When the process occurs in a nontraumatic way, one is able to come to terms with the true essence of things and move on. Indeed, this is considered to be paramount for psychological growth. Generally, an adaptive mourning process takes place when the loss is gradual and not devastating. Some people weather the inevitable loss of their illusions relatively smoothly, without extreme disruption to their maturational development. For others the relinquishment of a needed illusion can be traumatic, and they may struggle against the currents of reality in order to preserve their illusions. For these people, the task of giving up their illusions, mourning their loss, and working through the ensuing disillusionment engenders unthinkable anxiety. This is addressed in Chapter 3, which deals with illusion and disillusionment in connection with defenses.

Hence, accurately perceiving and dealing with the true nature of things both with regard to oneself and in relation to one's world can be a painful process. The wish to avoid emotional pain prompts many individuals to attempt to perpetuate their illusions and/or to ward off the awareness of disillusionment, and they circumvent the need to mourn the loss of cherished illusions. Chapters 4 and 5 explore the power of illusions and the role of illusion as an organizing principle.

The role of illusion and disillusionment is especially central in our understanding of the diagnostic entities of depression and narcissism. Depression frequently is a function of the loss of an exalted, idealized, and illusory view of oneself and one's specialness, which is replaced by the painful awareness of the true nature of one's vulnerability in the world. Depression emerges from being forced to relinquish certain illusions about oneself in relation to the world. The need to preserve and sustain illusions about oneself is seen in its most virulent form in narcissistic personalities. These individuals most prevalently display the inability to mourn the loss of the illusion that "the world is my oyster." These issues are addressed in Chapters 6 and 7.

Chapter 8 cites examples of illusion and disillusionment from the fields of politics, sports, literature, movies, theater, and songs. These areas, tangential to the book's core issues, are nonetheless of general appeal and interest.

Chapter 9 discusses illusion and disillusionment in the psychotherapeutic relationship. It is typical of many patients to enter therapy with illusions about what will transpire in the treatment process, as well as illusions about the therapist as a magical healer. Mental health practitioners themselves have illusions and disillusionments about what they can accomplish with their patients. Therapeutic failures often occur as a result of the unsuccessful resolution of the inevitable development of disillusionment in the relationship between patient and therapist. Therefore, it is desirable to closely monitor this dimension of the treatment process.

The thorough and systematic analysis of illusion and the management of working-through disillusionment are of central importance in successful psychoanalytic psychotherapy. This is particularly crucial given the changing patient population in which therapists' caseloads include an increasing number of people who come to treatment with early unresolved life issues, issues that assign a pivotal role to the dimensions of illusion and disillusionment.

1

Illusion and Disillusionment
in the Life Cycle

Rob the average man of his life illusion, and you rob him of his happiness at the same stroke.

Henrik Ibsen
The Wild Duck

The course of our lives is punctuated by a series of illusions and disillusionments. Illusions are an inherent part of normal development; hence, we may refer to them as necessary illusions. The management of disillusionment is a crucial dimension of adjustment. Maintaining central illusions and relinquishing them in the face of reality and its accompanying disillusionment is an ongoing aspect of growth.

What is an illusion? It is defined in the *Oxford American Dictionary* as follows: "1. something that a person wrongly supposed to exist. 2. a false belief about the nature of something." The supposition in this book is that an illusion is a false belief carved out of wishes, needs, and fantasies that are not rooted in reality. It can be said that an illusion is based on a misperception of the true nature of things. The verb *disillusion* is defined in the dictionary as "to set free from pleasant, but mistaken beliefs." *Disillusionment* is the process that springs from the realization that one's wishes, beliefs, expectations, and assumptions are not going to be fulfilled. In extreme situations disillusionment may be felt as devastating and demolishing to one's belief systems. To let go of an illusion in which one remains invested is a painful experience that requires a tolerance for disillusionment. In this way the processes of illusion and disillusionment are entwined.

There are distinctions between illusion, delusion, and hallucination. *Delusion* is defined as "a false belief held in spite of invalidating evidence" (*American Heritage Dictionary*) and "a persistent false belief that is a symptom or form of madness" (*Oxford American Dictionary*). To the degree that one's sense of reality is eroded and a fantasy or illusion is experienced as reality, one enters the domain of delusion. An *illusion* contains a distortion or error in perception or assumption that can be modified with intervention, in contrast to a delusion, which is more extreme, persistent, and unmodifiable. *Hallucination* is defined as a "false or distorted perception of objects or events with a compelling sense of their reality, usually as a product of mental disorder or as a response to a drug" (*American Heritage Dictionary*). The distinction between hallucination and illusion is best captured by Maurois (1968): "Hallucination is somewhat different from illusion. In an illusion the error stems from the interpretation. In a hallucination it is the sensation itself which is garbled" (p. 25).

The earliest illusions in life are promoted by as yet undeveloped cognitive and ego capacities, so that children function with what we might consider to be a set of false beliefs about themselves and their world. The definition of illusion generally includes an aspect of self-deception and lack of validity. In "The Future of an Illusion," Freud (1927) took things a bit further in suggesting that wish fulfillments play a central role in the formation of many illusions: "We call a belief an illusion when a wish fulfillment is a prominent factor in its motivation, and in doing so we disregard its relation to reality" (p. 31). Similarly, Chasseguet-Smirgel and Grunberger (1986) define illusion as "a belief motivated by a wish-fulfillment requiring no confirmation from reality" (p. 221).

The degree of investment that individuals have in their illusions can be understood as being generated by this wish-fulfillment aspect.

Disillusionment can be described as a process in which one comes to the realization that one's wishes, beliefs, expectations, and assumptions are not going to be fulfilled. Adam Phillips (1998) describes "growing up as a process of disillusionment" (p. xiv). There is usually an element of disappointment involved, which fuels a significant emotional response within the individual. It is noteworthy that in the German language the word for disappointment is *Enttäuschung,* which is also used to mean disillusionment. Disillusionment may come about in a more or less gradual way that paves the way for a relatively smooth acceptance and reorganization of one's belief system, or it may occur in an abrupt or traumatic way that has a long-lasting impact on an individual's personality development and character structure.

It has been postulated in various schools of psychoanalytic thought (see Chapter 2), that the earliest illusion in life revolves around the child's perception that *he brings about* the good feeding from the mother's breast. The primary needs of the infant have to do with the establishment and maintenance of physiological homeostasis. If he is fed when he is hungry, picked up and held when he is distressed, gets his diaper changed after bowel movements, and is generally responded to during his awake states, which are substantially shorter than his sleeping states, he is believed to experience a phase of blissful satisfaction. During this early period of development there is a considerably limited awareness on the part of the child of the distinction between self and other; therefore, that which comes from within and that which comes from the outside is not clearly delineated. In a sense the child functions to a significant degree as if "mother and I are one"; the pleasurable excitations from within, as well as the tension reducing ministrations provided by the mothering one, are for a time commingled in the experience of the child. Thus, it can be said that for a while, in the earliest months of life, the child proceeds with the illusion that the tension-reducing ministrations of the mother, such as feeding, holding, comforting, and changing, are events brought about by the child himself. Such a belief is a forerunner for the development of a sense of optimism as one navigates through the course of life. Later on, with additional maturational development, which allows the child to differentiate further between self and other, he finds ways to attempt to get his caregivers to respond to his needs. To the extent that these strivings are responded to in a healthy way, that is, one that creates a suitable balance between gratification and frustration, which is necessary for optimal growth to take place, the child can acquire a highly adaptive and valuable ego function known as the capacity to extract supplies from the environment.

Recent infant–mother research has indicated that the infant has an earlier sense of differentiation than previously believed (to be discussed in Chapter 2). Nevertheless, the infant and young child generally function as though the significant other feels, thinks, and acts as he does. Thus, on a psychological level the child operates under the narcissistic illusion of "twinship," that is, a belief in the sameness of the self and the significant other. This state, sometimes referred to as a phase of need gratification, involves the illusory expectation that the role of the other is to serve and satisfy the needs of the self. Furthermore, in this state one is not expected to give of oneself to the other, and the other is viewed as not possessing needs, wishes, or demands of his or her own. Some individuals carry this illusion into their adult lives, because these needs were either overly gratified or insufficiently attended to at the phase-appropriate time in early development. They pattern their adult relationships around this theme. As we shall see, many relationships fail as a result of illusions that cannot be fulfilled. To the extent that the child's illusion that the significant other mirrors oneself is responded to in a generally nondisruptive way, the child acquires a feeling of well-being, safety, and control over his or her world. This is part of normal development. In essence the child needs his or her illusions about others in order to sustain an ideal state of well-being, and, to a certain degree, this remains true throughout life.

The illusion of harmonious sameness between self and others must eventually be modified if one is to achieve healthy adult relationships. However, the relinquishing of cherished central beliefs about oneself and/or the world can be a painful process. As the child becomes increasingly aware of the true nature of things, he is usually able to let go of his illusions in favor of reality, and he moves forward. Under the influence of reality factors, disillusionment intervenes, and the child experiences conflict between his cherished illusory beliefs and reality awareness. Optimal disillusionment occurs in a gradual and smooth manner. Under these conditions the child is able to make the adjustment in a nontraumatic way, and earlier illusions are replaced by an acceptance of the true essence of things. It can be said that the management of inevitable disillusionment is a major developmental task. It is not so much the magnitude of the disillusionment but rather the point in time at which it occurs that determines the child's ability to accept the loss of core illusions. When adequate development of ego functions has occurred, and the illusion is not punctured prematurely and excessively abruptly, adaptation and accommodation to the new awareness of reality will take place.

This is not to suggest that this process occurs painlessly. Quite the contrary. The realization of psychological separateness on the part of the child is considered to be the first major disillusionment in the life cycle. This perception of separateness is accompanied by an awareness of the self as a small, vulnerable, and relatively helpless and dependent individual in a large, frightening, and overwhelming world. This aspect of early development assumes a prominent position in the work of many psychoanalytic writers (e.g., Mahler et al. 1975, Rothstein 1980). Erich Fromm (1941), a humanistic psychoanalyst, viewed man's state of aloneness as the primary dimension of the human condition. For Fromm the gradual awareness of one's separateness is a painful and frightening discovery. In other words, the loss of the illusion of blissful existence through the psychological connection with a significant other creates a source of existential anxiety in the developing child. What follows is a sense of disillusionment and a conflict between a gradual acceptance of reality versus solutions that attempt to restore the lost illusions. When the child grasps his true state of vulnerability in the world, he may attempt to compensate for his lost illusion by investing in the belief that he is attached to something or someone who is big and strong. Thus, the acceptance of reality ushered in by cognitive development is accompanied by a sense of disillusionment, which triggers another sequence of illusions needed to ward off anxiety about the true nature of things. In essence illusions about oneself and the world are often followed by reality awareness, which leads to disillusionment, which in turn may be accompanied by renewed efforts to find illusions that are designed to allow oneself to feel safe and secure.

The awareness of the anatomical differences between the sexes, which occurs between the second and third year of life, truncates another illusion in normal childhood development. This paves the way for the development of castration anxiety and the Oedipus complex, two central concepts in psychoanalytic theory. Prior to this point little boys and girls pay little attention to these distinctions, even though they may be socialized to assume contrasting roles. The awareness of the anatomical fact that males possess a penis and females do not is believed to have far-reaching implications in psychosexual development. In classical psychoanalytic theory this discovery is purported to usher in the awareness of castration and differentially promotes the relationship between castration anxiety and the Oedipus complex in boys and girls. Freud (1925b) maintained that when the little girl realizes she is without a penis, she suffers from penis envy, and blames her mother for her castrated state. In so doing she now turns away from mother, her original love object, and instead turns her libidinal investment toward her father, who possesses the wished-for organ. Thus, in the case of the little girl, it is castration anxiety that leads to the development of the Oedipus complex. According to Freudian theory, for the little boy the situation is quite the opposite. It is suggested that the little boy shows minimal concern upon first discovering the absence of a penis in females. Only later, when he is struggling with incestuous impulses toward the mother and murderous wishes toward the father, does the little boy experience anxiety about potential castration. Under the influence of the talion principle, he comes to fear that his father will retaliate for his oedipal feelings by destroying his own sexual organ, which has become a source of pleasure. Hence, as Freud (1925b) states:

> In girls the oedipal complex is a secondary formation. The operations of the castration complex precede it and prepare for it. As regards the relation between the Oedipus and castration complexes, there is a fundamental contrast between the two sexes. Whereas in boys the Oedipus complex succumbs to the castration complex, in girls it is made possible and led up to by the castration complex. [p. 256]

The awareness of the anatomical differences between the sexes is part of an ever-growing set of realizations that the young child encounters. In discussing the existentialist Norman O. Brown's (1959) exposition in his book *Life Against Death*, Becker (1973) states, "The horror of sexual differentiation is a horror of 'biological fact,' as Brown so well says. It is a fall out of illusion into sobering reality. It is a horror of assuming an immense new burden, the burden of the meaning of life and the body, of the fatality of one's incompleteness, his helplessness, his finitude" (p. 41).

As part of normal development, children in our culture are encouraged by their parents to believe in Santa Claus and the Tooth Fairy as benevolent figures who bestow timely gifts and rewards. It is striking to note that these illusions are maintained for an extended period of time. Several years ago a *New York*

Times poll of 261 children indicated that between the ages of 3 to 10, 87 percent of the children interviewed believed in Santa Claus. All of the 3-year-olds in the survey expressed a belief in Santa, as did two-thirds of the 10-year-olds. Hence, it must be comfortable to continue to hold on to this illusory belief long after the reality testing of the latency-age child suggests otherwise (e.g., that Santa Claus cannot really climb down the chimney or walk through locked doors to deliver presents). In preadolescence and adolescence the appeal of pen pals reflects another way in which our culture encourages the formation of illusions. It can be exciting for young boys or girls to attribute all sorts of idealized qualities to their special pen pal.

Another core illusion that needs to be dismantled during the course of normal development is the child's belief that he is protected from the dangers of the world by his parents. When the 2-year-old child becomes increasingly aware of his vulnerability, his sense of omnipotence is shattered. He then increases his investment in believing in the omniscience and omnipotence of his parents, and he restores a feeling of security and safety through his connection with them. Gradually, in the course of development, he comes to recognize the imperfections in his parents. It must be emphasized that this disillusionment needs to occur in a gradual way in order for the child not to feel overwhelmed and traumatized by the loss of his idealized image of his parents. If this occurs too abruptly or too early, the child may suffer long-lasting damage in his ability to sustain trust in his relationships.

This process of establishing a more realistic appraisal of the parents' strengths and weaknesses is usually accomplished by early adolescence.

One adult patient in the course of his psychoanalysis recalled how much he admired and idolized his father when he was a young boy. However, during latency, somewhat prematurely at age 9, he was forced to see his father as a man with limited knowledge and clay feet. This occurred when the patient went to his first football game with his father and a friend and the friend's father. The boy was excited over this event, and he and his friend talked about it for days in advance. He anticipated that he would finally learn about football. When a touchdown and place kick resulted in a 7–0 score being posted on the scoreboard, the boy turned to his father and asked how many points are for the touchdown and how many points for the kick after the touchdown. The father quickly replied that the touchdown counted for three points and the place kick for four points. At this point the friend's father laughed and in a knowledgeable and mocking tone, indicated that a touchdown and place kick counted for six points and one point, respectively. The patient recalled feeling devastated, embarrassed, and most of all humiliated by this exchange. He suddenly realized that his father, the adult he had put on a pedestal, had clay feet. This was a profound blow to his illusion about his father's omniscience, and he was unable to recover from it. As his image of his father was prematurely shattered, his feelings of safety and security were correspondingly diminished. He entered adolescence with a great deal of despair, cynicism, and depression.

In contemporary America the prevalence of single-parent families has increased dramatically in the last two decades. It has been estimated that in more than 50 percent of American families there is an absentee parent. One of the consequences of this sociological phenomenon is that it is more difficult for children to maintain the illusion of feeling protected by their parents from the dangers of the world. Instead there occurs an earlier coming to grips with the realization of loss, emotional deprivation, and vulnerability. The men's movement of the 1990s has emphasized the importance of adult men needing to deal with their unresolved pain over having been failed emotionally by their fathers. One of the central theses in Sam Keen's (1991) popular book, *Fire in the Belly*, is the necessity for men to deal with their disillusionment in their absent or emotionally unavailable fathers.

It has long been recognized that divorce can have a deleterious effect on the emotional development of young children. The ability to commit to future long-term relationships may be particularly impaired by the shattering of the illusion of growing up in a happy family. It is now believed that children who are young adults at the time of their parent's divorce may also be left with scars. A 1984 study on the effects of divorce on college-age children (Cain 1990) found that even young adults often suffer a deep sense of loss when their parents divorce at midlife. A surprising finding was that over half the students surveyed had maintained the illusion that their parents were the "ideal couple," despite evidence to the contrary. While some of the students expressed disillusionment in their revised views of love and marriage, it was noteworthy that most of them developed a replacement illusion of future happiness. The author of the study concluded, "Most of these youngsters unsuccessfully disguised a deep and abiding wish to marry, to have children, and to recapture the family of childhood—the one in the picture frame, animated, intertwined and inseparable" (p. 54).

It was pointed out above that when the young child of 2 or 3 realizes his state of vulnerability in the world, he attempts to replenish his lost sense of grandeur by sharing in the powers of his parents, whom he perceives as omniscient and omnipotent. To protect himself from anxiety related to navigating an overwhelming world by himself, a necessary idealization of the parents takes place. This is a normal evolution that allows the child to feel secure through his connection with his loved ones. Ultimately, a divestment in this idealization takes place, brought about by repeated disillusionment with the power and perfection of the parents. Thus, although disillusionment with one's parents is a part of normal development, many children subsequently experience the need to recapture the feelings of a vanished secure and more blissful time. This may account for the phenomenon of hero worship. As children turn away in disappointment from their parents, they may need to search for a hero as a parent substitute with whom they can regain the joyous feelings that go with idealization. The psychoanalyst Otto Rank (1957) describes this process in *The Myth of the Birth of the Hero*. In discussing hero worship, Rank states, "The entire endeavor to replace the real father by a more distinguished one is merely the expression of the child's longing for the vanished happy time, when his father still appeared to be the strongest and greatest man, and the mother seemed the dearest and most beautiful woman" (p. 67).

PARADISE LOST

The realization that one is a relatively vulnerable organism in a complicated world where others are not always welcoming is a disillusioning experience that replaces earlier illusions about one's specialness. As the child advances developmentally, as a result of the pressure of reality awareness, he must also mourn the loss of his earlier innocence and obliviousness to the more frightening aspects of his existence in the world. It is difficult to relinquish the satisfaction of the earlier, more blissful era, and, while one moves forward, there is also a corresponding pull toward recapturing the secure feeling of the past. Rank points out that in searching for a hero, the child is attempting to reexperience the feelings of attachment to the parent as he once believed mother or father to be, that is, prior to discovering the flaws in the parents and the ensuing disillusionment. In discussing the need for heroes Rank (1957) states, "The child turns away from the father, as he now knows him, to the father in whom he believed in his earlier years, his imagination being in truth only the expression of regret for this happy time having passed away. Thus the overvaluation of the earliest years of child-hood again claims its own in these fancies" (p. 67).

In normal development even as the confrontations with re-ality propel the young child to relinquish his early illusions of omnipotence, lack of separateness, and lack of anatomical dif-ferences between the sexes, he nevertheless continues to attempt to recapture the more blissful state of existence in which illu-sion prevails. Thus, with the thrust of maturation, the child's development goes forward, while another part of him seeks to regain an earlier feeling of satisfaction and safety.

The construct of the transitional object is useful for under-standing how the child accepts the reality of greater separate-ness from mother than previously acknowledged, while simulta-neously being able to utilize her maternal functions. This is achieved through the process of internalization, in which the child gradually takes into himself the nurturing functions pro-vided by the mothering one. Through the use of a transitional object, like a blanket or some other object associated with the nurturing mother, the child is able to re-create for himself the sense of blissful union and its soothing qualities. The child learns to regulate the dosage of self-soothing derived from the transi-tional object, and in a sense he can control and supply his sooth-ing needs even better than the way in which they are provided by the "good-enough" mother (Winnicott 1965). The involve-ment with the transitional object paves the way for the acquisition of internal psychic structure, which becomes the foundation for a secure sense of self. As the child increasingly internalizes the soothing functions of the mother, via the transitional object, the need for the latter eventually disappears. Nevertheless, for many individuals the need for some external representation of a tran-sitional object, in the form of a teddy bear, for example, may persist through later childhood and into their adult years. The capacity for self-soothing is thus considered to be an essential function for an individual to rely upon, particularly in times of stress, throughout the life cycle.

Many individuals go through life with a yearning to recapture what they imagine to have been a more blissful era in which they felt that their needs were exquisitely taken care of. Whether or not this state truly existed, these individuals react as if they have lost something essential to their happiness, and they pursue the illusion of finding the perfect relationship in which their needs, wishes, and desires will be fully met. It is as if they are driven by a sense of a paradise lost and a quest to restore the equilibrium that corresponded to their feeling state prior to the expulsion from the Garden of Eden.

The idealization and pleasure that adults derive from seeing the spontaneity, exuberance, and enthusiasm in young children may be related to an identification with the innocence of youth prior to the awareness of the realities of life. It might be viewed as an unconscious vicarious attempt to recapture an era in which a blissful love affair with the world prevailed before we experienced a sense of deflated omnipotence as a result of the limitations imposed upon us by reality considerations.

Sydney Smith (1977) refers to "the golden fantasy" to describe a secret fantasy that permeates the treatment of many patients in psychotherapy. According to Smith, the core of the fantasy is "the wish to have all of one's needs met in a relationship hallowed by perfection . . . . It is always tied to the conviction that somewhere in that great, unbounded expanse called the world is a person capable of fully meeting one's needs" (p. 311).

I believe that this is a prevalent fantasy that people harbor to different degrees. In those for whom such a wished-for state may be dominant in their ways of interacting in the world, the issues of illusion and disillusionment are perpetual themes that they must navigate. Smith considers the ubiquitous nature of these longings by posing this question: "Is it possible that 'the Fall,' if it is a metaphor referring to the loss of the oceanic pleasures of infancy, represents nothing more than a developmental stage in us all, namely separation from the all-giving mother,

[and] is that eviction from Paradise that sets off—at least in some—the endless repetitious efforts to restore this faintly remembered idyllic state?" (p. 311).

In these passages Smith is employing the literary metaphor of Milton's *Paradise Lost* to highlight the developmental struggle that occurs when there is an awareness of the loss of the illusion of a perfect union with a nurturing figure, and the ensuing disillusionment that must be negotiated. For some the magnitude of the lost illusion is experienced so intensely that they need to invest their efforts in attempting to restore a sense of paradise and thereby ward off the pain of disillusionment.

To relinquish an illusion that has provided a source of safety and a sense of well-being can be a wrenching experience. At different stages of life people are invested in maintaining phase-appropriate illusions and may fight against surrendering them to what they experience as the harsh demands of reality. This struggle occurs for a number of reasons. Foremost among these are the gratification received through adherence to one's illusions (e.g., a sense of blissfulness, enhanced self-esteem, feelings of closeness and connectedness with others) and the anticipation of anxiety about what they would need to contend with without their cherished illusions (e.g., a lesser view of oneself and a greater sense of one's vulnerabilities and limitations). If illusions are central to one's existence, then we might think about the role of illusions from different vantage points, such as necessary illusions, special illusions, shameful illusions, secret illusions, sanctioned illusions, punctured illusions, and so forth (discussed in further detail in Chapter 3).

ADOLESCENCE

Although adolescence is generally a period of considerable turmoil, some adults look back nostalgically on that phase of their lives as a time when hopes were high and horizons were boundless. The future held promise and one's options in life were limitless.

Among the hallmarks of the adolescent phase of normal development are illusions about one's invulnerability and disillusionment with parents and other adults. As ego capacities become consolidated and strivings for greater independence are achieved, the adolescent characteristically becomes impressed with his new strengths and freedom. The peer group becomes a powerful force that serves to dilute the influence of the family. Adolescence is sometimes referred to as the second period of separation-individuation insofar as it recapitulates, on a higher level, some of the earlier sequences in the development of the child. Most notable are the periods of elation and deflation common to both eras. Just as the young child exudes an air of excitement when the maturational spurt allows him to walk, run, and freely move away from his caregiver, so, too, does the adolescent experience an excitement about his growing independence and his being more accountable to himself and his peer group and less accountable to his parents. Like the toddler the typical adolescent also portrays an obliviousness to the potential dangers in the world. On a surface level the adolescent self-image is characterized by feelings of immortality and invulnerability. Adults' warnings about the future health repercussions of smoking, drinking, and excessive sunbathing fall upon deaf ears, because adolescents feel invulnerable and immortal, and these behaviors are socially accepted and reinforced by the peer group. The role of illusion in the adolescent experience is exquisitely captured in the movie *Fame*, in which the expectation of living forever and learning to fly are prevalent and repeated themes.

To the extent that an adolescent's functioning is governed by erroneous beliefs about himself in relation to the world, his judgment may be colored or even significantly impaired. The sense of invulnerability and immortality can lead to reckless behavior such as taking drugs or speeding while driving. The leading cause of death for individuals up to age 39 in the United

States is auto accidents, to which, it seems highly likely, a contributing factor is adolescents' feeling of invincibility.

But, along with the sense of invulnerability, adolescence is also filled with turmoil and disillusionment. Adolescents may feel vulnerable as they stand more on their own and experience the true nature of the world. A profound sense of disappointment and despair may occur as teenagers acquire a greater awareness of the flaws and foibles of adults who were previously venerated. The impact of parental divorce, their own failures in relationships, news of political scandals and corruption, and athletes and other heroes who fall from grace serve to deflate the optimism and elation of adolescence. In extreme cases, the realization of life's limitations, conflictual emotions, confusion over evolving sexual identity, and feeling misunderstood by significant others can lead to suicidal ideation and behavior. Adolescent suicidal behavior can be viewed as a response to feelings of deflation related to the awareness of the vulnerability of the self vis-à-vis the unresponsively experienced and disillusioning outside world. Some adolescents are unprepared to deal with this trauma and seek a way out through suicide, which is simultaneously an attempt to escape the painful feelings of vulnerability and an attempt to strike back at and hurt others whom they perceive as having failed in the task of protecting them against the awareness of this vulnerability.

MOURNING

The realization that one is a relatively vulnerable being in a complicated world in which others are not always welcoming is a disillusioning experience that replaces earlier illusions about one's specialness. The management of inevitable disillusionments is a primary developmental task throughout life. Beginning in early childhood a sense of paradise lost must be dealt with, when the toddler is no longer oblivious to the fact that he is an organism with a separate identity from his mother. This theme occurs time and again in life and may take many forms, as for example when one searches for a hero as a substitute for a disillusioning parent; or when a physical illness or disability punctures the illusion of immortality; or when a spouse finally relinquishes the belief, hope, and expectation that the connection to another person will restore the feeling of blissful well-being in a permanent way; or when one comes to realize that time is the enemy of illusions.

Thus, the ability to mourn the loss of paradise is a necessary and recurrent developmental milestone. Under the influence of the reality principle most individuals are able to gradually mourn the loss of their illusions and move on. The task at hand, as with any experience of mourning, is to recognize the loss, deal with the pain, and gradually come to terms with the new reality.

One patient came to psychotherapy in a deep depression when his illusion of striking it rich collapsed. He had invested his moderate life savings in marketing an invention, with the expectation that it would generate many millions in profits. He proceeded to pursue a lifestyle of a very wealthy man, and built up considerable personal debt. In his childhood his self-worth was derived from academic achievement, which garnered his mother's approval. It was also ingrained upon him that he had to overcome his background of poverty and live a life of affluence, which his parents had yearned for but never had. When his under-capitalized business venture failed, he plummeted into a sea of despair and sought professional help. His early sessions revolved around the working through of his disillusionment, and he gradually came to accept the position that "I now can live within my means, instead of having to live within my dreams."

A precursor to the capacity to mourn is the ability to tolerate feelings of sadness. When adequate mothering in the preoedipal stages of development has allowed the child to acquire sufficient ego strength, the child will be able to tolerate sadness in connection with his psychic awareness of separateness from the caregiver. Mahler and colleagues (1975) describe this process as "low-keyedness," and it represents a form of normal developmental mourning. In addressing this issue Kavaler-Adler (1994) states,

> Such normal developmental mourning, during the separation period, can then lead to later states of developmental mourning, as seen during the oedipal period and adolescence, and even later during middle and old age . . . . If the preoedipal state of mourning is not reached, incremental stages of mourning during these later developmental stages will not be done. [p. 77]

For some individuals the pain of mourning and the resistance to mourning is so great that they may take the opposite path and insist on re-creating, refinding, or holding on to the lost illusion in total disregard of reality. For others the disillusionment is experienced in such a powerful way that they need to avoid situations in which they might feel vulnerable. It is as if the ego requires a prolonged recovery time before it can allow for further experiences that may elicit or arouse anxiety. The following case exemplifies this point.

> Janine was an attractive, intelligent professional woman in her fifties, who had never married. She had very much wanted a husband and children, and one of her chief reasons for seeking psychoanalysis was to better understand why she had not fulfilled these goals. She was the youngest child in a Southern family with parents who doted on her and encouraged her to find a man who would be worthy of her, and not to settle for somebody ordinary. In her twenties and

thirties she had had many romances, but these came to an end when she would discover some defect in the man that she could not tolerate. There were many oedipal and dependency dynamics that were revealed in her continuing competition with her mother for her father's attention, and the ways in which she perpetuated allowing herself to be taken care of by her family.

During the course of treatment we uncovered a central fantasy in which she would find and marry a man who was perfect. She was carried by the illusion that he would be flawless and would respond to all of her needs in a most sensitive way. While in analysis she developed several successive liaisons. Invariably, the pattern was that she would be drawn to a man who was handsome, worldly, paid her a lot of attention, and made her feel special. She would quickly idealize these men and place them on a pedestal. Eventually, she would find a chink in their armor, and even though the perceived flaw might be seen objectively as something relatively minor, she could not sustain her interest in these men. In effect she would overly value them in an impulsive and unrealistic manner in order to fulfill the requirements of her illusion, and then excessively devalue them in reaction to her first feelings of disillusionment. Her investment in these unrealistic relationships was so strong, and her disappointment was so great, that when these liaisons ended she went through extensive periods of mourning in which she berated herself for her blind spots in how she perceived these men, and berated them for misrepresenting themselves and encouraging her to see them as more perfect than they were.

Subsequently, she needed prolonged periods of recovery in which she avoided situations in which she might meet a new man. It was during these times that she was most amenable to exploring the power of her illusion and her part in setting herself up for repeated disillusionment. She complained often about how difficult it was to meet available men and how men in her age range were interested in much younger women. While these concerns were undoubtedly valid, we came to see that the greater problem for her was not about meeting eligible men, but rather what got set in motion once she did meet a new man. Accordingly, the focus of the treatment shifted toward her developing more successful ways to appraise the strengths and weaknesses of her partners along with persistent analysis of her core illusion about finding Mr. Perfect. Anxiety about intimacy and oedipal guilt were significant dynamics that hampered her attempts to establish a permanent relationship, and were signficant foci of the working-through phase of treatment. In addition, however, I believe it was the systematic analyses of her central illusion and its defensive function, along with continuing attention to the ways in which she participated in bringing about failure in her relationships and subsequent disillusionment, that ultimately helped this woman to move forward.

In a recent paper Gaines (1997) has extended our understanding of normal mourning to include a process of "creating continuity" along with the process of detachment from what has been lost. Traditional psychoanalytic theory has highlighted the detachment aspect of mourning in which the chief tasks involve the acceptance of the permanence of the loss and incremental decathexis of what has been lost. Thus, in terms of lost illusions it becomes necessary, if healthy adjustment is to proceed, that the loss is appropriately mourned and the individual moves on to new sources of satisfaction. Gaines states, "Coming to terms with a loss must involve some relinquishing of hopes, dreams, and other future expectations, some acceptance of possibilities that will never be" (p. 553). This is what is meant by disillusionment. Gaines adds, "The idea of detaching reflects this aspect of mourning" (p. 553). In considering the loss of a relationship Gaines states,

Emphasis on the need to detach from the lost object has obscured another aspect of the work of mourning which is to
repair the disruption to the inner self-other relationship
caused by the actual loss. The individual needs to reconnect
the severed bond, now on an exclusively internal basis, and
to maintain the availability of a sustaining inner relationship.
[p. 549]

This is referred to as the task of creating continuity. In
applying this notion to the loss of illusions, a different kind of
creating continuity often takes place: the capacity for transformation of lost illusions into progressive new spheres of illusion.
To the extent that we all need some illusions in order to exist,
lost illusions need to be decathected and corrected in accordance
with reality, and old illusions sometimes need to be replaced with
new illusions.

NOSTALGIA

Nostalgia plays a role in illusion and disillusionment. Adults look
back on the "good old days" when life seemed simpler, less stressful, and more promising. Personal insecurities that existed at an
earlier age may be obfuscated and one's recollections may be
colored by the memory of a feeling state in which hopes ran
high. The idealism characteristic of adolescence and young adulthood promotes the formation of dreams about personal accomplishments, as well as beliefs about attaining unity and brotherhood throughout the world. When the normal disillusionments
of later adulthood take root, such as periods of marital disharmony or issues in midlife crises, there is a tendency to yearn for
the feeling state of an earlier era, and to recapture moments or
relationships that belonged to that era. One middle-aged patient,
who spent a lot of his time in therapy dwelling on the lost opportunities of the past, described how rejuvenated and invigo-

rated he felt when he joined his friends from high school for their annual reunion weekend. He remembered his adolescent years longingly as a time when "we could just be ourselves, and we all accepted each other's craziness."

Another middle-aged man came to therapy to deal with his problems around the aging process. His chief anxiety was that he would die of a heart attack as his father had at age 55. He lived in dread of each new birthday, which meant that he was getting closer to his anticipated demise. In the course of therapy we uncovered a compromise formation in which he could be a successful professional, far more successful than his father, provided he did not outlive his father. To achieve the latter represented to this man the ultimate oedipal victory. At the same time it was also his secret wish to live longer than his father, but this very wish filled him with guilt and anxiety. As a result he could take no pleasure in any of the richness in his family life or professional activities. He could only allow himself to enjoy things from the past. He went through the motions of everyday life with severely constricted affect, but he was very emotionally involved with nostalgic reminiscences. He would collect old records and old baseball cards because they reminded him and connected him with bygone days when life seemed more carefree. In sessions he frequently spoke wistfully about his lost happy times during his twenties. Following upsetting arguments with his wife, he would have a recurrent dream about accidentally running into a girlfriend from more than thirty years ago. In the dream they were both 20 years old and were attracted to each other once again. This had not been a significant romantic relationship for this man and he never thought about this woman in his waking life. His associations led him to the time he was a counselor at camp, where he had met this young woman, when summers were full of fun and it seemed life would last forever. This dream became pivotal in his beginning to work through his sadness over his lost youth and to experience satisfactions in his present-day accomplishments. He continued to hold on to some pockets of nostalgia, but he also allowed himself to become more alive with new interests and to plan for a meaningful future after the age of 55.

For many individuals the normal developmental phase of the midlife crisis stirs up anxiety about the future. Fears about losing our physical attractiveness and mental capacities often impel us to yearn longingly for the past. In essence, this type of nostalgia may be a way of warding off anxiety about the unknown future and about death. Our culture provides many outlets for people to immerse themselves in nostalgia. Memorabilia has become a growing industry, as have baseball fantasy camps, in which middle-aged men can spend a week at a training camp playing ball and reminiscing with former stars from the national pastime. The Broadway theater has become replete with musical revivals that take the audience back to earlier times and wistful memories. When one has become thrown by the inevitable disillusioning acids of life, it can be comforting to cushion such blows through nostalgia. Dwelling on the past and a strong investment in nostalgia may serve as a way of avoiding facing one's anxieties about the future.

Nostalgic memories serve to put us in touch with an earlier affective state that has been embellished. As noted by Wolfenstein (1966), "Probably nostalgic memories generally preserve something from very early childhood . . . . The theme of such memories, more or less disguised, is of the self as a greatly loved small child. As Wordsworth says, in his great nostalgic poem on recollections of early childhood: 'Heaven lays about us in our infancy' " (p. 115).

ILLUSION AND DISILLUSIONMENT IN
LOVE RELATIONSHIPS

In the earliest months of life the child experiences the mother's love through her ministrations of his physical needs and via the emotional attunement she provides. The psychoanalyst Michael Balint (1959) describes this as the state of primary love. Balint states, "Primary love is a relationship in which only one partner may have demands and claims; the other partner (or partners, i.e., the whole world) must have no interests, no wishes, no demands, of his or her own. There is, and must be, a complete harmony, i.e., a complete identity of wishes and satisfaction" (p. 22).

Winnicott (1965) developed the concept of the "good-enough mother" to describe the reliable and consistent nurturing supplies provided by the caregiver in an environment that is characterized by a predictable balance and rhythm of gratification and frustration. Out of these repeated experiences the child builds illusions about himself as omnipotent and invulnerable, and about the world as a satisfying place that is sensitive and responsive to his needs. Hence, one consequence of good-enough mothering is that the child gradually comes to approach the world with a sense of optimism and trust.

In a similar vein Kernberg (1976) stipulates that in normal development the child acquires an internal world that includes "a stable world of integrated, internalized object representations," which enables him to feel loved and promotes the foundation for the formation of basic trust. In Kernberg's words, "Basic trust . . . . ultimately derives from the first internalization of a gratifying, reliable mother-representation in relation to a loving, gratified self-representation" (p. 73).

Ultimately, with the psychological development that takes place in the first three years of life, the child comes to value the qualities of the caregiver over and above, and independent of, his state of need. This process is referred to as object constancy (Hartmann 1952), which means the child has reached a point in emotional maturation at which he is able to maintain his positive, loving feelings toward the caregiver, even at times when she is frustrating or unresponsive to his needs.

Joffe and Sandler (1965) introduced the concept of "an ideal state of well-being," in which the object is seen primarily as a vehicle for the attainment of this state. In other words, one needs to have a loving connection in order to feel optimally good within oneself. This view might explain the tendency toward overestimation of the positive qualities of the love object frequently noted in the state of being in love. Thus, through the connection with an idealized love object one can enhance the ideal state of well-being. Joffe and Sandler believe that even after object constancy has been reached, the object is not loved for its own sake, but only as a vehicle for the attainment of the ideal state. Hence, object love is seen as a roundabout way to acquire this exalted self state. When a love object is lost, one experiences not only its loss, but also the loss of the object-complementary aspect of the self. In this view, individuals need to develop and sustain illusions about the attributes of their partners and the relationship itself, in order to derive an optimal sense of well-being. When the relationship is lost, often as a result of unrealistic expectations and faulty assumptions about the partner, the ideal state of well-being fizzles.

Gabbard (1993) takes a similar position in alluding to the role of illusion and disillusionment in relation to the Oedipus complex:

> In addition to giving up the fantasy of having the real opposite-sex parent for oneself, the resolution of the Oedipus complex also involves renouncing an idealized version of the self as a partner to an idealized version of the opposite-sex parent. A crushing disappointment, associated with lingering bitterness, accompanies the resignation to the reality that such a relationship will never exist. [p. 235]

Illusion and disillusionment are prevalent in marriage. In our contemporary society one out of every two marriages ends in divorce, and to a great extent this staggering statistic might be attributed to the consequences of unfulfilled illusions and subsequent disillusionment in these unions. Shor and Sanville (1978) in their book *Illusion in Loving* postulate about the underlying reasons for disenchantment with marriage. As discussed earlier in this chapter, during the course of normal development the growing child comes to recognize the flaws and failings of his parents, and gradually relinquishes his illusion that the parents are omniscient and perfect. While emotional development moves forward, a part of the child remains angry and resentful about the loss of his illusion, and this sets the stage in many individuals for the formation of the "golden fantasy," which was described earlier. The wish to restore the feelings of a blissful relationship in which one's needs were exquisitely taken care of leads people to anticipate marriage as the great restoration. The work of Shor and Sanville relates to this theme:

> We projected on to the institution of marriage all our dreams of self-repair. Our parents were imperfect, imperfectly reared us.... We looked to marriage as to a healer; it was to be our salvation. Specifically, the chosen spouse was to be all that the former caretakers and mentors had failed to be, and such perfection would of course cure all our deficits and perfect us. On an unconscious level, we took with utmost seriousness the myths that we would marry and live happily ever after. With such high hopes and elaborate expectations it is no wonder that we set ourselves up for the inevitable fall, for disappointment in relationships and despair about ourselves.... That to which we looked as the source of goodness and restoration, capable of rendering us whole and sound, has instead, like the parents, failed us, left us feeling still bad, still flawed. [p. 9]

Many people approach marriage with an underlying fantasy that one's connection to another person will restore the feeling of blissful well-being in a permanent way. This need may be met through the repeated experience of mutual caring interactions. At times a sense of well-being can be derived simply through ongoing continuity with the chosen object, while involved in a solo activity. Many couples describe how they feel secure by having the spouse present, even silently in the next room. No interaction or direct contact is required at these times; just the awareness of the presence of the significant other is experienced as comforting and soothing. In contrast some of these individuals describe feelings of emptiness and anxiety when they are engaged in their solo activity (e.g., reading the newspaper, watching television), and the partner is not nearby. This state can be viewed as a reactivation in adulthood of the normal needs of the practicing phase of preoedipal development in which the child is able to pursue autonomous functioning in a climate of emotional availability provided by the mother.

The illusion of finding a partner with whom one will live happily ever after belies the reality that partners are flawed (just like the original attachment figures), and that conflicts, misunderstandings, and a certain amount of insensitivity to one another's needs is inevitable. When the hopes, beliefs, and expectations about the perfect union are unfulfilled to a large degree, or are even shattered, the foundation of the marriage may crumble and divorce may follow. Storr (1968) states, "It may be our idealization of interpersonal relationships in the West that causes marriage, supposedly the most intimate tie, to be so unstable. If we did not look to marriage as the principal source of happiness, fewer marriages would end in tears" (p. xiii).

Marital disharmony often results from frustrations and resentments about unfulfilled expectations. Sadomasochistic engagement may follow as an acting out of the disappointments and resentments. It is at this point that couples often seek professional counseling in an attempt to get one or the other partner to change so that the earlier expectations can be met. This agenda is generally unproductive, and experienced counselors will often attempt to get the participants to examine their underlying assumptions and fantasies about the relationship. Bringing these things out sometimes allows the couple to bridge and mend the chasm in their relationship. At other times the wounds have been too hurtful and the chasm is too great. However, even in these situations many couples break up, only to reconcile at least two or three times with illusions about how things will be different, in order to avoid the painful reality of a failed relationship.

In *Intimate Terrorism: The Deterioration of Erotic Life*, Michael Vincent Miller (1995) takes the position that when illusions in love relationships give way to disillusionment, abuse can follow. For some individuals the loss of the needed illusion is shattering and idealization is replaced by reactions that go beyond devaluation to demonization of the other. In these relationships disillusionment does not lead to a more realistic acceptance of the partner's assets and liabilities, but rather to a need to destroy the other through character assassination or other direct and indirect undermining acts of "intimate terrorism."

The feelings of despondency that often accompany a divorce are usually viewed as a reaction to the loss of the attachment figure. What I am suggesting here is that it is the loss of the dream, as much or more than the loss of the particular relationship, that creates this feeling of despondency. In other words, one needs the relationship in which certain needs are assumed to be fulfilled, in order to sustain the ideal state of well-being. One man in his thirties, who came to therapy to deal with the breakup of his marriage after twelve years, described his depression as follows: "My depression is not about the relationship, but about the loss of what she provided. I feel like a 4-year-old. She gave me a sense of safety, security, and permanence, all the things that a 4-year-old needs. As long as I knew she was there, even if she was in the next room, I felt safe. Getting divorced, because of all of our conflicts, was like a struggle to get out of jail; but feeling divorced and dealing with being divorced, and the loss of my hopes, is something very different."

It can be postulated that the experience of loss in divorce is related to one's developmental level of object relatedness. For those individuals who have not attained a sufficient degree of object constancy, divorce represents the loss of the need gratifying object. In this stage of development it is the supplies provided by the partner, rather than the person in his or her own right, that is most important. In effect the individual requires the supplies rather than the person in order to feel complete or good about oneself; loss of the relationship means loss of the supplies. In these cases, which are very prevalent in contemporary society, there is an incomplete definition of self and the self as defined through a wished-for type of connection with the object. The obsessive love syndrome is an extreme example of an individual's need to define himself through a fantasied involvement with another. In this situation one is consumed with gaining the affection of an idealized person, who is usually unavailable, in order to feel whole. The obsessive pursuit is driven by the belief that one needs to feel special, worthwhile, wanted, and lovable. Reality considerations are often cast aside under the power of the need to pursue the object at all costs.

MIDLIFE CRISIS

Midlife crisis has been recognized as a developmental stage that is characterized by a more or less painful examination of one's past, present, and future. The realization that certain dreams, hopes, and fantasies may not be able to be fulfilled, coupled with the loss or diminishment of certain capacities in one's functioning that were heretofore taken for granted, ushers in the midlife crisis. Time becomes the enemy of illusions about oneself, and illusions begin to crumble. In fact, it can be argued that it is the breakdown of illusions about one's immortality and endless time to pursue life's goals that generates and crystallizes the midlife crisis. The awareness of the finiteness of time is shattering to many illusions and leads to disillusionment. The midlife crisis involves the ability to mourn the loss of certain cherished hopes for one's life.

Daniel Levinson (1978) describes the role of reappraisal of one's illusions at midlife, which is accompanied by a process of acceptance of limitations that he calls "de-illusionment":

> As he attempts to reappraise his life, a man discovers how much it has been based on illusions, and he is faced with the task of de-illusionment. By this expression I mean a reduction of illusions, a recognition that long-held assumptions and beliefs about self and world are not true. This process merits special attention because illusions play so vital a role in our lives throughout the life cycle. [p. 192]

The emphasis here is on the reduction of certain illusions, rather than a giving up of all illusions, since it is recognized that it is part of normal adaptive functioning to sustain some form of illusion in order to enrich our lives. Levinson views the loss of illusions during midlife as developmentally desirable and an indication of maturity.

Middle age is generally thought of as a stage in life, a transitional era between adulthood and old age. There is a normal reluctance in this period to contemplate the phase of old age and the accompanying implications of physical decline and the impending shadow of death. We can also think of middle age as a state of mind related to how one perceives oneself. If we ask midlife individuals to identify what age they perceive themselves to be internally, invariably they cite an age significantly younger than their chronological age. Thus, most people maintain a younger self-image, which is a way of avoiding the anxiety that accompanies the awareness of aging. The loss of the illusion of "forever young" may be experienced as catastrophic. As Modell (1989) says,

> If one seeks to identify the state of mind that transforms a young adult into a middle-aged person, one thinks of the re-

nunciation of illusions and the acceptance of limitations . . . .
In youth and young adulthood many share the illusion of
immortality; the actuality of one's own death is unthinkable
or is postponed to a distant, actually unimaginable future.
[p. 19]

It is psychologically difficult to relinquish such illusions as
time is endless and forever young that govern people's daily functioning, but the forces of reality often serve to puncture the
bubble. Freud (1915b) stated, "We welcome illusions because
they spare us emotional distress and enable us instead to indulge
in gratification. We must not then complain if now and again
they come into conflict with some portion of reality, and are shattered against it" (p. 280).

This may take numerous forms at midlife. For some it is the
waning of their physical attractiveness and/or others' reduced
acknowledgment of their attractiveness. For others it may be the
awareness of lessened energy, reduced sexual activity, or declin-
ing athletic ability. The illusion of invincibility, immortality, and
invulnerability is sometimes shattered during midlife when one
experiences a breakdown in bodily functioning, for example the
beginning onset of chronic disease. Liebert (1989) has pointed
out that "the middle years demand an acceptance that we cannot achieve all we had hoped and planned and cannot hold on
to all we have achieved" (p. 154). This requires the process of
mourning the loss of illusions about oneself and one's aspirations and the coming to terms with disillusion over our unfulfilled dreams.

One of the chief anxieties of the midlife crisis involves the
loss of the illusion of immortality. While this increasing awareness of the inevitability of one's own death frequently leads to a
greater appreciation of life in the here and now, and attending
to goals in the present, at the same time many individuals up
the ante in their fight against relinquishing their illusion of
immortality. There is a conflict here between a growing conscious
awareness and a pervasive unconscious wish for immortality.

Freud (1915b) highlighted this in a well-known statement: "No one believes in his own death . . . . In the unconscious everyone is convinced of his own immortality" (p. 289). Along these lines Oldham (1989) states, "Yet there is a midlife collision between this wish for immortality and the growing awareness of the fact of mortality . . . . The unconscious conviction of one's immortality is challenged by the decline and death of one's parents. For the first time in one's life one can no longer secretly cling to the belief that it is still someone else's turn to die" (p. 92).

There appears to be general agreement in the psychological literature that middle age is a time when certain basic illusions about oneself begin to crumble. In a study by Lewinsohn (1987) middle age is described as "a point in life when you realize that you may never become what you dreamed—famous, rich, whatever" (p. 69). The author utilizes this observation to explain his position that there is a significant increase in depression in midlife.

The theme of loss generally is heightened during midlife and may coalesce around such circumstances as the loss of one's youthfulness and attractiveness, and the loss of one's parents.

As the average life span increases, it has become more usual for people to be confronted with the death of the second parent during midlife, at a time when they are already experiencing concerns about their own mortality. This intensifies the anxieties evoked by the midlife crisis. Among the themes most frequently expressed by midlife adults in this situation are "Now I am an orphan," "I am most likely the next in line to die," and "You feel young as long as one of your parents is alive." The death of the last surviving parent signals the need to come to terms with the inevitability of one's own mortality. Prior to this point it is common to avoid thinking about one's own death because of the discomfort and anxiety associated with such thoughts.

To the extent that individuals are invested in warding off a sense of their own mortality, they are harboring an adaptive illusion insofar as it allows them to function with less anxiety, an illusion that is typically dismantled during the course of the midlife crisis.

Elliot Jacques, in his celebrated paper, "Death and the Midlife Crisis" (1965), has referred to the awareness of personal death as the crux of the midlife experience:

> The entry upon the psychological scene of the reality and inevitability of one's own eventual personal death, that is the central and crucial feature of the midlife phase—the feature which precipitates the critical nature of the period. Death— at the conscious level—instead of being a general conception, or an event experienced in terms of the loss of someone else, becomes a personal matter, one's own death, one's own real and actual mortality. [p. 506]

Jacques describes individuals who respond to the midlife crisis with an intensification of activity that is designed to counteract the implications of the aging process: "The compulsive attempts, in many men and women reaching middle age, to remain young, the hypochrondrical concern over health and appearance, the emergence of sexual promiscuity in order to prove youth and potency . . . they are attempts at a race against time" (p. 511).

In normal development these attempts at what Jacques calls the "evasion of awareness of death" ultimately give way to a sense of resignation and adaptation to the limitations and finiteness of life. The working-through process in the midlife crisis involves the ability to mourn one's own eventual death.

Ernest Becker (1973), in his Pulitzer Prize-winning book, *The Denial of Death*, discusses the terror of death as an acquired fear that human beings need to counteract through the development of illusions. To exist with an ongoing awareness of one's true state of vulnerability and mortality is intolerable, and so we build defensive walls to insulate ourselves from these truths. Becker points out that developmentally the child is unaware of the knowledge of death prior to the age of 3 to 5, and that only gradually thereafter does he reach a full recognition of the meaning of death as something that eventually takes everyone away. This process can take up to the ninth or tenth year of life. Becker draws from the writings of Zilboorg in connecting the fear of death and the instinct of self-preservation.

> The fear of death must be present behind all our normal functioning, in order for the organism to be armed toward self-preservation. But the fear of death cannot be present constantly in one's mental functioning, else the organism could not function . . . . [There is] the ever-present fear of death in the normal biological functioning of our instinct of self-preservation, as well as our utter obliviousness to this fear in our conscious life. [p. 16]

Becker views this as an ongoing paradox in life.

Hence, as we get older the acids of life force us to recognize unpleasant truths about the human condition such as aging, decline of functioning, illness, and mortality. Thus it becomes increasingly difficult to maintain one's illusions about endless time to attain future goals and to ignore one's limitations.

The role of illusions about immortality and the impact of disillusionment that occurs in response to life-threatening illnesses is central to the writings of Elisabeth Kübler-Ross, who is best known for her work with terminal cancer patients. In *On Death and Dying* (1969) she describes the characteristic stages that individuals traverse in dealing with their own impending death. Kübler-Ross delineates five stages that many individuals experience in their reaction to the diagnosis of advanced cancer that will probably result in death: (1) denial, (2) anger, (3) bargaining, (4) depression, and (5) acceptance. It is not meant to imply that these are discrete stages without overlap from the adjacent stages, but rather that there is a predictable succession of reactions on the way toward acceptance of death. In effect the first stage involves the puncturing of the illusion of immortality and the utilization of the primitive defense of denial to counteract the unwanted truth. As reality gradually takes hold, the defense of denial weakens and is replaced by the affect of anger, which generally is experienced in some variation of "Why does this have to happen to me!" In the next stage, bargaining, the individual attempts to exert some control over the course and outcome of the disease by striking a deal with the powers that be: "Let me live until my daughter's wedding next year" or "If I follow good nutrition and adhere to my medical regimen, I can defy the statistical odds." It is in this stage, when the bargaining doesn't work, and is exposed as illusory, that the ultimate experience of disillusionment sets in. The recognition of the true state of affairs and the inability to alter them leads to the stage of depression. This is followed by the final stage of acceptance, in which one comes to terms with the inevitability of death and there are no further illusions. Although these stages were outlined by Kübler-Ross from her observations with patients with terminal illnesses, it appears likely that they are applicable to the process of dealing with other life-threatening diseases in the era of AIDS, in which there may be a prolonged course from the time of diagnosis to the point of death.

2

The Themes of Illusion and Disillusionment in Psychoanalytic Theory

To endure life remains, when all is said, the first duty of all living beings. Illusion can have no value if it makes this more difficult for us.

Sigmund Freud
"Thoughts for the Times on War and Death"

While various psychoanalytic theories give some attention to the role of illusion and disillusionment, they vary widely in the extent to which they draw upon them as explanatory psychodynamic concepts. Some theorists place greater emphasis on the role of illusion, while others are more intrigued with the impact of disillusionment on personality formation and psychodynamics. Thus, Freud stressed the central role of illusion in his understanding of the perversions, Winnicott gave great importance to the role of illusion in early development, and Kohut highlighted the role of early disillusionment in the resistance to the establishment of what he refers to as selfobject transferences. Mahler's developmental theory, perhaps more than any other, revolves around the child's experience of illusion and disillusionment during the first three years of life. Other psychoanalytic writers, such as Jacobson, Modell, Fromm, and Mitchell, have also discussed the role of illusion or disillusionment in their work, in varying degrees of importance, and these theorists are also considered in this chapter.

SIGMUND FREUD

The concept of illusion was crucial in Freud's discovery and development of psychoanalysis. Much of Freud's early work evolved around his conviction that prevailing assumptions about the human psyche needed to be challenged. In the culture of late nineteenth century Vienna it was believed that children were devoid of sexuality. Through the painstaking study of his patients' dreams, uncovered repressed longings, and symptom formations, Freud came to the conclusion that this belief was an illusion. In formulating the libido theory, Freud took a position quite radical for that era, that sexuality was a basic human instinct from birth on, and that this instinct sought expression in various ways throughout the earliest years of life. Freud's discovery of infantile sexuality, which was scorned for many years by the medical community, was gradually accepted and became the basis of his formulation about psychosexual stages of development, which culminated in the child's resolution of the Oedipus complex.

Freud (1927b) maintained that "what is characteristic of illusions is that they are derived from human wishes" (p. 31). For Freud it is errors in perception driven by a wish fulfillment component that constitute illusions. Hence, the need to view children as nonsexual was, according to Freud, the basis for that widely held false belief, that is, illusion.

In Freud's (1911) view, a milestone in early development occurs when the supremacy of the pleasure principle gives way to the reality principle. This is a transitional process that culminates in the transformation from a pleasure ego into a reality ego. Where id is, there ego shall be. For Freud, the core of neurosis is the avoidance of reality. One of the goals of psychoanalytic treatment is to facilitate the relinquishing of illusions about the self and the world and to enable the individual to deal appropriately with reality, which was formerly too threatening to encounter.

However, there is a universal tendency, especially at times of increased stress, to perpetuate illusions designed to obfuscate the discomfort of unpleasure. As Strenger (1989) points out, "Human beings are always drawn back to the state in which they can disregard the nature of reality as it is, and hence the battle against the pleasure principle is never won for good" (p. 596). Freud equated maturity with the acceptance of the reality principle, and classical analytic technique involves exhorting the patient to relinquish the gratifying distortions of reality. Thus, for Freud illusions are often manifestations of infantile functioning and need to be renounced in favor of mature functioning, which adheres to the dictates of the reality principle.

Freud was interested in exploring the connection between illusion and the need for religion. In his monograph "The Future of an Illusion" (1927b), Freud proposed that religion "comprises a system of wishful illusions together with a disavowal of reality" (p. 43). It was Freud's contention that the need for religion was rooted in an ongoing longing for the strong father. For Freud the awareness of vulnerability and helplessness as part and parcel of the human condition leads to a need for protection, which in turn is transformed into a belief in religion, with God as the representation of the powerful father. Freud maintained that although the child's first love object is the mother who also provides the first "protection against all the undefined dangers which threaten it [the child] in the external world—its first protection against anxiety . . . in this function [of protection] the mother is soon replaced by the stronger father, who retains this position for the rest of childhood" (p. 24). Hence, it is the sense of helplessness and the need for protection from a powerful parental figure that propels us to embrace religion. Freud refers to religious doctrines as illusions that allow us to reduce anxiety about the meaning of life and death.

In formulating his views on the basic nature of human beings, Freud was strongly influenced by the world events of his era. The massive destructiveness of World War I and the rise of communism in the Soviet Union served to further the development of his dual-instinct theory. In proposing the libido theory,

Freud emphasized the life-affirming and pleasure-seeking side of human organisms, but he also believed that there was a counterpoint to man's loving nature. His early dual-instinct theory, which highlighted sexual instincts and self-preservation instincts, was gradually revised and eventually replaced by his drive theory based on the primacy of sexual drives and aggressive drives. The importance of sexual drives (infantile sexuality and psychosexual stages of development) preceded the subsequent equal emphasis given to the role aggressive drives in Freudian theory.

The destruction to human life in World War I was particularly distressing to Freud, and had a significant effect in shaping his formulations about the uncivilized, aggressive, destructive forces inherent in human nature. The themes of illusion and disillusionment are heavily underscored in a paper published by Freud in the midst of World War I, in which he sharpened his thinking about the role of aggression as a basic drive. In this thoughtful but relatively underrecognized paper, entitled "Thoughts for the Times on War and Death" (1915b), Freud discussed the disillusionment of war and the illusion of man's basic goodness. Freud was horrified by the brutality of the soldiers representing the nations at war. This led him to consider that it is an illusion to have the belief that in civilized countries the process of socialization and the influence of education is sufficient to transform man's inherent evil tendencies into altruistic ones. Freud argued that although it is a prevalent assumption that the process of socialization promotes the attainment of a higher plane of individual morality, "In reality, there is no such thing as eradicating evil tendencies" (p. 295). Thus, for Freud, the brutality of World War I, the most destructive war in the history of mankind up until that point, forced us to acknowledge the power and persistence of the aggressive instinct in humans. For Freud disillusionment related to the destruction of an illusion:

> Our mortification and our grievous disillusionment regarding the uncivilized behavior of our world-compatriots

in this war are shown to be unjustified. They were based on an illusion to which we had abandoned ourselves. In reality our fellow citizens have not sunk so low as we feared, because they had never risen so high as we believed. [p. 285]

In this passage Freud conveyed his pessimism about man's capacity to sustain only loving, caring, and civilized connections with one another. The inference is that it is illusory to view man as basically good, moral, and altruistic without considering his potential for uncivilized behavior emanating from one's aggressive drives. Such thoughts were instrumental to Freud in his evolution of the dual-instinct theory.

As his analytic investigation progressed, Freud (1932) became increasingly committed to the position that there is an inherent death instinct that "turns into the destructive instinct if . . . it is directed outwards, on to objects" (p. 211). He maintained the view that to attempt to eliminate human aggression was indeed an illusion. In a letter written in his later years to Albert Einstein, Freud stated,

> The Russian Communists, too, hope to be able to cause human aggressiveness to disappear by guaranteeing the satisfaction of all material needs and by establishing equality in other respects among all the members of the community. That, in my opinion, is an illusion. . . . There is no question of getting rid entirely of human aggressive impulses; it is enough to try to divert them to such an extent that they need not find expression in war. [1932, p. 211]

Thus, Freud had come to view war as an unfortunate and overdetermined expression of man's aggressive instinct, and it was an illusion to think that nations could coexist in ongoing peaceful harmony. The best that could be hoped for was to divert the aggressive instincts of man into channels that did not necessarily lead to war and its horrific consequences.

Freud regarded difficulties in the resolution of the Oedipus complex as the cornerstone of all psychoneuroses. He postulated that boys and girls initially harbor the illusion that there is no difference between the sexes in their anatomical makeup. Subsequently, with the advent of the realization of the existence of anatomical differences, castration anxiety exerts a powerful impact on development. According to classical psychoanalytic theory castration anxiety is a prelude to the Oedipus complex in girls, while it is the Oedipus complex that leads to castration anxiety in boys. In both situations there occurs a profound disillusionment that must be negotiated. For the boy it is the loss of the illusion that he can possess his original love object (the mother). Freud did not emphasize the illusion–disillusionment aspect of this process, but rather the necessary adaptation the boy must make after taking into account the true nature of the situation— that a bigger, more powerful rival exists whose claim on the mother takes priority over his own. Thus, the boy, under the impact of fear of retaliation for his sexual longings and wishes for the mother and aggressive impulses toward the rival father, comes to relinquish his oedipal strivings. In effect in normal development the boy under the sway of the reality principle resolves the conflict by identifying with the father and later seeking out a woman of his own who is similar to the mother.

For the little girl the situation is somewhat different. She must contend with the disillusionment of not having the prized possession bestowed to boys, that is, a penis. Freud and his followers took the position that there are three main alternative pathways for the resolution of castration anxiety in girls. The predominant route is for the girl to relinquish her wish for a penis, that is, penis envy, and to assume passive-feminine receptive attitudes and roles. In Freud's times this was considered to be the most adaptive and most common resolution. The second alternative is for the girl to deny her castrated state and to compete with boys as if she has an illusory penis. She does not accept her more limited position and instead may express her continuing penis envy by pursuing a professional career or by assuming the role of a woman in a man's world. This view seems highly outdated in the 1990s in light of the prevalence of women who succeed in professional life without compromising their femininity. Moreover, it is this aspect of classical theory that has most enraged the community of the feminist movement, and has led to extensive anti-Freudian sentiments and reactions. The third pathway is toward lesbianism, in which, according to the theory, the girl does not shift her libidinal attachment toward the father in an attempt to restore her missing organ through her connection with him, but instead remains pathologically attached to other females.

Within the Freudian framework the classical position does not sufficiently consider the mourning aspect of the loss of the illusory penis in girls, and the loss of the oedipal attachment to the mother in boys. This is because these Freudian formulations are couched largely in terms of the anxiety related to the unacceptable and dangerous drives attendant to this phase of development and the fear of retaliatory consequences.

Many individuals do not resolve their conflicts around castration anxiety and the Oedipus complex in traditional ways. Psychoanalysts have increasingly recognized such entities as the "oedipal winner," reflecting those people who bask in the glory of oedipal victory by virtue of having been preferred by the parent of the opposite sex and having dethroned the same-sex parent, and the so-called phallic woman, who unconsciously is unable to acknowledge her lack of a penis. For Freud, resolutions that take the form of perversions were most strongly generated by illusions that serve the purpose of temporizing castration anxiety.

It is in the syndromes of fetishism and transvestism that the role of illusion is most fully described. Freud maintained that every neurosis contains an element of wish-fulfilling falsifications, that is, illusions. He was particularly impressed with this feature in cases in which fetishism was a prominent symptom. Fetishism is generally viewed as a perversion in males, in which the individual requires the presence of a specific object in order to perform sexually. Among the typical fetishes are shoes, earrings, and long hair, which Freud regarded as penis symbols. Other common fetishes are women's underwear and lingerie. Freud emphasized that adult fetishism has its roots in the boy's illusion that females also possess a penis. In his highly regarded paper entitled "Fetishism," he stated, "What had happened, therefore, was that the boy had refused to take cognizance of the fact perceived by him that a woman has no penis. No, that cannot be true, for if a woman can be castrated then his own penis is in danger" (1927a, p. 153). Hence, in the adult fetishist an illusion is created in which the inanimate object stands for (symbolically) the woman with a penis. This illusion of the female penis is designed to counteract anxiety about castration. "[Fetishism] remains a token of triumph over the threat of castration and a safeguard against it; it also saves the fetishist from being a homosexual by endowing women with the attribute which makes them acceptable as sexual objects" (p. 154).

Greenacre, who follows in the Freudian tradition, presents a similar formulation about fetishism:

> This object, the fetish, clearly represents the penis and is necessary to ward off the intense and incapacitating castration panic which the patient would otherwise suffer. [1960, p. 191] . . . Its function is a focal one to represent the female phallus and thereby through visual, tactile, and olfactory incorporating to insure the fetishist of his own possession of it. [1969, p. 162] . . . Both fetish and transitional object are security props which serve to bring the current anxiety-provoking situation under the illusory control of the individual infant or man. [1969, p. 150] . . . It is this capacity for illusion . . . which is of special importance in the forming of both the transitional object and the fetish. [1969, p. 157]

In different terms it can be said that the fetishist, as is true of other types of perversion as well, develops an outlet for erotic gratification that enables him to fortify his uncertain genitality. Consequently, for such individuals resorting to repeated fetishist activity is usually ego syntonic, and it is rare for them to be uncomfortable enough to seek treatment for this as a problem. Freud pointed out that fetishes usually appear belatedly in the course of an analysis, and without a great deal of anxiety in the patient about this aspect of his functioning. As a rule such patients are not especially inclined to give up their fetish, and become motivated only by shameful feelings around the fear of exposure and ridicule.

Although Freudian theory asserts that fetishism is based on the need for the illusion of a female penis in order to counteract intense castration anxiety, it is important to note that in such individuals this illusion coexists with the awareness of the reality that women do not possess a penis. In other words, the fetishist functions as if he knows reality on one level and denies reality on another level. Insofar as he simultaneously knows reality and acts as if he doesn't know reality, it can be said that the need for connection with the woman's illusory penis (through the fetish) outstrips adherence to the reality principle. Fenichel (1945), a follower of Freud, described this apparent contradiction in terms of splitting and denial:

> The ego of such persons is actually split into a conscious part that knows reality and an unconscious part that denies reality. [p. 131] ... Fetishism as an attempt to deny a truth known simultaneously by another part of the personality presupposes a certain split of the person's ego. Persons whose childhood history has enabled them to make an exceptionally intense use of the defense mechanism of denial are, therefore, predisposed for the development of fetishism. [p. 343]

In transvestism, or cross-dressing, as it is currently described, the role of the illusory penis and castration anxiety is also central. Freud viewed this as a disorder in men who function with the false unconscious belief that women possess a penis, and they identify with this "phallic woman" through cross-dressing. The transvestite, according to Freud, is consumed with castration anxiety, and he allays this dilemma by concealing his penis beneath his feminine appearance (i.e., dressed in women's clothing). In essence, cross-dressing becomes a way in which he can act out the illusion of a woman with a penis and simultaneously avert the threat of castration by secretly hiding his penis. Male transvestites are often not homosexual, inasmuch as the goal is to identify with the powerful phallic mother, but not necessarily to emulate her object choice. The central dynamic in cross-dressing is to refute the danger of castration by masquerading as a woman.

Female cross-dressing is a woman's attempt to make believe she is a man with a penis. By identifying with the image of a man, she is able to deny her unwanted femininity and its implications of being castrated. Freud viewed cross-dressing in women as a displacement of penis envy to an envy of appearing masculine. He distinguished male and female cross-dressing by way of pointing out that the male can reassure himself that he retains his penis in the course of playing the game, while for the female no such corresponding reassurance can take place. As in the situation with fetishism, Freud took the position that transvestism is a perversion aimed at proving that there is no castration. Such proof, illusory as it might be, often serves as a precondition for the attainment of sexual gratification.

The following case describes the struggle of a young man who was heavily involved in cross-dressing.

Kevin, a handsome and very masculine looking 23-year-old college student, sought psychotherapy because of his anxiety that he would be seen when he went out in the street dressed in his mother's clothes. He was aware that he turned to cross dressing as a way to ameliorate feelings of anxiety, but he did not understand the source of these feelings. He referred to this cross-dressing as his "fix," and he was concerned that "I don't run my fix, my fix runs me." He expressed the wish that he could have greater choice over "doing my fix," and the attainment of choice over compulsion in this matter was established as a goal of the therapy.

Kevin grew up in an Irish Catholic family. He had one sibling, a sister three years his senior. He described his mother as dominant and his father as more of a buddy than a parent. His earliest memories included seeing his father lying across his mother's knee being spanked by her, and Kevin felt terrified that she was hurting him. At the time he came for treatment, Kevin was engaged to a young woman whom he described as being "soft and fluffy." He was attracted to her but was fearful of sexual intercourse. The intensity of his castration anxiety was revealed in the initial consultation, when he several times made a slip of the tongue by referring to the woman's "wound" instead of womb.

Kevin's cross-dressing was usually accompanied by a fantasy of a man being subjugated by a woman and being forced to wear women's clothing. He would masturbate under these conditions about ten times a week. He felt secure and feminine when dressed as a woman, but he was not attracted to other men. Thus, to be a passive victim, to be a man in women's clothing, and to identify with his phallic mother were all ways of denying the presence of his penis, and thereby circumventing the danger of castration. In other words, to act as if he was an unassertive male with his penis concealed beneath women's clothing was a way of saying, "You need not take my penis away, since I already appear to be castrated!"

In the course of therapy we were gradually able to connect his castration anxiety and his need for his "fix." He described his worries about being "kicked in the balls" and "catching my penis in my zipper." He stated that he didn't want to be a woman, but that there is something threatening and dangerous about being an assertive man. We came to see how it felt safer for Kevin to be a man when to outer appearances he looked like a woman, but down deep he knew he was really a man. Along with this his abhorrence of the vagina was profound. He experienced the vagina as an insatiable orifice, and he blatantly stated his fear that "a woman's cunt can cut my prick off." His association of contact with the vagina and damage to his genitals was further illustrated in his description of "skinning" his penis when he "dry humped" his fiancée.

The working-through phase of treatment involved Kevin's growing awareness that his compulsion to cross-dress was based on the need to rely on the illusion that he could successfully masquerade as a woman with a hidden penis. As he gained insight he came to recognize that by dressing up in his mother's clothing he was identifying with her, and at the same time making a statement that "you can't take away my penis because it looks like there's none there." These realizations made it increasingly difficult for Kevin to comfortably resort to his "fix." His cross-dressing episodes became less and less frequent, and when he did resort to his "fix" he assumed greater responsibility for doing so. He reported in one session, "Something is changing. I did it this week, but got no kick." In another session he stated, "The thoughts of putting on my mother's clothes is stimulating. The only thing that keeps me from doing it is knowing how I'll feel afterward." Several months later he said, "The 'fix' isn't worth it. I feel bad afterward and I gotta tell you about doing it." The utilization of positive transference feelings and the acquisition of higher level ego functioning, that is, the capacity to anticipate consequences, are reflected in these statements. However, his gains did not accrue linearly and without setbacks. A part of Kevin did not wish to give up his "fix," which had both provided him with sexual satisfaction and assuaged his castration anxiety. With increased understanding about the source of his anxiety he had less need for the "fix" and he sustained longer intervals between "fixes." At the same time he described how much he resented the loss of excitement that accompanied his reduced investment in cross-dressing. He lamented that "feeling better is somewhat depressing."

Ultimately, Kevin married his fiancée and with the help of continued psychotherapy he was able to work through his castration anxiety to a moderate degree. His interest in cross-dressing became drastically reduced, but along with this he felt a tremendous void in his life. For some time he experienced the pain of being in no-man's land, which is a phase in psychotherapy in which the patient gives up a major defense and feels lost without it until he finds some new source of satisfaction to take its place. Eventually, it was the joy of fatherhood that allowed Kevin to find an ongoing source of genuine satisfaction, although he continued to miss the excitement of the world of cross-dressing.

In summary, the concepts of illusion and disillusionment are encompassed in several ways in Freud's psychoanalytic thinking. His early work on infantile sexuality debunked the prevailing illusion of the times that children were devoid of sexuality. In his formulations about the need for religion, Freud took the position that religious doctrines are illusions aimed at reducing anxiety about issues in life and death that instill feelings of helplessness. His theory of an inherent death instinct were shaped by the disillusioning impact of the human destructiveness seen in World War I and his concomitant recognition that the belief in man's basic goodness is indeed an illusion. Freud maintained that unresolved issues in the Oedipus complex were the basis for the development of all psychoneuroses, and the loss of the illusion, in the preoedipal phase, of the lack of anatomical differences between the sexes ushers in concerns about castration anxiety, which is intricately related to the Oedipus complex. The role of illusion is most thoroughly adumbrated by Freud in his writings about perversions. This is especially depicted in his studies of fetishism and transvestism.

EDITH JACOBSON

Edith Jacobson was at the center of the second generation of classical Freudian theorists known as ego psychologists. Spearheaded by the concepts of Anna Freud, who elaborated on the role of specific defense mechanisms, and Heinz Hartmann, who developed the view that autonomous functions of the ego were present from the beginning of life, rather than part of an ego that emerged from the id, ego psychology became the mainstay of American psychoanalysis. Accordingly, a shift took place in psychoanalytic practice in which the analysis of defenses and the building up of sturdy ego functions became a chief focus alongside of the analysis of sexual and aggressive conflicts emanating from the id. Jacobson's contribution coalesced around the development of the self and the object world and the understanding of depression.

Jacobson viewed disillusionment in one's love objects as a central trigger of depression. A predisposition toward depression occurs, according to Jacobson, when disillusionment in one's parents as omnipotent figures takes place at time when the ego functions are not yet well established and resilient. In a classic paper entitled "The Effect of Disappointment on Ego and Super-ego Formation in Normal and Depressive Development" (1946), Jacobson related the role of disillusionment and ego development. She discussed the German word for disappointment, *Enttäuschung*, which translates in English as disillusionment, and pointed out that the gradual disappointments and frustrations provided by the parents are necessary for healthy ego development to take place. Jacobson was concerned about the timing and dosage of such disillusionments and she emphasized that disillusionments that occur too early can be traumatic and have an adverse impact on ego development. By this she meant that the gradual disillusionments experienced by the child can be expected to have a constructive impact on the child's ego development in general, and more specifically on his acquisition of reality testing:

> If the child meets with decisive disappointments at a time when the infantile ego has asserted itself to some extent, disillusionment in the parents results in a realistic evaluation of parents and object world as well as of himself, which is the prerequisite of normal ego formation. [p. 131] . . . [On the other hand], if such an extreme deflation in the parental images sets in early, the ego of the child is affected deeply by it. Since for the child the magic power of the parents is, at this stage, the main source of narcissistic support, deflation of their images must necessarily tear down the infantile ego at the same time. [p. 132]

Thus, Jacobson believed that early disillusionment affects ego growth, and is the precursor of depressive problems in adults. She adhered to the position that in early childhood it is essential for healthy development that the child maintain the illusion that his parents possess magical and omnipotent powers. As differentiation proceeds, the child recognizes that sources of nurturance and protection come from outside himself, and he remains, for a while, invested in the magic omnipotence of his parents: "After having lost his belief in his own omnipotence, the child is convinced of and participates in the fantasized magic omnipotence of his parents" (p. 130).

When the expected gratifications for the child are not forthcoming, as in the case of early maternal deprivation, the child at this stage experiences disillusionment in his object. This may lead to the withdrawal of libidinal attachment and, in turn, with the devaluation of the object at a time when the child's ego still requires the illusion of the magic power of the parents as a primary narcissistic support. To the extent that the child's self image at this stage is still substantially entwined with his image of his significant objects (bad mother = bad me), disillusionment in others is tantamount to self-deprecatory affects.

According to Jacobson, when disillusioning experiences in the preoedipal stage of development results in the deflation of self and other, "The ego reacts with various attempts of self-restoration which are the more successful the more advanced the ego-development is at the time of injury" (p. 142). Thus, for Jacobson it is not the severity of the child's disillusionment in the parents as much as the point of development when it occurs that is crucial for emotional development. When the child has had the opportunity to acquire sufficient ego strength, he can weather disillusionment provided it is not excessively severe or abrupt. In the first few years of life the ego of the child is insufficiently formed to be able to withstand the assault of disillusionment in his idealized objects. Hence, truncated ego development is frequently the result of premature disillusionment.

We can see from the above that in Jacobson's thinking the role of illusion, and especially disillusionment, are intricately related to ego development.

D. W. WINNICOTT

The role of illusion in psychological development is most prominent in the writings of the British object relations theorist D. W. Winnicott. He formulated such concepts as the good-enough mother, the holding environment, and the transitional object, which have become integral ideas in the training of psychodynamic psychotherapists. It is Winnicott's thinking about the function of transitional objects in the first year of life that draws upon the importance of illusion. As the child experiences the initial waves of differentiation of self and object (which is a very gradual process), he needs to find new ways to soothe himself particularly at times of distress and discomfort. With the beginning awareness of separateness the child starts to recognize that his needs are satisfied by something outside of himself, that is, the ministrations of the mother. At the same time there occurs a growing awareness that these soothing ministrations are not ubiquitously available.

Winnicott defined the transitional object as the first "not-me possession." Specifically, the transitional object is usually a blanket or some other soft object that the child latches onto in a special way, and it is used by the child as an early defense against anxiety. In essence the transitional object stands in as a representation for the comforting ministrations of the caregiver. It is not an internal object, but rather reflects a transition from a state of being merged to a state of being in relation to the caregiver as something outside and separate from oneself. Hence, it is a way that the child discovers to soothe himself when separate or apart from mother. One could say that it is a primitive way of being with mother in the absence of mother. Winnicott regarded the transitional object as a necessary step in healthy emotional development.

Prior to the formation of the transitional object, good-enough mothering, according to Winnicott, involves an almost complete adaptation to the needs of the infant. This promotes in the child the illusion of omnipotence and magical control over mother. The mother, by being responsive to the basic needs of her infant, provides an experience in which an illusion flourishes. Since differentiation has not yet occurred, and the state of merger prevails, the infant experiences the nurturing supplies from the mother as something that he himself brings about. When the good-enough mother anticipates the infant's needs and is responsive to them, the infant feels that he brings the breast into being. Winnicott (1951) called this "the moment of illusion." Thus, in normal early development the natural maternal ministrations foster a climate in which the infant creates the illusion that the breast, and its forthcoming supplies, are part of the infant.

The transitional object becomes the heir to the earliest illusion of omnipotence and magical control over the breast. As differentiation begins the infant achieves the capacity to perpetuate the illusion of omnipotence and control over her environment in increasingly complex ways. For Winnicott illusion refers to a self-soothing activity, what he called "a resting place of illusion," which is essential for growth and can be activated throughout the course of life.

The construction of a transitional object, and cathecting onto it, represents the child's attempt to bridge the gap between the illusion of oneness (the state of merger) and the beginning awareness of separateness. It is a phase of psychological maturation that is literally in transition between these two states of mind. Eventually, with the acquisition of greater ego structure, the child arrives at a more realistic appraisal of self and object, but during this period the child forges a compromise between illusion and reality. For Winnicott transitional experiences and transitional objects represent a place between subjective omnipotence and objective reality. Through his investment in the inanimate transitional object, the child affords himself the opportunity to retain the illusion that the soothing functions supplied by the mother are still present and under his control, while at the same time he demonstrates that he is on the way toward acknowledging the reality of separateness. This reality can only be accepted as a gradual process, so for a time the child needs to cushion the psychic pain of separateness through this newly discovered illusion of omnipotence. In essence he imagines that the benefits derived from contact with the transitional object serve as a substitute for those previously received from the mother, which the child believes himself to have created. Winnicott maintained that the transitional object does not "go inside," that is, it is not internalized. Rather, according to Winnicott, the fate of this important construct is that it gradually loses meaning for the child as he acquires stronger ego functioning. However, it seems to me that the experience of creating and utilizing a transitional object sets the stage for the acquisition of an aspect of psychic structure; that is, the child recognizes on some emotional level that he has the capacity to discover soothing functions for himself that can be employed throughout life in different forms at times of stress.

This point of view is echoed by Marian Tolpin (1971), who suggests that through his connection with his transitional object the child can control the dosage of self-soothing to a degree that may be even more satisfying than that which the "good-enough" mother can supply. In her classic paper, "On the Beginnings of a Cohesive Self," Tolpin states, "Circumscribed losses of the mother in her role as need-satisfying soother and regulator not only are inevitable and unavoidable during infancy; they are also necessary in optimal doses if mastery of separation from her and individuation of the psyche are to occur" (p. 328). This is facilitated through the transitional object, for example the blanket, which in turn is decathected gradually as its soothing functions undergo internalization.

In considering the relationship between internalization and the transitional object, Tolpin, who is aligned with the self psychology school of thought, takes a position that is quite different from Winnicott's. She argues that through the use of the blanket as a transitional object the child experiences cathexis, optimal loss, and internalization of supporting maternal function, which build the ego during infancy. Tolpin concludes, "When the soothing functions of the mother and blanket are effectively internalized, a normal phase of relative structural insufficiency has passed. The fate of the outgrown transitional object is to 'pass away' because it does 'go inside' as soothing psychic structure" (p. 333).

Winnicott (1951) recognized that in order for emotional growth to occur, the good-enough mother must also provide disillusioning experiences for the child:

> The mother, at the beginning, by an almost 100% adaptation affords the infant the opportunity for the illusion that her breast is part of the infant. It is, as it were, under magi-

cal control. . . . The mother's eventual task is gradually to disillusion the infant, but she has no hope of success unless at first she has been able to give sufficient opportunity for illusion. [p. 238] . . . The mother's main task (next to providing opportunity for illusion) is disillusionment. . . . If things go well in this gradual disillusionment process, the stage is set for the frustrations that we gather together under the word *weaning*. [p. 240]

In this way Winnicott envisioned the role of disillusionment (subsequent to the opportunity for illusions of omnipotence) to be a central precondition for the child's ability to build up frustration tolerance and reality testing, which are essential ego functions. Thus, the task of the mother is to introduce disillusionment, after providing the opportunity for illusions, so as to promote the gradual acquisition of reality testing. In Winnicott's view, healthy emotional development involves the ultimate relinquishing of illusions in favor of the acceptance of reality.

Winnicott's elaboration of the concept of the transitional object has had a substantial impact on the field of psychotherapy. Many therapists have utilized the concept in creative ways in dealing with their patients. The following vignette is illustrative.

Penny, an attractive 28-year-old dance therapist, came to therapy after a series of unsuccessful relationships in which she felt mistreated. Her pattern of involvement was to become quickly available in a new relationship with men who would then behave in an unreliable and distancing way toward her. She would ultimately feel taken advantage of and emotionally abandoned, and the relationship would falter. She would subsequently repeat this pattern in her next relationship. These issues highlighted her dependency and masochistic features, and they became the central focus of the treatment. She gradually came to understand her powerful identification with her mother and the way she played out her mother's ways of relating to her father. Penny was able to utilize the insights gained in her therapy, and she married a man who provided stability and sensitivity to her needs. Part of what had enabled Penny to turn things around, and to find a constructive and reciprocally caring involvement, was the impact of the therapeutic relationship. She felt valued by her male therapist, and he demonstrated his willingness to relax the frame of treatment with regard to her periodic financial constraints and scheduling problems. This allowed her to feel that she had a meaningful impact in the therapeutic relationship and to experience the therapist as genuinely responsive to her legitimate needs.

Six months into the marriage her husband was awarded a writing professorship in England for one year. Penny committed herself to going with him, but she was very upset at the prospect of having to disrupt her therapy. Many sessions were devoted to dealing with her anxiety about losing her connection to the therapist. Even though she was the one to be leaving, she experienced it as an abandonment from a necessary object. It was clear that her dependency and separation issues had not been sufficiently worked through. As the time neared for her departure, the therapist offered to give her a small ceramic animal that he kept on the table next to his telephone. He suggested that she could take this with her as a reminder of their relationship. His plan was to provide her with a transitional object that she could use to soothe herself in his absence.

Penny was delighted by her therapist's offering, and she gladly accepted the inanimate object. This paved the way for her being able to separate in a less frantic way. While she was in England, she wrote several times and described how comforted she felt by holding on to the ceramic animal during periods of loneliness and anxiety. She reported that the surface had a tactile grainy feel to it that was especially comforting. Eventually, she returned to continue and complete her therapy.

In this vignette the therapist was able to apply his understanding of Winnictott's concept of the transitional object in a way that was particularly valuable for this patient. One could cite many other examples in everyday psychotherapeutic practice. For instance, it is frequently reported by patients with structural defects that it is helpful to them, at times of stress, to be able to call into the therapist's answering machine at a time that they know she is not there and hear her voice on her recorded message. Thus, the answering machine serves as a transitional object that may also be used by certain patients as a way of maintaining the connection to the therapist during periods of separation such as vacations.

MARGARET MAHLER

Margaret Mahler's work built upon Freud's drive theory. She is best known for her infant observation studies and her formulations about child development in the first three years of life. While Freud emphasized instinctual aim, and source, along with object cathexis during the psychosexual stages, Mahler focused on the nature of the interplay between child and caregiver during normal development. In this vein she is regarded as a pillar of the American object relations school of thought. She outlined three phases that the child negotiates in the first three years: autism, symbiosis, and separation-individuation. To the extent that the mothering one provides an atmosphere in which the child experiences illusion and optimal disillusionment at the phase-appropriate junctions, normal growth and development occur. When there is maternal misattunement to the child's need for illusion and disillusionment, the conditions are set for pathological outcomes that usually carry over into adulthood.

According to Mahler, as the infant moves from the normal autistic phase of the first two months of life toward the overlapping phase of normal symbiosis, he begins to be aware that the satisfaction of his needs comes from outside himself. Nevertheless, at this junction his mental image of himself continues to be primarily fused with that of his mother. Differentiation is a gradual process, and so the illusion of oneness prevails for some months to come. There is a blissfulness that accompanies the exquisite emotional attunement of the phase of symbiosis, and although the maturational spurt pushes the child along to the next developmental phase, there is a part of the child that yearns to recapture the earlier bond between himself and the mothering one. Growing up entails a step-by-step moving away from the normal state of human symbiosis, that is, of oneness with the mother. This moving away is a lifelong mourning process, and many adults search for relationships in which they hope to experience unconditional love, akin to the blissful era of symbiosis. The chief developmental need during the phase of symbiosis is the illusion of a satisfying sense of oneness between what in reality are two separate organisms. The expression of unresolved problems of the symbiotic phase is seen in individuals who are forever patterning their object relationships on the search for the good, need-satisfying (preoedipal) mother, yet at the same time dreading the prospect of reengulfment in symbiosis. There are many clinical examples of such individuals who are in conflict between the wish to re-create a symbiotic-like experience with a new person as a representation of the early (good) mother, and the fear that such closeness would lead to being engulfed and losing one's separate identity.

During the practicing subphase of the stage of separation-individuation, from approximately ages 10 to 18 months, the evolving autonomous functions, particularly upright locomotion, usher in a period of elation, and the child's "love affair with the world" (Mahler et al. 1975, p. 70) is at its height. During this period the junior toddler is more or less oblivious to the true nature of the realities of the world. His activities are guided by the illusion of his own sense of greatness, and he functions as if the world is his oyster. The illusion of merger has waned under the influence of the child's excitement in being able to crawl, walk, and run, which allows him fuller exploration of the environment. In essence, the illusion of merger has now been replaced by the illusion of "the world is my oyster." This state of unbridled well-being is often reactivated in late adolescence and early adulthood before the responsibilities and realities of life bring about disillusionment.

The child at this point does not as yet grasp his limitations in relation to the world, and so for a while he rides the crest of the wave of elation and omnipotence. In his relationship to the mother, he establishes the best of two worlds. On the one hand he uses the mother as a stable home base from which he freely launches in his forays into the world. He is engrossed in his explorations to the point of being oblivious to the whereabouts of his mother. On the other hand, when he is ready to return for "refueling" (Mahler et al. 1975, p. 69), he requires a climate of maternal emotional availability.

The attitude and behavior of the mother at this crossroad in the practicing phase have considerable significance for the further psychological development of the child. If all goes well and the mother of the practicing phase is attuned to the evolving needs of the child for autonomy and refueling, the child moves smoothly forward to the next subphase in separation-individuation, which Mahler referred to as rapprochement. There are two major potential pathological outcomes that result from maternal misattunement during the child's practicing phase. In one direction are those mothers who derive so much gratification from the symbiotic attachment to the child that they are unready to let go and to encourage and support the child's emerging independence. When the mother at this phase is excessively overprotective and infantilizing, it is detrimental to the child's normal need for disengagement and individuation beginning in the second year of life. These children often grow up with conflict around assertiveness and success, which represent destructive attacks on the internal representation of the mother from this stage of development. Another form of misattunement occurs in those mothers who prematurely abandon their toddler and do not make themselves available for refueling at this stage. For the child's development to flourish he requires the best of both worlds (disengagement and refueling) at this time. Children who have experienced premature emotional abandonment during the practicing phase often develop adult relationships that are punctuated by the suffocating need to ensure the emotional presence of the partner, or conversely, punctuated by the illusion of self-sufficiency.

The next subphase in the separation-individuation process, rapprochement, which occurs generally from 15 to 24 months of age, is characterized by the child's increasing intrapsychic awareness of separateness from the mother. The earlier refueling type of contact with the mother, intrinsic to the practicing phase, is now replaced with a need for constant involvement on the part of the child with his mother. The child at this point has begun to experience his own limitations and to increasingly recognize the obstacles that lie in the path of his being on top of the world. The gradual realization that he is a relatively helpless, small, and separate individual in a world that is large, threatening, and unsafe is a painful experience for the toddler. Mahler described this developmental process as follows:

> We found that in the practicing subphase a mood of elation seemed subphase specific, obligatory, and dominant. In addition, this mood often manifested itself in a quasi-delusional but age-adequate sense of grandeur, omnipotence, and conquest. This mood of the junior toddler—at the crest of mastery of many of his autonomous functions, the paradigm of which is locomotion—necessarily had to give way to a more relative appraisal of his smallness in relation to the outside world. A gradual recognition of the disproportion of his illusion of grandeur and the obstacles in the way of successful adaptation to the exigencies of reality has to take place from the fifteenth to eighteenth month onward. [Mahler et al. 1975, p. 213]

The core affective experience of the child during the rapprochement subphase is disillusionment. A powerful sense of deflation occurs as the toddler's ego development allows him to take stock of the true nature of things. As a consequence of his revised picture of himself and the world, in greater congruence with reality, the child attempts to reengage with the mother in an intense, demanding, and dependent fashion. Many mothers find it difficult to accept what on the surface seems to be regressive behavior on the part of the child, and are unable to provide a climate of support that allows the child the opportunity for optimal disillusionment about his previously held beliefs. This creates a pattern of disharmony between child and mother, which Mahler refers to as the rapprochement crisis. In a sense, with the increase in intrapsychic awareness of separateness, the child temporarily recoils from going forward in his maturation, and attempts to reinstate the safe, secure, and more blissful feelings of symbiosis. Mahler (1972) concluded:

> One could regard the entire life cycle as constituting a more or less successful process of distancing from and introjection of the lost symbiotic mother, an eternal longing for the actual or fantasized "ideal state of self," with the latter standing for a symbiotic fusion with the "all good" symbiotic mother, who was at one time part of the self in a blissful state of well being. [p. 338]

To a considerable extent Mahler draws upon the role of illusion and disillusionment in her theoretical formulations. Central to Mahler's theory of separation-individuation is the notion that the child's illusion of an identity based on merger is gradually disconfirmed by reality, and the subsequent internal awareness of separateness is absorbed and accompanied by the experience of disillusionment. In the practicing phase of normal development the child's attitudes, behaviors, and experiences are characterized by an illusion of invulnerability. For Mahler, the subsequent disillusioning collapse of the toddler's belief in his own omnipotence, which occurs during the rapprochement phase, triggers a basic depressive mood within the developing child. The favorable resolution of this depressive response involves grief and sadness as part of a mourning of the loss of the good, need-satisfying symbiotic mother. At the same time there is a pull throughout life, particularly during periods of extreme stress, for symbiotic longings to reemerge.

In the last two decades there has been increased attention to the treatment of patients with preoedipal pathology. Patients with borderline and narcissistic problems, as well as those with other characterological difficulties, have come to represent a substantial portion of the practice of most psychotherapists. These patients often have persistent conflicts around the self in relation to others, and these difficulties are generally rooted in pathology stemming from the early mother–child (preoedipal) relationship. The treatment of these cases often focuses on exploring and addressing certain core illusions and disillusionments that permeate their interpersonal relationships. This is particularly true in cases in which narcissistic illusions about the self and the world prevail. In this regard the theoretical contributions of such theorists as Winnicott, Mahler, Kohut, and Modell have been invaluable in working with these individuals. Clinical cases abound of patients whose core conflicts revolve around the yearning to re-create the exquisite attunement of symbiosis, and others whose search for the all-giving mother leads to repeated disillusionment. In many others the sense of self is deficient and their need for a significant other for completion of the self is fueled by illusions about finding need-gratifying objects who provide unconditional love.

The growing interest in preoedipal pathology has led to an increased focus on the early mother–child dyad, and what has been internalized by the child from this period of development. The listening perspectives of psychotherapists have been strongly influenced by this shift in attention toward developmental deficits. Are the patient's difficulties attributable to early deprivation or overindulgence? Was disillusionment in the child's belief in his own omnipotence and that of his parents too abrupt? Was the rapprochement crisis successfully negotiated? Did the patient as a child internalize a chaotic and erratic holding environment? These are among the conceptual frameworks that modern psychotherapists utilize as they listen to and sort out their patients' material. Presenting problems that heretofore were assumed to be derivatives of unresolved oedipal conflicts are now being considered in the light of preoedipal theories. For example, let us consider the patient who has conflicts around being successful. It is possible that these conflicts emanate from oedipal anxiety about fulfilling the wish to outperform the same-sex parent. It is equally possible, however, that the patient's fear of success has to do with earlier pathology in the mother–child dyad such as the belief that to become too autonomous is to risk premature abandonment and the loss of love from the mother. Similarly, an issue such as fear of retaliation from others for being assertive may derive from unresolved oedipal wishes or the preoedipal discouragement of too much separateness. Only thoughtful attention to the patient's material over a substantial number of sessions will direct us to the central roots of the problem.

Numerous early infant development research studies in the last twenty years (Beebe and Lachmann 1994, Lichtenberg 1983, Stern 1985) have provided mounting evidence that the infant's capacity for differentiation from the mother takes place considerably earlier than Mahler believed. The findings of these studies have called into question Mahler's assumptions about the phase of normal symbiosis, which is based on the illusion of merger as the primary experience of the infant from 2 to 12 months.

Pine (1994), who collaborated extensively with Mahler, has suggested that separation-individuation theory needs to be amended to accommodate the compelling findings of infant research. Pine maintains that in light of these studies we can conceptualize this phase of early development as one in which "merger moments," in which symbiotic feelings hold sway and influence the infant's development, coexist alongside of differentiated moments in the infant's experience. Pine concludes:

> Given what we now know about infant cognition, I would propose that the infant has moments of the experience of boundary-lessness or merger-moments, not an ongoing state lasting weeks or months. That is the modification in Mahler's view that the infant research compels. My prime candidates for such moments of merger are those when the infant, in the mother's arms, having sucked vigorously at breast or bottle, progressively calms and falls into sleep as body tonus relaxes and he or she "melts" into the mother's body . . . . there is clearly no contradiction between the presence of moments of merger in the post feeding drowsy state and the presence of more articulated cognition in other states. [pp. 17–18]

In accepting the critique offered by the infant research studies, Pine attempts to preserve the utility of Mahler's theory by emphasizing the importance of moments of symbiotic merger experience in contrast to the earlier view of symbiosis as an ongoing state in this phase of development. Accordingly, Pine arrives at "a different conception of the symbiotic phase from the one initially presented by Mahler. The findings of the infant research literature certainly have affected this conception. Moments of merger are different from a symbiotic totality" (1994, p. 22).

Pine (1994) has also pointed out that the concept of separation-individuation has been misunderstood to mean that it pertains to separation anxiety. Even many therapists have misapplied it in this way. In fact Mahler utilized this term to convey the toddler's growing *awareness* of separateness, which replaces an earlier belief or assumption about oneness and merger (i.e., an undifferentiated state). It is the relinquishing of the illusion about oneness with mother, under the prevailing forces of reality, at some point between the practicing and rapprochement subphases that characterizes the (waxing and waning) process of separation-individuation.

Galatzer-Levy and Cohler (1993) have criticized Mahler's formulations about the developmental process in the first three years of life on the grounds that it places separateness and autonomy as developmental goals that highlight the attainment of independence at the expense of the need for what they refer to as "the essential other." This criticism seems excessive insofar as it polarizes the need for self-sufficiency versus the need for others. In separation-individuation theory it is not that the need for the significant other is given up; rather, the functions needed from the significant other change according to the shifting developmental needs of the child.

ERICH FROMM

Erich Fromm was one of the forefathers of the school of interpersonal psychoanalysis, which challenged the premises of classical drive theory and placed the ways in which individuals relate as its central concern. Fromm's contributions have been underrecognized outside of this school of thought, but it is noteworthy that he applied the concept of symbiosis to human interaction (1941) more than a decade before Mahler began utilizing this notion as an integral part of separation-individuation theory. Fromm's work took an existential direction in which he viewed man's awareness of his vulnerability, impotence, and mortality as the central source of anxiety. According to Fromm, the child's blissful state of safety and security in utero is disrupted at birth, and this is followed by a gradual awareness of one's separateness and fundamental state of aloneness in the world. As a result the individual responds to the human condition, in which frightening feelings of aloneness and isolation prevail, by developing illusory escapes aimed at re-creating blissful and harmonious attachment to others. For Fromm all neuroses represent in some form an attempt to fortify the illusion of merger with significant others. He describes different personality orientations, each of which is designed to allow the individual to maintain core illusions about blissful security and avoid dealing with the awareness of the reality of separateness.

In his book *Beyond the Chains of Illusion* (1962), Fromm takes the position that mental health involves coming to terms with the existential anxiety about separateness and the sense of aloneness that is characteristic of the human condition: "Man must get rid of illusions that enslave and paralyze him; that he must become aware of the reality inside and outside of him in order to create a world which needs no illusions. Freedom and independence can be achieved only when the chains of illusion are broken" (p. 181).

In essence Fromm arrives at a position similar to Mahler and other developmental theorists in that the quest to revive blissful feelings of symbiotic merger (especially at times of heightened anxiety) is a periodic issue from the cradle to the grave. The therapeutic process is conceived as helping the individual to recognize his anxieties about the human condition and the illusions he has created to cope with them. The goal of treatment for Fromm is to correct interpersonal distortions (i.e., relinquish illusions) in accordance with an accurate appraisal of reality. The assumption in Fromm's writings is that the patient is helped to let go of his illusions and to accept reality. However, it seems to me that insufficient attention is given to techniques for dealing with the pain engendered by disillusionment.

HEINZ KOHUT

The concepts of illusion and disillusionment are woven throughout Kohutian theory. Central to Kohut's thinking is the role of necessary illusions, optimal disillusionment, and defenses against experiencing repeated disillusionment when underlying selfobject needs and longings are reactivated.

Kohut practiced for many years as an eminent classical psychoanalyst before he came to believe that the classical method was not effective in working with certain types of patients with developmental deficits. The treatment of narcissistic patients, for example, was often unsuccessful because in the traditional approach the analyst's interactions were geared toward exhorting the patient to relinquish his pursuit of infantile narcissistic gratifications in deference to the reality assessments made by the ego. Kohut discovered that a more effective approach to these patients was to allow them to establish what he called selfobject transferences in which the patient's early needs, which had been dealt with in an insufficiently responsive manner, could now be reactivated.

As other psychoanalysts came to recognize that they had an increasing number of these type of patients in their practice, and that alternative approaches were needed, they embraced Kohut's formulations and techniques that were central to what he called the self-psychological model. Today the self-psychological approach has a large following and its basic concepts are utilized in the treatment of many different types of disorders.

For Kohut (1971) normal developmental needs during childhood include (1) the need to have illusions about one's self importance and a sense of specialness, what Kohut refers to as "the grandiose self" (p. 107), which is supported by the empathically attuned parent; and (2) illusions about the parents as omnipotent and perfect (replacing an earlier view of the omnipotent and perfect aspects of the self, characteristic of the normal stage of primary narcissism), which Kohut refers to as the idealized other, or "idealized parent imago" (p. 25), and which occur in a climate of acceptance by the parents. Wolf (1993), an early collaborator with Kohut, states, "Such blissful illusions of unique and superlative excellence are not only common but a necessary experience in the developmental history of firm and cohesive selfs" (p. 680).

According to Kohut (1971), when the mirroring needs of the child's grandiose self and the merger needs with the idealized other are met, the foundation is established for the child to move on with a cohesive sense of self to a higher level of functioning:

> Under favorable circumstances (appropriately selective parental response to the child's demand for an echo to and participation in the narcissistic-exhibitionistic manifestations of his grandiose fantasies), the child learns to accept his realistic limitations, the grandiose fantasies and the crude exhibitionistic demands are given up, and are pari passu replaced by ego syntonic goals and purposes, by pleasure in his functions and activities and by realistic self-esteem. [p. 107]

Thus, under optimal conditions the experience of disillusionment over the loss of cherished illusions about the self and others is worked through in a systematic, nontraumatic, and smooth fashion. Under the gradual impact of expanding reality testing, more accurate appraisals of the limitations of the self and significant others evolve and are integrated in a healthy way. However, when less than favorable conditions prevail, when these basic needs for mirroring of the grandiose self and merging with the idealized parent imago are not sufficiently met, pathological outcomes often occur. As adults these individuals may continue to exhibit grandiosity, a need to be seen as special, and a need to merge with an idealized other in order to derive a more exalted sense of self. Developmental arrest with regard to these processes is most vividly seen in patients described as narcissistic personality disorders. Kohut understood that these needs, with their accompanying illusory aspects, were yearnings that appropriately belonged to certain phases of infancy and childhood that were unfulfilled in these patients.

A central tenet in Kohut's theory of self psychology is the idea that when the parents lack empathy with the child's basic needs for responsive mirroring, merging, and an idealized other, defenses are built up to protect against further injury to the (developing) self. The goal in psychoanalytic treatment is to work through these defensive structures so that the underlying needs can reemerge in the form of selfobject transferences that ferment in a therapeutic atmosphere in which they can be understood, interpreted, and responded to with attunement. Kohut's approach is based on the assumption that one needs to have illusions about a grandiose self and an idealized other as part of normal development, and that the psychoanalytic situation in and of itself stimulates reactivation of that developmental point in time when these needs were arrested. The analyst, in self psychology, allows these needs to emerge spontaneously and to build for a time without interruption. Through the empathic connection with the analyst, it is assumed that the patient gains a certain satisfaction of these needs, a satisfaction that was not adequately provided in infancy and childhood. In addition the analyst gradually and increasingly interprets the genetic source of these powerful unfulfilled needs. Thus, an empathic therapeutic atmosphere is provided along with interpretations that address the fear of new injury and the ways in which the patient defends against this danger. As stated by Wolf (1993), this approach "will gradually lead to a mobilization of the defended against childhood wishes for a self-enhancing selfobject experience" (p. 684).

In Kohut's view the concept of resistance to the psychoanalytic process is understood not in terms of obstacles to the uncovering of sexual and aggressive drives and their derivatives, but rather as a reluctance to reactivate these core needs with an accompanying feeling of vulnerability. Kohut believes patients are resistant to the experience of the mirroring and idealizing illusions, that is, to the articulation of these specific illusions and the concomitant transference manifestations. Resistance to the establishment of selfobject transferences is expressed through a reluctance to experience the empathic analyst as empathic, which is rooted in a fear of retraumatization. Casement (1991) refers to this as "the pain of contrast." There is considerable anxiety about allowing oneself to need (the analyst) and to be vulnerable, which opens up the danger of further disillusionment in relation to an attachment figure. This fear of disillusionment and of retraumatization, in which needs for merging, mirroring, and idealization will be reactivated and unmet once again, is intense and profound in these patients. The understanding of these resistances and techniques for addressing them is described by Ornstein (1974).

For Kohut the effectiveness of psychoanalytic treatment with these patients also involves what he calls the process of transmuting internalization, in which the patient gradually and incrementally internalizes "the anxiety assuaging, delay tolerating, and other realistic aspects of the analyst's image" (1977, p. 32), along with a growing ability to metabolize his/her disappointments in the inevitable errors, flaws, and failings of the analyst that create disruptions in the analytic relationship (Wolf 1993) and disillusionment in the analytic process itself. Developmentally, optimal disillusionment is necessary for emotional growth. Thus, under favorable circumstances little by little the mother provides failures in her mirroring functions, and disappointment follows. It is the gradual series of these relatively small failures and doses of disappointment that lead to optimal disillusionment. The child integrates these experiences along with the more satisfying responses provided, and arrives at a fuller and more appropriate appreciation of the relationship. Something akin to this occurs in transmuting internalization in the treatment of narcissistic disturbances. For Kohut, as for Winnicott, mental health involves learning how to mediate the demands of the real world while, at the same time, never fully relinquishing one's illusions. Illusions are central to the development of the self. This is in contrast to the view of theorists such as Freud and Fromm in which illusions are seen as defenses against aggression, helplessness, despair, and existential reality.

ARNOLD MODELL

The writings of Modell draw heavily on the concepts of illusion and disillusionment. In concert with other psychoanalytic theorists, especially Mahler, Winnicott, and Kohut, he views the analytic setting as representing a play space where illusions prosper.

In an early paper, Modell (1975) drew attention to the "narcissistic defense against affects" in patients who were fearful of feeling close to their analyst. According to Modell this type of defensive constellation is accompanied by an illusion of self-sufficiency that belies the underlying dependency on the analyst: "Their state of non-relatedness is paradoxically associated with that of intense involvement" (p. 276). In effect, such patients often harbor grandiose and omnipotent images of themselves in order to sustain the illusion that they need nothing from other people. Modell urged analysts to utilize their countertranference reactions of affective withdrawal as a useful way to key in to this type of characterological defense mechanism. This defense of nonrelatedness is particularly prevalent in narcissistic personalities and is attributed, by Modell, to early developmental failures in which the child accurately perceives the mother's faulty judgment and emotional unreliability, becomes disillusioned with the mother, and may prematurely separate from her. For Modell the origin of narcissistic pathology occurs in the preoedipal period, at age 2 or 3, when the child recognizes with mortification that the mother's judgment is off and that he cannot rely on her. His response is to feel disillusionment with mother and to build compensatory grandiose illusions about his self-sufficiency. Modell contrasts this defense of nonrelatedness characteristic of narcissistic personality disorders with the extreme intensity of affects seen in borderline states, and he views the latter diagnostic group as suffering from more severe environmental traumas. What stands out in the narcissistic personality disorder is the precocious sense of self, which is accompanied by an illusion of self-sufficiency and a denial of needing object relatedness.

Although Modell values Kohut's contributions to our understanding of preoedipal development, he criticizes Kohut's theory as portraying a self that is too exclusively reliant on a selfobject for survival, rather than a more balanced view that includes a self-generating self that can fuel itself from within. For Modell (1993) the "private self" stands alongside, and is as important as, the need for selfobjects in establishing a cohesive sense of self. Like Kohut, Modell emphasizes the role of idealization as a central ingredient in normal development. Modell sees disillusionment as the failure of idealization, and when this occurs precociously the child "may need to preserve an illusion of the 'goodness' of his parents by taking their 'badness' into himself" (p. 109). In this regard Modell aligns himself with the object relation theorists who advocate that bad object relationships are internalized so that illusions about good objects can be retained.

THE PRIVATE SELF VERSUS THE RELATIONAL SELF

Modell maintains that the importance of a self-generating aspect of the self, what he refers to as the private self, has been vastly overlooked in psychoanalytic theory in favor of an emphasis on relatedness in establishing a cohesive self. The private self "refers to that portion of the self that we keep hidden and which we do not usually share except with those with whom we are intimate. There is an aspect of the private self that may never be communicated to others" (1991b, p. 732). When basic early developmental needs are unmet, what Modell calls environmental failure, it may be adaptive as well as necessary for emotional survival to retreat to the private self. Under adverse environmental conditions, disillusionment can be cushioned and illusions can flourish in an unattenuated fashion in the private space of the private self. Modell states, "For some who face dreadful environments, private space is the place in which one can retreat to alternative worlds of fantasy, worlds which may guarantee psychic survival in an unsupportive environment" (1992, p. 6).

Illusions and fantasies are by and large territory that belong to the private self. Ethel Person (1995), who has studied the role of fantasy in people's lives, has pointed out that it is customary to be very proprietary about one's conscious fantasies. Most people guard them with secrecy and conceal them as private property. Freud (1908) recognized this aspect of the private self early in his writings: "The adult . . . is ashamed of his phantasies and hides them from other people. He cherishes his phantasies as his most intimate possessions, and as a rule he would rather confess his misdeeds than tell anyone his phantasies" (p. 145).

Person observes that people are much freer about relating their dreams than their fantasies. This is an interesting phenomenon that can probably be explained on the grounds that people feel less responsible for their dreams, which are further removed from conscious control and regulation.

Modell stresses that the need for private space involves more than the need for nonrelatedness. It involves the need to draw upon structures within the self that are self-generating and self-healing. It is fueled from within and provides a sense of mastery. The establishment of the private self and private space is a normal developmental process and needs to be safeguarded throughout life. Infant research studies have discovered that as early as the first month of life the infant requires periods of active disengagement from the mother, during which he can pursue his own interests, along with incremental periods of involvement and engagement with the mother (Sander 1983). Modell (1992) draws from these studies, as well as from the work of Winnicott, to propose that this is an inherent healthy need for time-out from relatedness, that disengagement is equally as important as engagement, and that "this natural rhythm of a balance between alternate periods of relatedness and disengagement persists throughout life" (p. 8).

In psychotherapy practice there has been a growing recognition that certain patients need to periodically take a break from treatment, and return later on to further address their unresolved issues. Such a pattern may reflect an appropriate or necessary expression of time-out from relatedness, and a need to retreat to the private self when the treatment is experienced as too threatening. In some situations taking a break may be understood as adaptive rather than as resistance or acting out.

Modell takes exception to the self-psychological position that "it is the analyst who provides, through a mature selfobject relation, that which is missing in the patient's experience" (1992, p. 21). Whereas Kohut has proposed that the self cannot survive without the emotional oxygen obtained from selfobject affirmation, Modell counters with the view that the self cannot survive without space for the private self. The private self, fueled from within, is the only place to which one can retreat to ensure personal survival in an unsupportive world.

As a proponent of the relational self, Mitchell (1988) builds on the view that there is a primary inherent need in all individuals to find a pathway to connect and relate to others. The analytic experience is seen in the relational model, chiefly as an interactive encounter between two individuals, and the exploration of the ways in which they impact on each other is central to the treatment process. The relational self is seen as having both yearnings and anxieties about connecting, but what is always of paramount importance is how relationships are being negotiated. Thus, Mitchell points out that in the relational model "the pursuit and maintenance of human relatedness is the basic maturational thrust in human experience" (p. 289). Mitchell divides the relational model theorists into two groups: those who espouse a relational-conflict model, and those who adhere to a relational-developmental arrest model. In the former view an emphasis is placed on the ways in which the nature of disturbances in early relationships are repeated in subsequent (adult) relationships. Adhesive attachments to archaic objects and illusions that are superimposed upon new relationships prevail. According to Mitchell, "Operating with old illusions and stereotyped patterns reduces anxiety and provides security not simply because the illusions and patterns are familiar, but also because they are familial and preserve a sense of loyalty and connection" (p. 291).

In the relational-developmental arrest model, Mitchell describes a "developmental tilt" (p. 152), in which the provisions
of relatedness supplied by the interventions of the analyst enable the patient to have "past omissions corrected and developmental gaps plugged up" (p. 152). In this model the patient is
seen as "an infantile self in an adult body, fixed in developmental time and awaiting interpersonal conditions which will make
further development possible" (p. 170).

In this view psychoanalytic treatment represents a second
chance to obtain the necessary growth enhancing supplies derived from a core relationship, what Mitchell refers to as "developmental remediations" (p. 152). This is in contrast to Modell's
position, which emphasizes that developmental gaps created by
experiences such as the noxious impact of intrusiveness or
misattunement in the fit between child and mother need to be
dealt with by solidifying the "private self" in which conditions
are safe and self-generating. The common ground in both
groups of relational-model theories is the view that disturbances
in the early dyadic relationship between mother and child creates a predisposition for pathological forms of relatedness in subsequent relationships.

An additional criticism of the relational developmental arrest theories is that they place a one-sided emphasis on the problems emanating from developmental deprivation. By accentuating
the importance of explicating and repairing earlier deprivation,
such theories overlook those individuals whose problem has to
do with too much gratification and indulgence from their
caregivers. As a result, these people fail to acquire the ego
strength of frustration tolerance and they continue to function
with the illusion that the world is supposed to be there for them
in ever-gratifying ways. Their interactions reveal a perpetual
search for "the world is my oyster," and the experience of a
blissful relatedness in which their primary needs are taken care of.

Galatzer-Levy and Cohler (1003) address the need for relationships versus the need for independence. In contrast to

Modell's point of view that most current psychoanalytic theories overlook the importance of the private self in favor of a bias toward the importance of the relational self, these authors maintain that a bias exists in psychoanalysis toward seeing the capacity to stand alone as a measure of optimal mental health. Drawing largely from Kohutian theory, they posit that interdependence rather than self-reliance (independence) is a more mature form of healthy functioning, and that the former is central to a sense of well-being in every stage of development. Galatzer-Levy and Cohler develop the concept of "the essential other" to describe "our experience of other people, and entities in the environment, that supports the sense of a cohesive and vigorous self and its development" (p. 3). In my view the chief contribution of these authors lies in their interest in extending the meaning of essential others beyond significant people in our lives. Thus, such things as books, movies, and inanimate objects can provide a source of sustenance and serve as an essential other. I believe that it can be argued that there exists a bias in our culture and among mental health practitioners that the utmost healthy state is one in which the individual cultivates an intimate relationship with a significant other. In seeking a balance between the needs of the relational self and the private self, it can be useful to think of one fulfilling the need for an essential other both through relationships as well as in other ways such as a meaningful connection with hobbies, books, causes, and projects of one's own creation. For example, the essential other could be another aspect of oneself such as the benign superego or, conversely, the critical superego with which one is in constant connection and influences one to perform and produce.

SUMMARY

This chapter discussed the way in which the themes of illusion and disillusionment are considered in each of the major psychoanalytic theories. Among the points highlighted were (1) Freud's view that the loss of the illusion of the lack of anatomical differences between the sexes paves the way for the development of the Oedipus complex; (2) the emphasis of classical theorists such as Freud and Fenichel on the central role of illusion, which underlies perversions such as fetishism and transvestism; (3) Winnicott's elaboration of the importance of the baby's illusion of omnipotent magical control of the breast in maturational development, as well as the role of illusion in the capacity to be alone and the formation of transitional objects; (4) Mahler's emphasis on the central role of illusion during the phase of normal symbiosis, and the role of optimal disillusionment as a precondition for a smooth resolution of the rapprochement crisis; (5) Kohut's view that an optimal sustaining of illusions is essential for the development of a cohesive self, and that metabolized disillusionment leads to transmuting internalizations.

The prominence given to the role of illusion and disillusionment in the understanding of various pathological syndromes was explored. With the increasing shift in psychoanalytic interest toward preoedipal conditions such as narcissistic and borderline personalities, the dimensions of illusion and disillusionment have assumed increasing importance in the conceptualization of listening perspectives and treatment approaches. In this regard the work of such theorists as Jacobson, Fromm, Modell, and Mitchell was considered. The impact of illusion and disillusionment on the need for relatedness (Mitchell), versus the needs of the private self (Modell) was also discussed.

3

Illusion, Disillusionment, and Defenses

Illusions are protective coatings against the disillusions of life.
—A patient in psychoanalysis

Defensive illusions are developed and maintained in the service of protecting the individual from painful truths. These illusions may relate to such things as invulnerability, immortality, control and mastery of one's environment, and misperceptions in love relationships. People often maintain their illusions because they are afraid, or feel ill equipped, to deal with the feeling of disillusionment that would ensue if these illusions were relinquished.

Thus, illusions are developed to protect oneself from painful truths. In this sense they may be considered as defense mechanisms. Just as the infant would be overwhelmed by the awareness of his helpless vulnerable position in the world and thereby requires, for a time, illusions about omnipotence and merger, so too do individuals throughout the course of life require illusions to ward off awareness about the true nature of things.

Let us focus further on the interconnection between illusion and disillusionment. It was highlighted in Chapter 1 that in the course of normal development illusions about oneself and the world are gradually eroded and the individual then needs to deal with the disillusionment that follows. Thus, for example, with incremental cognitive development the toddler comes to realize that the world is not his "oyster" and that he is a vulnerable organism in a threatening world. He experiences a certain amount of disillusionment and then comes to acquire and accept a more realistic appraisal of himself and his world. This sequence is repeated at other junctures in life (e.g., the outrageous sense of omnipotence in adolescence, the realization of life's finiteness in middle age). This task is generally not accomplished in a linear fashion, but rather with a considerable amount of turmoil and struggle. The struggle is characterized by alternating states of holding on and letting go of the illusion. Under the sway of anticipated anxiety or despair, people may consciously choose to hold on to an illusion, even though they know it is an illusion, until they feel more ready to deal with the feelings that accompany disillusionment. The following vignette from a psychotherapy session is illustrative:

> Gary, a middle-aged man, suffered with anxiety and depression after his marriage of twenty-five years ended in divorce. He had no living family members and no friends. He felt it was essential to find a new woman with whom he could establish a loving relationship. He pursued this goal by going to many singles functions and arranging numerous blind dates. After many disappointing encounters with a variety of new women, he ultimately connected with someone who became very special to him. They dated for several months and when he pressured her for a more romantic and sexual relationship, she rebuffed him. Although she liked spending time with Gary, she made it clear that she was not physically attracted to him, and did not want to have a romantic involvement with him. Gary had already imagined himself in a permanent love relationship with her, which he now recognized was a fantasy that could not come true and was therefore an illusion. In his next therapy session, he expressed his feelings of devastation, while at the same time wanting to hold on to his dream of fulfilling his wished for relationship with this woman.

Gary: It's better to have an illusion than nothing at all!

Therapist: What you are saying is that if you are to give up the illusion of having something special with Vivian, you would be left with the pain of dealing with strong feelings of emptiness and nothingness, and you don't feel ready to do that.

Gary: Yes. I know that it's not real, it's wishful thinking, but it's better than having nothing.

Therapist: So it's hard to let go of wanting something that you know cannot happen.

Gary: Another part of me knows that I have to find something that is real. But the women I meet turn out to be unattractive or uninteresting. It's so hard to find someone to connect with so I hold on to my illusion about Vivian.

Under ordinary circumstances the individual metabolizes the pain of disillusionment and reconstitutes his mental organization with a progressively greater adherence to the true nature of things. However, even in the face of reality many individuals are reluctant to give up their illusions, because to do so would necessitate dealing with the discomfort and pain that accompanies disillusionment. There are numerous situations in which an individual may be threatened, traumatized, disorganized, or devastated by the loss of a much-needed illusion and is unable to deal effectively with the accompanying disillusionment. In such instances the individual may need to institute new illusions in order to restore a sense of emotional homeostasis. I refer to these processes as compensatory or secondary illusions. For example, an attractive young woman with an abrasive, hostile personality finds it intolerable to deal with the repeated rejections from desirable men she expects to connect with in the singles scene. In lieu of examining her interpersonal deficits, she may develop the compensatory illusion that she will find Mr. Right when she loses ten pounds.

Yet another pattern involves those individuals who are so fearful about contending with potential disillusionment that they have a powerful investment in not allowing themselves to harbor illusions. This may operate on a conscious or unconscious level. In these cases the need to protect oneself, often because of earlier trauma and/or unintegrated disillusionment, supersedes the yearnings that give vent to the formation of illusions.

All schools of psychoanalysis recognize the importance of defense mechanisms in mental functioning. In some cases the goal is to analyze the individual's defenses in order to remove them as constricting impediments to productive functioning. In other cases an aim of treatment may be to bolster defenses when the patient's level of functioning is more fragile. Defense mechanisms are generally unconscious and belong to the province of the ego. They were first described by Freud as mental mechanisms that are developed to ward off unacceptable impulses and wishes emanating from the id. The first defense mechanism discovered by Freud was repression, in which threatening feelings, wishes, impulses, and memories are blocked from awareness.

In the early days of psychoanalysis, many patients presented with physical symptoms that Freud thought reflected unconscious psychic conflict that was being expressed through the body. The primary goal in the treatment of these patients was to make the unconscious conscious, that is, to lift the intervening repression and thereby expose the underlying conflicts and make them accessible to exploration and resolution. In the patient population of the 1990s there are fewer so-called symptom neuroses than heretofore, and a much greater prevalence of character neuroses, but the necessity of understanding and working with the patients' defense mechanisms continues to be paramount. All psychoanalysts from Freud to this day work in some way with the interacting concepts of defense and anxiety in their treatment approaches. Freud was intrigued with the connection between anxiety and repression. At first he believed that repression, with its accompanying damming up of libidinal forces, was the catalyst for anxiety. Subsequently, he revised his theory (1926), and posited the reverse—that it is anxiety and the unpleasant affect associated with it that leads to repression.

Prior to the formulation of his structural theory of the mind in which id, ego, and superego are in ongoing negotiation, Freud (1911) described the pleasure principle and the reality principle as the central components in mental functioning. The seeking of instinctual gratification (the pleasure principle) is gradually replaced by the reality principle in which the child has acquired the ability to assess the appropriateness and implications of his behavior. The acquisition of the reality principle also provides a defensive function in that it allows the individual to protect himself from painful sensations emanating from the external world. Freud (1911) viewed neurosis as a pathological alternative to dealing with reality: "We have long observed that every neurosis has the result, and therefore probably the purpose, of forcing the patient out of real life, of alienating him from actuality. . . . The neurotic turns away from reality because he finds it unbearable" (p. 218). To deal with a reality that one may experience as oppressive and painful, an individual may turn to defensive illusions, that is, illusions designed to protect oneself from painful awareness. Freud (1930) recognized this: "Men know that with the help they can get from 'drowning their cares' they can at any time slip away from the oppression of reality and find a refuge in a world of their own where painful feelings do not enter" (p. 78).

As was pointed out in the situation with fetishists (see Chapter 2), there are many instances in which the individual realizes on one level that his beliefs are illusions, while simultaneously behaving as if they are not unrealistic. Freud (1930) noted that for many individuals "satisfaction is obtained through illusions, which are recognized as such, without the discrepancy between them and reality being allowed to interfere with the pleasure they give" (p. 80). Taking this a step further Freud goes on to point out that in neurotic individuals reality is regarded "as the source of all suffering, as the one and only enemy, with whom life is intolerable and with whom therefore all relations must be broken off if one is to be happy in any way at all" (p. 81).

The existentialist Ernest Becker (1973) pursues this same line of thinking in pointing out that "the neurotic symptom is a communication about truth: that the illusion that one is invulnerable is a lie. . . . The neurotic opts out of life because he is having trouble maintaining his illusions about it, which proves nothing less than life is possible only with illusions" (pp. 188–189). Becker recognizes the need for defensive illusions and anxiety about disillusionment: "We protect ourselves and our ideal image of ourselves by repression and similar defenses, which are essentially techniques by which we avoid becoming conscious of unpleasant or dangerous truths" (p. 51). Thus, without defenses against the awareness of the true nature of reality, we would be neurotic, or in more extreme situations psychotic. Becker paraphrases Searles's views about schizophrenia as "a failure to confidently deny man's real situation on this planet" (p. 63).

These views related to illusion, reality, and neurosis may help us to understand why certain patients need to repeatedly act out their impulses, which are fueled by powerful illusions. In these cases the seeking of pleasure, the avoidance of anxiety, or the need to cling to a particular perception of themselves in relation to the world is so central that it outstrips good judgment and reality testing.

> Sara, a promiscuous 35-year-old single woman, sought out sexual encounters with men in order to sustain the illusion that she was a femme fatale. Although she was a successful attorney, she derived no satisfaction in her work, and defined herself essentially in terms of her sexual attractiveness. In truth she was obese and quite unattractive, but if she could get men to go to bed with her, she could believe that she was desirable. On some level she knew that men were just using her as a sexual object, and more often than not

she was treated poorly in these encounters. Nevertheless, her need to fuel her illusion about her desirability led her to continue to seek out one night stands, in spite of her recognition of the fact that it was highly dangerous to do so in the age of AIDS. Several years of psychotherapy were required before Sara was able, bit by bit, to dismantle her illusion and reroute her self-destructive pattern of behavior.

Sara's case represents an example of a necessary misperception of reality, of the true state of things, in order to safeguard an intact sense of self and to avoid a painful truth. Here again it is useful to quote Freud (1937):

> The psychical apparatus is intolerant of unpleasure and strives to ward it off at all costs and, if the perception of reality involves unpleasure, that perception, i.e., the truth, must be sacrificed . . . hence the ego's defensive mechanisms are condemned to falsify the inner perception. . . . The purpose of the defensive mechanisms is to avert dangers. It cannot be disputed that they are successful . . . but it is also certain that they themselves may become dangerous. Not infrequently it turns out that the ego has paid too high a price for the services which these mechanisms render. [p. 237]

To the extent that defenses lead to the falsifying of inner perceptions, they are promoting illusions. We can see how defensive illusions may serve to insulate the individual from psychic pain and are therefore needed in that regard. At the same time, defensive illusions can be costly to one's overall functioning, as the case of Sara demonstrates.

Illusions are needed as defense mechanisms in order to provide the individual with a sense of well-being, safety, and security, and to insulate us from the pain of disillusionment. We might correlate disillusionment and illusion with the psychodynamic concepts of anxiety and defense. For many individuals the experience of disillusionment, especially if it occurs in an abrupt fashion, can provoke unthinkable anxiety, and secondary illusions are needed to protect oneself from being overwhelmed. In other situations there is a readiness, which has been gradually developed, to experience the disillusionment that follows the loss of cherished false beliefs.

An example of the former situation is the following case:

Rona, a single college student, sought therapy because of her difficulty in sustaining relationships. She was the youngest child of three girls, and she grew up in the shadow of her intellectually gifted sisters. Rona's pathway for gaining some attention within the family was through performing in school sports and plays. As an adult her excessive neediness for acknowledgment and affirmation alienated many of her peers. In college she made the varsity women's tennis team and she expected to bask in the spotlight of celebrity status. Others were put off by her need for attention, and they turned away from her. The result was that she was not popular on campus. She curried special attention from the tennis coach and she nurtured the belief that she was his favorite player. Although he treated each member of the team equally, Rona harbored the illusion that she held the inside track to his affections. This was a repetition of her childhood attempt to become her father's preferred child through her performance accomplishments in sports and on stage.

In a therapy session Rona was distraught because of two recent incidents in which she passed the coach in the hallway and he walked in the other direction without acknowledging her. Her heightened sensitivity to rejection led this to be a shattering experience for Rona, and it rocked the illusion of her specialness. The pain of disillusionment was too difficult for her to absorb at this time. Consequently, she needed to establish a face-saving illusion, that is, secondary illusion, that the coach must not have seen her, rather than to consider the painful alternative that he chose not to acknowledge her. This is a common example in everyday life of the pull toward defensive illusions in order to ward off varying degrees of unthinkable anxiety. It is understandable that people need their illusions in order to ward off anxiety about what they would have to deal with if they were stripped of their defenses.

Henry Ezriel (1973), a renowned British group psychotherapist, conceptualized a useful schema for understanding the relationship between anxiety and defense. He outlined a paradigm of positions that people are obliged to enact in their interpersonal relationships. He described three basic roles in this schema: (1) the required position, (2) the avoided position, and (3) the calamitous position. Ezriel maintained that when unacceptable unconscious fantasies are inadequately repressed (and threaten to break through into conscious awareness), a defensively fueled required relationship is set in place that serves to reinforce the repression. For example, a man who cannot tolerate dealing with his underlying hatred of women and/or his latent homosexuality might become a Don Juan. The required position thereby assuages the anxiety that would accompany the breakthrough of unacceptable unconscious feelings or wishes; it allows the individual to preserve control over the corresponding unconscious fantasy. Another example might be the situation in which a woman assumes a required position of idealization in relation to certain other women in order to ward off her unacceptable competitive and devaluing feelings. In Ezriel's formulation, people pursue the required position in their relationships in order to circumvent being in the avoided position. The anticipated consequence of being in the avoided position is to be in the calamitous position. Thus, we can see how assuming the required position allows one to avoid the anxiety that would emerge if one were in the avoided position. The required position is therefore a defense against the anxiety attendant to the avoided position. Furthermore, if one does not steer clear of the avoided position, it could lead to one's being in the calamitous position, in which intense anxiety prevails.

In applying his paradigm to clinical cases, Ezriel highlighted the importance of uncovering the illusions that accompany the calamitous position. There is often occasion to explore this in the course of the therapeutic process. In the evolution of the transference the patient is afforded the opportunity to test out his beliefs about the consequences of his feelings and actions toward the therapist. For example, a female patient may maintain a distancing stance toward her male therapist (the required relationship), because she fears that if she allowed herself to get close to him she would become sexually excited and make advances toward him (the avoided position), which might result in his terminating her treatment, or, even worse, in his responding to her sexually (the calamitous position). Another example would be that of the male patient who needs to be solicitous and compliant toward his male therapist (the required position) in order to ward off his unconscious rivalrous and murderous oedipal transferential feelings (the avoided position), which might result in retaliation by the therapist (the calamitous position). Well-trained therapists do not generally succumb to their patients' sexual advances or retaliate against their patients' aggressive feelings. These are illusions that are frequently harbored by patients about the calamitous position, and are tested out and dismantled during the course of effective psychotherapy. Utilizing Ezriel's approach, patients can be understood in terms of these formulations. Most common is the situation in which the patient assumes a deferent or passive stance in relation to the therapist (or to significant object relationships) in order to avoid the expression of unacceptable aggressive feelings and the accompanying illusion that the expression of these feelings would lead to irreparable harm to the needed object or incur his/her retaliation. Another frequently seen pattern is that in which the patient assumes a hostile, combative, required relationship in order to ward off his unacceptable passive, or affectional needs, lest they lead to feelings of overwhelming vulnerability and/or ridicule from others.

Ephraim, a 40-year-old criminal lawyer, was highly successful in his career, but was inept in his personal relationships.
He was combative, assertive, and sarcastic, and he utilized
these qualities to his advantage in his professional life, where
he was perceived as a skillful and dangerous "shark." However, these personality traits were curiously absent in his interpersonal life. He was severely traumatized at age 6 when
he came home from school one day to discover that his
mother had committed suicide by hanging herself. He was
then raised by his depressed father, and subsequently by a
stepmother who ministered to his basic physical needs but
was emotionally distant. In psychotherapy sessions (as an
adult) it quickly became evident that Ephraim felt starved
for emotional supplies. We gradually came to understand
that his interpersonal pattern of stumbling and bumbling
and generally appearing to be socially incompetent (the
required position) belied an unconscious motivation. This
pattern, in which he played up his boyishness, his naïveté,
and his vulnerability, was designed to get a nurturing and
rescuing response from women. In effect he was perpetually seeking the all-good mother who would be there for him
and take care of him in the way his mother had before she
died. Ephraim's illusion was that the only route to attain
these emotional supplies (and to master the earlier trauma)
was to come across in this lost, bereft, disorganized, and
needy way. He held the internal belief that if he functioned
as a competent and effective partner in a relationship, he
could not get his nurturing needs met.

  While many women were responsive to Ephraim's way
of relating, they could not respond to the magnitude of his
neediness, which belonged to the original mother–child relationship. Invariably his relationships would fail as a result
of his excessive need for maternal supplies, but he did not
allow himself to mourn the loss of these attachments (the
avoided position). To do so would have exposed himself to

renewed rounds of pain over abandonment, which would reactivate the original traumatic loss of mother and arouse intolerable affect (the calamitous position). Instead of working through the disillusionment related to the loss of the illusion that he could truly and fully replace the absent mother, he steadfastly sought out new opportunities in his never-ending search for the all-good mother of childhood. The therapeutic goals in this case were to (1) explore the unconscious meaning and purpose of Ephraim's passive-dependent stance; (2) challenge his assumptions about how to get his needs fulfilled and the viability of success; (3) work through feelings of disappointment, loss, and abandonment, that is, the mourning process; and (4) encourage Ephraim to take risks in allowing himself to relate in a more adult fashion.

Many people, like Ephraim, have never acquired the ability to fully integrate the positive and negative attributes of their partners. They require that others fulfill their wished-for expectations as nurturer, provider, lover, and exquisitely attuned other, and they become anxious, rattled, disappointed, resentful, and angry when lapses occur in the availability of these provisions. Such individuals function at the need-gratification level of object relatedness and have not attained the higher level of functioning known as object constancy. In object constancy one is capable of valuing the object for his or her personal qualities over and above one's state of need at any given point in time. It is not the services rendered that are of paramount importance so much as the ongoing connectedness to the whole person. At this level of object relatedness, one recognizes that the object who gratifies one's needs may also at times respond in a way that is disappointing and insensitive. But one accepts the fact that the world and its inhabitants are imperfect. For those who function predominantly at the level of need gratification, there is a tendency for idealization and devaluation to taint the nature of their relationships. In idealization, illusions about the magnificence of the other person abound, and the connection one has to such a person serves to bolster feelings of well-being and security. In this sense, idealization, with its illusory component, often serves as a defense against underlying feelings of vulnerability and inadequacy. In essence by hitching one's wagon to the star of the idealized other, one derives a sense of safety, worthwhileness, and specialness. Thus, idealization may be viewed as a defense designed to avoid coming to terms with the difficult feelings that accompany the awareness of one's vulnerability.

The psychoanalyst Louise Kaplan (1978) highlights this point in noting that "the unending search for a perfect partner whose comings and goings can be magically coerced is one way to cover up inner emptiness and feelings of vulnerability" (p. 43). These individuals have difficulty in accepting the fact that soaring with exhilaration and falling with disappointment are inherent aspects of the human condition and characterize the functioning of self and others: "They idealize those whom they can coerce into becoming the all-giving, perfectly holding partner who will sustain their image of self-perfection. Although they idealize their partners . . . they use them in order to experience the pride that comes from possessing a perfect partner" (p. 42).

When the object fails to consistently provide the needed supplies (e.g., holding, mirroring, praising, nurturing, attunement, etc.), they may quickly fall from grace and become devalued. Like Ephraim, the person functioning at the level of need gratification may experience brief, or sometimes extended, periods of blissful idealization in their relationships, and then move on, in a serial way, to the next person who might be able to fulfill and sustain one's illusions about a primary relationship. Idealization contains an element of illusion insofar as it allows one to overestimate certain qualities of others. Through one's real or imagined connection to the idealized object, the individual enhances his own level of self-esteem. Idealization may be durable for a prolonged period of time, or it may collapse abruptly after the first indications that there are chinks in the armor of the object. When the object falls from grace, one loses not only the object as one perceived it to be, but also the exalted and exhilarated sense of self based on one's connection to the idealized object. The well-known phenomenon of being in love with love exemplifies this point. In the process of being in love one loves the chosen object, whose positive qualities are generally magnified and overvalued to the exclusion of his or her negative qualities, but the individual is simultaneously exhilarated by the feelings of being in love. When reality considerations undermine the illusions that promote idealization of the significant other, disillusionment is bound to follow. Oftentimes the pendulum swings to the other extreme in which anger and hurt over the loss of the idealized object lead to devaluation. Having failed to continue to measure up, the object is now considered to be worthless and useless.

ILLUSION AND FANTASY

Fantasies are part of our everyday life and involve mental images that contain unfulfilled desires. They are usually an expression of wish fulfillments. For example, the young woman who yearns for a romantic relationship may nurture a Cinderella fantasy in which she is discovered and swept off her feet by a charming prince. The fantasy of becoming instantly rich is what generates the purchase of millions of lottery tickets. Similarly, many people play the stock market in the hopes of becoming wealthy, but also as an expression of the fantasy that they are smart enough to make the best stock picks. The psychoanalyst Ethel Person (1995) has made a comprehensive study of the role of fantasies in everyday life: "The goal of fantasy is to achieve an overall change in state—a change in how one feels. [p. 38] . . . It has been recognized that many underlying wishes and motives operate in fantasy, including the need for the regulation of self-esteem, the need for a feeling of safety, the need for regulating affect, and the need to master trauma" (p. 63).

Like fantasies, illusions also contain a wish-fulfillment aspect and serve the purpose of protecting one from threatening truths; they enhance the sense of well-being. The chief distinctions are twofold: the basic connection to reality is not obscured in fantasy, and there exists the possibility that a fantasy could come true. Illusions, in contrast, are based on false beliefs, and it is their lack of fruition in the face of overwhelming odds that defines them as illusions. For example, a man who writes a novel may harbor the dream of winning the Pulitzer Prize in literature. It is a fantasy that might possibly be accomplished, although the chances of its fulfillment are quite remote. However, if the writer is of average intelligence and limited creativity, he is harboring an illusion, since the probability of fulfilling the dream is virtually zero.

On the other hand, a man who is determined to marry an heiress, or a woman who is determined to marry a captain of industry, may have some remote possibility of enacting the fantasy. If the individual is particularly attractive, has a very charming personality, establishes the right social connections, and devotes his or her full-time energies to pursuing the dream, the possibilities are somewhat enhanced. An example would be Eva Perón, who came from poverty and ultimately united with the popular dictator of Argentina. This would be called a fantasy rather than an illusion. A successfully enacted fantasy is not an illusion. Both fantasy and illusion contain an element of wish fulfillment, but the chief difference is that fantasies can sometimes come true, while illusions are always based on a misperception of reality. In some situations there may be substantial overlap between fantasy and illusion, and the line of demarcation needs to be based on how far removed from reality the fantasy lies in order for it to be considered an illusion.

To a certain extent hopes and dreams belong to the same family as fantasies. It can be said that hopes and dreams always contain a wish-fulfilling aspect. When hopes and dreams are derailed or lost, we may think of the corresponding affective state as that of disappointment. However, fantasies may exhume a positive or negative valence. Although we are more accustomed to thinking about fantasies in a positive direction, they can also have a negative direction. For example, a man who avoids sexual intercourse may have the underlying unconscious fantasy that if he were sexually aggressive, some damage to his genitals would follow. If he allows himself to attempt intercourse and discovers that the anxiety is unconfirmed, his negative fantasy may diminish. Over a period of numerous successful sexual experiences, the fantasy may wane even further. In addition, the root of this negative fantasy may be explored and addressed successfully through psychotherapy.

One might raise the question as to whether the term *disillusionment* can be utilized to describe the affective state when fantasies, dreams, and hopes have been lost. I would propose that disillusionment be reserved, by definition, to the loss of an illusion. Another term is needed to describe the state in which negative fantasies have been relinquished or dissolved. Perhaps a word such as *de-fantasied* would be useful in this regard.

Fantasies and illusions may occupy a central or peripheral place in an individual's functioning. They may also operate on the conscious as well as unconscious levels. Psychoanalysts have recognized the importance of uncovering and analyzing the role of unconscious fantasies and illusions in mental life. As the renowned psychoanalyst Jacob Arlow (1969) pointed out,

> The most powerful influence distorting the images of the past and contributing to the misperception of the present is the intrusion of unconscious fantasy thinking. During our busy wishful life, dominated by the reality principle, we are only intermittently aware of the persistent intrusion into our conscious experience of elements of fantasy thinking. [p. 32]

Arlow was particularly interested in how seemingly inappropriate reactions and responses on the part of his patients made sense in terms of an inner unconscious fantasy, rather than according to reality. Thus, patients' seemingly unrealistic wishes and fears need to be understood "as a misperception of reality in terms which are appropriate for the contents of the unconscious fantasy" (p. 34). This is a basic tenet in psychoanalytic work.

Many individuals secretly harbor a fantasy or illusion in which they will find a relationship with a partner who is exquisitely attuned to them, available with unconditional love, and totally sensitive and responsive to all of their needs. The acknowledgment of this fantasy or illusion often exposes a feeling of vulnerability. To avoid experiencing this threatening feeling of vulnerability, one may invest considerable energy in warding off and pushing down this fantasy or illusion. In psychotherapy it is often productive and freeing to help the patient get more fully in touch with their illusions centering around unconditional love, dependency, and immortality, and then to work on the process of mourning the inability to fulfill the wish and coming to terms with the true nature of things and the human condition.

ILLUSION AND DENIAL

Denial is a defense mechanism that involves a refusal to believe or accept a painful or unwanted reality. It includes an investment of energy devoted to changing the choreography of real-life events. Denial can best be described as a defense in which the individual tunes out some aspect of reality that is objectively evident in order to circumvent the unpleasant implications and affects incumbent upon dealing with the truth. Most psychologists view denial as an unconscious and sometimes conscious defensive reaction to unacceptable events in the external world. Through denial the individual effectively attempts to alter reality. Denial has been differentiated from avoidance, a related defense that emanates primarily on a conscious level. In avoidance there is usually a determined effort not to deal with the stressful event, but the existence of the event is not denied (Lazarus 1983). Denial is often employed as a necessary defense to protect the ego from being overwhelmed at times of crisis or trauma, as, for example, when a sudden or unexpected death occurs.

Denial is considered to be a very primitive defense mechanism because of the extent to which it involves distortions of reality. However, in adjusting to sudden, very threatening events such as the loss of a cherished relationship or the diagnosis of a terminal illness, it can serve as a useful mode of reacting. In dealing with trauma, denial may be a valuable defense that allows the individual to confront the event in a gradual way in manageable doses. In those people who experience more extensive psychological damage, denial may be a pervasive defense employed to numb and gain distance from emotional pain.

Selectively confronting a patient's denial system is frequently a primary intervention in the work of a psychotherapist. As patients are increasingly confronted with the maladaptive aspects of their denial system, they often experience an upsurge of anxiety over the potential loss of a favorite defense. They feel that something important is being taken away from them, and they resent having to deal more with their underlying emotional turmoil. One patient in the throes of this process quipped, "You mean da Nile is not just a river in Egypt?" When the denial mechanism is attacked assiduously, as is recommended in some psychotherapy approaches, there is a danger of personality fragmentation. In contrast, when a more titrated technique is employed, based on an assessment of the patient's capacity to mourn and to tolerate the loss of a core defense, it is likely that the patient will stabilize at a more advanced level of emotional functioning and with other, less primitive, defense mechanisms at his disposal.

Denial can be thought of as an adjunct to illusion. An illusion is a misperception, rather than a denial of reality, that also places emphasis on a hope, wish, or dream that is felt to be necessary for one's emotional survival. In essence, denial can be utilized as a defense that allows one to perpetuate an illusion. Positive self-esteem may be preserved by illusions that are accompanied by denial. For example, a man might need to continue to harbor the belief that his wife is faithful to him, in spite of the fact that he discovers love letters from a suitor. Denial enables him to tune out the implications of these letters and retain his much-needed illusion. In a similar vein, a young woman may nurture the belief that her philandering boyfriend will soon marry her. While he acts lovingly toward her, she must tune out all of the ways in which he repeatedly conveys that he is unavailable and a happily unmarried man who intends to remain single. Here again denial facilitates the preservation of the illusion. To the extent that individuals invent illusions as necessary for their emotional survival, they may need to utilize denial as a mechanism to fortify their false beliefs.

In distinguishing illusions from defenses such as denial and repression, the psychologist Shelley Taylor (1989) takes the position that "defenses distort the facts, leading people to hold misperceptions of internal or external reality. Through illusions, on the other hand, people make the most of bad situations by adopting a maximally positive perspective . . . repression and denial alter reality, whereas illusions simply interpret it in the best possible light" (p. 126). Taylor's view is somewhat divergent from the position held here, which is that illusions also involve false beliefs and misperceptions of reality. Whether or not these serve a positive or adaptive purpose is another matter. Therefore, I believe that it is more parsimonious to think of defenses such as denial and repression as available to the individual for the purpose of aiding and abetting the preservation of illusions.

ILLUSION-DISILLUSIONMENT AND IDEALIZATION

Idealization involves an overestimation of human attributes in which the self or other is regarded as perfect. It is an unrealistic assessment in which illusions of perfection prevail. The affective state of being in love characteristically entails the idealization of one's partner, and, via the connection to the partner, an idealization of the partnership. Freud (1925a) held the view that initially the young child "tries to interject into itself everything that is good and to reject from itself everything that is bad" p. 237). He referred to this as the "purified pleasure ego" (p. 237), and in this way the child idealizes himself. However, as a consequence of the confrontations encountered in dealing with the world of objective reality, the child's illusions about his own perfection become unsustainable. In a sense the child becomes disillusioned with himself in the face of discovering his limitations. The child then turns to his parents as objects of idealization. Thus, through the relationship with an idealized other, the child retains a feeling of perfection about himself. The experience of perfection of the ideal self is now derived through the satellite-like connection to the idealized other. In Mahler's terms we might say that the child compensates for the loss of the illusion that "the world is my oyster" by "hitching his wagon to a star," and he derives a sense of power and perfection from the perceived omnipotence of his parents. Many adult relationships are also patterned around the attempt to complete oneself through connecting with an idealized other. When the chinks in the armor of the loved one are exposed, the idealization falters, devaluation follows, and disillusionment in the relationship often occurs. This cycle may be repeated over and over again in individuals who are driven to seek a sense of perfection through an idealized relationship. In psychotherapy the idealization of the therapist as a magical healer is a common phenomenon. This will be discussed more fully in Chapter 9.

In normal development the child continues to maintain illusions about his parents' perfection, and this idealization culminates toward the end of the period of latency or during early adolescence. Through the idealization of one's parents during these formative years, the child basks in the glow of perceived perfection of the parents, and also feels safe and protected from the dangers of the outside world. When the illusion of parental perfection is punctured abruptly, or in some cases prematurely, the individual's ego development suffers. The psychoanalyst Arnold Modell (1993) describes the failure of idealization as disillusion:

> To lose one's belief in the parent as a protective presence is to face catastrophic disillusionment. Children need to believe in parents' fundamental altruism—need to believe that parents will place the child's interests above their own. In many families . . . the child cannot count on this parental altruism; in such cases if the relation with the parent is to be maintained, it can be maintained only by virtue of denial and idealization. [p. 111]

When the idealized view of the parent as a protective caregiver is punctured by confrontations with reality, the child, in order to ward off an overwhelming experience of disillusionment that he is not ready for, may maintain his tie to the parent as a good object through the formation of compensatory illusions about the parent fueled by denial. Thus, a defensive idealization may emerge based on the need to ward off dealing with disillusionment. In other situations, when the reality of the parental flaws and limitations are too strong, the child may adopt an attitude of contempt toward the parent who abruptly or prematurely fails him as a way of circumventing the experience of pain in not being able to idealize the parent. This is the precursor of the attitude of devaluation seen in later relationships when the overestimation of the partner's qualities is unsustainable and disillusion in the relationship occurs.

One of the most prominent debates in the psychoanalytic literature over the last twenty-five years has centered around the meaning and function of idealization. The eminent theorists Heinz Kohut and Otto Kernberg have spearheaded this dialectic. According to Kohut, idealization is seen as a legitimate developmental need that in certain patients reemerges in the treatment process. It is viewed as a way of filling a gap in an area of arrested development, and the therapeutic strategy involves fostering this process until such time as it is no longer required by the patient. In an alternative approach, Kernberg views idealization essentially as the patient's defensive maneuver to ward off his intense aggressive feelings. The therapeutic strategy involves interpreting the defensive function of idealization and exposing the underlying rage, envy, and other concomitant aspects of the patient's aggression in order for the working-through process to take place. Kernberg proposes a schema in which different types of idealization, ranging from greater or lesser pathological significance, can be seen in different diagnostic categories.

TYPES OF ILLUSIONS

There are a variety of ways to think about illusion. To cite but a few, let us consider necessary illusions, persistent illusions, shattered illusions, adaptive illusions, and positive illusions.

Necessary Illusions

Necessary illusions are those processes by which people protect themselves from the true nature of things. To the extent that reality threatens to be overwhelming, we all develop defensive illusions as a way to insulate ourselves from excessive anxiety. For a certain period of time they are necessary for our psychic survival. Thus, an illusion serves as a defensive function insofar as it protects one from painful reality. This has long been recognized as a central dimension in human functioning. The writer Anaïs Nin (1967) summed it up by stating, "The caricature aspect of life appears whenever the drunkenness of illusion wears off" (p. 118).

Thus illusions about oneself and one's world are necessary or required, up to a point, as ubiquitous protective mechanisms in normal development. Pathologically necessary illusions occur when one's mental and emotional equilibrium is dependent on maintaining the false belief at all costs in defiance of reality. An example would be the characters of Martha and George in Edward Albee's (1963) play *Who's Afraid of Virginia Woolf?* whose marital relationship centers around the shared illusion of having a child, when in fact no such child ever existed.

In the course of psychotherapy many patients experience a phase of heightened alarm, when their defensive illusions are dismantled. It is common for such patients to describe this phase as a feeling of being in no-man's-land without their usual ways of functioning. It is often expressed "Therapy has taken my defenses away, without giving me anything to replace them." In essence this is an anxiety-arousing phase of the treatment, during which the familiar maladaptive illusions no longer work, and new, more adaptive, structures are not yet in place. It is essential that this phase be handled sensitively and skillfully by the psychotherapist.

This type of experience was described articulately by the patient in the following case vignette:

> Sheldon was in therapy for three years, in which his grandiose view of himself was gradually and incrementally addressed. Although his "quick to fix it" modus operandi was useful in his highly successful career as an investment banker specializing in mergers and acquisitions, it has substantially hampered him in his interpersonal relationships. More specifically, his wife and friends were repeatedly alienated by his problem-solving approach to conflict, which bypassed dealing with feelings—both his own and those of others. Uncertainty, ambiguity, and complexity were intolerable emotional states for Sheldon, who prided himself on getting everything under control. Gradually, he learned to tolerate uncomfortable affects, and along with this, he became less pressured to find immediate solutions to interper-

sonal conflict. His relationships improved, but he felt more endangered as he relinquished his illusion of invulnerability. As his necessary illusion diminished in the context of more gratifying personal relationships, he stated,

> I mourn the loss of the insulating mechanism. My illusion of invulnerability is waning and my defense of "fixing it" is no longer working. A part of me feels much happier in my personal life, but another part feels sad about losing what feels like a best friend. The bravado helped me to be very effective in my career. Now I realize how alive it is to have access to my feelings, but also I realize how potentially vulnerable I am, and that makes me insecure and scared.

This was a developmental milestone for Sheldon. The working-through process over many sessions involved (1) relinquishing his necessary illusion, (2) mourning the loss of a familiar defense, and (3) gradually replacing the loss with more solid internal psychic structure.

Persistent Illusions

Persistent or intractable illusions, like necessary illusions, are not easily dismantled. When false beliefs are clung to in spite of mounting evidence that they are not realistic, they take on a persistent or intractable quality. It is as if one's survival depends on holding on to a cherished illusion. In Greek mythology the tale of Sisyphus exemplifies a persistent illusion. As punishment for outwitting Hades, the god of the dead, Sisyphus was ordered to roll a huge stone to the top of a high hill. Each time Sisyphus reached the top of the hill with the stone, it rolled back down. Despite constant failure to achieve his goal, Sisyphus did not acknowledge the impossibility of the task, but continued to pursue an unattainable solution. In essence Sisyphus was given an eternal punishment in which dealing with disillusionment was not an available option, and he was doomed to chasing after a persistent illusion.

In clinical practice we see patients who have difficulties in sufficiently incorporating reality into their ongoing functioning. These patients are not psychotic in that they are not primarily out of touch with reality, but rather they are unrealistic about their expectations of themselves and others. Their emotional needs may selectively outstrip their sense of reality, and as a result their judgment may suffer. They are committed to pursuing their persistent illusions at all costs; it is much like insisting upon fitting a square peg into a round hole. No matter how often it doesn't work, like Sisyphus these individuals continue to try the same unproductive route over and over again. One patient defined insanity as "consistently doing the same thing and expecting a different outcome." An illusion is a mistake in interpretation. The question that arises is whether we change our interpretation after checking with reality, or do we need to insist on altering reality in order to retain and maintain our illusions. It is the latter course that people with persistent illusions attempt to follow, and in varying degrees it can be damaging to psychological health.

With therapeutic intervention many of these individuals can be helped to shift gears. In the early years of psychoanalytic treatment persistent illusions were generally viewed as expressions of unresolved infantile strivings. Patients were often admonished to relinquish their unrealistic approaches to the world and to develop more appropriate adult ways of functioning. To the extent that the underlying anxieties about letting go of much-needed belief systems were not fully explored, this technique was not overly successful. Subsequently, with the advent of ego psychology, therapeutic techniques were aimed at helping these patients develop more effective ego strengths such as utilizing memory to profit from experiences, anticipating consequences, tolerating frustration, and improving reality testing and judgment. This approach was helpful to many patients. In addition to this approach, current technique in psychotherapy places a greater emphasis on such factors as understanding why the patient has the need to hold on to persistent illusions, how it serves him, and what he would have to deal with without them. The application of Ezriel's schema, described earlier in this chapter, is relevant here.

Shattered Illusions

There are situations in which basic false beliefs are suddenly punctured by an overwhelming reality. We refer to these as shattered illusions and they may have a traumatic impact. A prime example of a shattered illusion occurs in *Who's Afraid of Virginia Woolf?* George's abrupt puncturing of the shared illusion about their fictitious son was devastating to Martha. This was the ultimate act of revenge on the part of the abused and humiliated husband, and Martha becomes unhinged and emotionally broken. As the play draws to an end a resilient aspect of Martha's personality emerges in which she begins to accept the necessity for relinquishing the shared illusion. In contrast to her contemptuous earlier interactions, she now relates to George in a calm and attached way and is taking the first tentative steps toward getting her life back together.

When people suddenly discover that their spouse is having an affair, or when youngsters abruptly perceive their idealized parents as having clay feet, they may experience a shattered illusion. Disillusionment occurs when the previously held illusion crumbles. Subsequently, the individual may gradually come to accept the reality of the situation, or may construct a replacement (compensatory) illusion to provide further protection to the wounded self. A more malignant outcome occurs when the individual is unable to process the feelings of disillusionment nor develop a replacement illusion.

Janoff-Bulman (1992) discusses the connection between trauma and shattered illusions:

> We have built our lives on assumptions that enable us to feel safe and secure. . . . Clearly the assumptions we hold about ourselves and our world provide us with illusions about our own invulnerability. . . . These assumptions derive from our earliest experience with "good enough" caregivers . . . . The ultimate impact of these illusions is . . . we approach the world with optimism and trust . . . . We fail to truly appreciate the reality of our fragility as physical creatures. [pp. 56, 60–61]

Janoff-Bulman describes cases of traumatic victimization in which illusions about oneself as invulnerable and one's world as safe are precipitously shattered, and the survivor-victims are left with the terror of being "forced to see the world as it really is" (p. 61).

Adaptive Illusions

Illusions may serve an adaptive function when they provide an individual with optimism and a sense of well-being and do not conflict with the demands of the external world. The viewpoint was presented in Chapter 1 that it is part of normal development to have illusions about oneself and the world, and there are typical illusions that correspond to different stages of the life cycle. There may be a fine line between man's investment in illusions that are useful and those that are destructive. For example, if one buys an occasional lottery ticket in the hope of striking it rich, this would most likely be a harmless expression of optimism about good supplies coming from the environment. If, on the other hand, one pursues the illusion of striking it rich by gambling large sums at casinos, this is likely to be a self-destructive way of managing the illusion, since the laws of probability indicate that sooner or later one is going to lose.

Under unduly stressful living conditions, one may develop an adaptive illusion in order to fortify one's capacity to carry on. A patient who was despondent over failures in her love life as well as her work life invented a fantasy city called Fenwick in which her illusions about a perfect society and receiving unconditional love would be indulged. By retreating to her land of make believe, she could summon up resources to deal with her present unhappiness and adaptively buy herself some time to consider alternative pathways of functioning. We might think of this as an example of regression in the service of the ego. Maurois (1968) follows a similar line of thought: " 'Mape' is the name that a little girl gives to the country she has invented in order to escape the harsh rule of her governess . . . . For every man after a certain age, happiness is found only in 'Mape' " (p. xv). These and other Camelot-type fantasies are prevalent in fueling adaptive illusions.

The "golden fantasy" described by Smith (1977) is a state of defining the self-in-relation-to-other in which one recaptures "the fantasied utopia perfectly attuned to our needs, where all is magically gratified" (Peebles 1986, p. 218). While Smith focused on the persistent yearnings reflected in the golden fantasy as obstacles to successful therapy, this fantasy also serves an adaptive purpose for many individuals, especially during periods of heightened stress. In patients who suffer from acute ego fragmentation, annihilation anxiety, or intense narcissistic injury, the accessing of a golden fantasy, however illusory it may be, may restore a feeling of cohesion to an otherwise shaky sense of self. In such cases the golden fastasy may serve as a bridge that allows one to sustain hope. At such critical periods the golden fantasy has adaptive value in that it "establishes an illusion of continuous environmental support and security, which the patient uses to protect himself against [the dangers of disintegration]" (p. 225). Thus, while golden fantasies exist in all of us to some extent, it is particularly important to recognize their potential adaptive value in the treatment of more disturbed patients (i.e., individuals with less well delineated psychic structure). In a similar vein, Peebles points out that, "the Golden Fantasy often shields a patient from an experience of bottomless dread and nonexistence. . . . Its purpose is to preserve life" (p. 233).

Positive Illusions

Positive illusions is a term coined by the psychologist Shelley Taylor to refer to those false beliefs that allow people to constructively enhance their view of themselves, the world, and the future. They serve an adaptive function, particularly in adjusting to life-threatening circumstances. In a critique of Taylor's work, Cella (1985) describes Taylor's contribution as a "cognitive theory of adaptation to cancer and other threatening events, based on the premise that 'illusion' and self-deception are effective against often uncontrollable external threat. Illusions provide a buffer and help establish personal meaning, self enhancement, and mastery" (p. 1275).

Taylor's (1989) work is dedicated to the view that, for some people in certain circumstances, illusions may be necessary and essential to a sense of well-being, requiring the distorting, exaggerating, or obfuscating of reality. In challenging the view that illusions are indicators of pathology, Taylor maintains that "illusions are not only normal, but are actually adaptive, promoting rather than undermining mental health" (p. 46).

Taylor designated three primary areas in which positive illusions are most apparent and adaptive: self-enhancement, an exaggerated belief in personal control, and unrealistic optimism. She was impressed with research studies on cancer patients that indicated that those patients who maintained strong illusions of personal control over the progression of their illness tended to survive longer than patients who were passive and deferent. Taylor extended these observations to other life situations, and concluded that "people's positive distortions often increase, not decrease, as matters become more important and consequential . . . . Positive illusions, then, are pervasive and not confined to the unimportant matters of life" (p. 45).

In everyday life we may think of positive illusions as constructive aspects in promoting a sense of well-being. Relatively small distortions of reality enable one to look at the facts in a more optimistic way. Giving the facts of a situation a positive spin often allows one to function more effectively. Although illusions involve a degree of self-deception, they often provide us with a sense of mastery, which in turn fuels a sense of well-being. This notion was also recognized by Baumeister (1989), who coined the term *optimal margin of illusion* to describe how illusions about oneself and the world can be self-enhancing on the one hand and self-damaging on the other. While relatively small illusions may increase one's sense of happiness and effectiveness, larger distortions can be harmful. Baumeister concludes, "Optimal health, adjustment, happiness, and performance may arise from overestimating oneself slightly. Departures from this optimal margin lead in opposite directions to different sorts of problems. It is depressing and maladaptive to see oneself too accurately, and it is dangerous to see oneself too favorably" (p. 188).

4

The Power of Illusions

Psychoanalysis teaches us how extraordinarily difficult it is . . . for objective reality to win out over the reality powered by wish and affect.

Fred Pine
"The Era of Separation-Individuation"

Core illusions can be powerful and central to the ongoing functioning of certain individuals. Through early experiences with caregivers, many people acquire illusions about themselves and the world. They become committed to these false beliefs, which may take on an enduring or adhesive quality. One's everyday functioning may be governed by such false beliefs. Some illusions may fuel poor judgment and maladaptive behavior, while others may be relatively harmless and even adaptive. A total absence of illusions is the mark of an empty and constricted existence. Some core illusions are conscious, while others may operate on an unconscious level. Weiss and Sampson (1986) discuss how unconscious pathogenic belief systems that are formed through early relationships with parents around dependency and trust can dominate one's way of functioning in the world.

It is striking to note that people may insist on holding on to their illusions, even after they have been debunked and exposed as false beliefs. In such instances the need for the illusion outstrips the need to adhere to the reality principle. André Maurois (1968) spoke to this point:

> We are victims of illusion when we believe that we see, touch
> and hear things that do not exist, that we have feelings we
> do not actually feel, that we understand. But we must im-
> mediately establish the difference between the mistake, which
> we correct as soon as we recognize it as such, and the last-
> ing illusion which persists even after we have understood its
> mechanism. [p. 3]

There is a phenomenon called the Müller-Lyer illusion,
which is described in introductory psychology college courses.
Subjects are presented with the two lines shown below.

$$\longleftarrow\joinrel\relbar\joinrel\relbar\joinrel\relbar\joinrel\longrightarrow$$
$$\longrightarrow\joinrel\relbar\joinrel\relbar\joinrel\relbar\joinrel\longleftarrow$$

When asked which line is longer, most people pick the bottom line. When it is suggested that these lines are of equal size,
some subjects accept this reality, while others may hold on to
their belief and question or challenge this new information. This
phenomenon highlights the power of illusions and raises the
question of under what circumstances do individuals change
their belief systems after reality intervenes versus insisting on
altering reality in order to maintain their illusions.

There are numerous medical myths that fall in the category
of illusions. According to scientific evidence, myths about physical health, such as that arthritis pain is related to changes in
barometric pressure, or one can catch a cold from being out in
wet weather without an umbrella, or eating chocolate and nuts
triggers acne in adolescents, have all been refuted (Kolata 1996).
Yet, in spite of research findings to the contrary, many people
continue to cling to these prevailing false beliefs.

World history is replete with examples of charismatic leaders who imposed illusory beliefs on willing followers. Hitler had
millions of Germans believing that they were the master race.
In the United States President Lyndon Johnson used the domino
theory of the spread of communism to gain popular support for

the escalation of the Vietnam War. The disillusionment in American political leaders that followed the debunking of this myth has permeated public sentiment for more than three decades. In earlier history, Maurois (1968) reminded us, "Napoleon was a madman who took himself for Napoleon. He had formed a certain image of himself and for fifteen years enforced this illusion upon Europe" (p. 29).

Illusions are a source of hope, and as a result many people become very connected to their illusions. The "American dream" is based on certain successful accomplishments and corresponding material possessions (e.g., owning a home with a white picket fence and a two-car garage). The illusion is that these accomplishments will bring real happiness. When these goals are achieved, and true happiness does not follow, then disillusionment sets in. Levinson (1978) describes the central illusion in American culture as follows: "If I attain the dream ... then life will be good and everything really important will come to me" (p. 246).

During midlife this illusion often unravels as one is faced with the reality of mortality. Until this time the sense of immortality with which we function is the most powerful illusion of all. It is the powerful wish for immortality that leads us to avoid and deny the reality of the human condition. This might explain why the recognition of our mortality at this stage of life can be so catastrophically painful. For those individuals who seek psychotherapy in midlife, a prevalent issue in the treatment is lost illusions and the wish to retrieve them. Milton Horowitz (1989), who works extensively with this population, remarks:

> "The patients want something more than mere relief of anxiety or depression; they want fulfillment of old wishes. Often they feel infuriated by the thought that they will be denied the "full life." [p. 7] ... Nowhere is the issue of the persistence of fantasy more poignant than in the analysis of the middle-aged patient. Many such patients have the idea that this is their last opportunity to make their wishes come true. [p. 8]

The powerful nature of illusions is often expressed poignantly in certain cases of sexually compulsive behavior.

John was the youngest of three brothers who grew up with an overbearing mother and a kind, but distant, father. His early attempts at autonomous functioning were squashed by his mother, and, although he felt safer with his father and brothers, his efforts to attain affectionate contact from them were interfered with and preempted by his controlling mother. He grew up with an abhorrence of women and a yearning for father love.

In his late teens John became actively homosexual and he pursued this way of life with a vengeance. Homosexuality for John represented a way to be deviant, and thereby to assert his will over that of his mother, who had harshly imposed her values onto him. At the same time it was a way through which he could satisfy his yearnings to feel close to a man. John's psychological damage had occurred very early, during the first three years of life (the preoedipal period); consequently he did not develop object constancy. As a result he never valued his sexual partners as human beings, but only for the sexual gratification he received from them.[1] His sexual behavior was driven by the illusion that he could incorporate another man's strength through performing fellatio. His preferred activity was to cruise subway toilets in search of older men. Although he selected attractive partners, he showed no interest in them other than in sucking their penis. He would feel temporarily gratified when he scored in this manner, but it did not last, and he would seek out several partners in the course of a day.

---

1. Bach (1994) discusses perversions as a way of functioning, sexually as well as nonsexually, in which the lack of capacity for whole object love is predominant.

The awareness that he was engaging in dangerous activity in a public place did not faze John. Even after he was arrested, he resumed this compulsive sexual acting out. The need to pursue the illusion that he could find father love indirectly through anonymous fellatio was so strong that it outweighed his ability to consider the realities of danger and disease.

After many years of this type of sexual activity John became depressed and sought psychotherapy. Over several years he acquired psychodynamic insights into the meaning of his type of homosexual activity. Nevertheless, these insights were not sufficient to overcome the gratification he derived from sustaining his sexual acting-out behavior. Eventually, as he came to experience a meaningful relationship with his therapist, he was able to find partners with whom he could form deeper object relatedness. It was a significant step forward that he was able to shift his sexual pursuits to less pathological (i.e., less dangerous) avenues of expression, but the powerful nature of his magical illusion that he could incorporate strength and gain closeness to his father through performing fellatio remained entrenched and continued to drive him.

Overindulgence of early developmental needs and/or a premature loss of such supplies accompanied with incomplete mourning are the soil from which dominant illusions may grow. Excessive gratification or deprivation sets the stage for the formation of unrealistic assumptions about how we can expect to be treated in the world. Thus, for example, an overly gratifying oral phase leaves one unsuited to deal with the realities of the slings and arrows of life in the real world. Individuals with such backgrounds are unprepared for relationships, which entail inevitable frustrations and mutuality, and they are often strongly invested in perpetuating their illusions and expectations about how the world should be there for them. Psychoanalysts have long noted how excessive oral gratification creates an "excess of optimism which is not lessened by reality experience" (Glover 1925, p. 136). In spite of repeated experiences of disappointment and frustration, such individuals continue to hold on to their cherished beliefs and expectations about being blissfully responded to in their adult relationships.

> Elissa grew up as an only child who was overindulged by both parents. Her mother accurately anticipated her needs and generally met them before the child expressed her wishes, and her adoring father lost no opportunity to treat her as his princess.
>
> Her adolescence was notable for its lack of sturm and drang. She did not go through a phase in which she became disillusioned with her parents, and the absence of turmoil and rebellious behavior reflected an atypical adolescence. This type of adolescence without apparent conflict is deemed to be pathological in the sense described by Anna Freud, since it is deviant from what normally occurs in this developmental phase.
>
> Elissa became a beautiful-looking woman who continued to rely on the indulgences of her parents. Although she was able to move out of their home and live in her own apartment, and earn her own living, she remained emotionally dependent on them. When she was invited to parties, her father would drive twenty miles from suburbia to the city in order to provide safe crosstown transportation. Such arrangements were characteristic of their relationship and were accepted and unquestioned as to their appropriateness. Elissa came to therapy as a 30-year-old who was unhappy because she could not sustain relationships with men. She had no difficulty meeting new men and beginning a relationship, but it seemed that they were always disappointing her in their lack of attentiveness and sensitivity. It was only through exploration in psychotherapy that she came to recognize that her personal life was a mess because of her

powerful illusion that others would treat her in the same manner as her overly indulgent parents had done.

For an extended period of time in her psychotherapy she thrived on an idealizing transference in which the therapist, like her father (and like herself in the eyes of her parents), could do no wrong. Even her therapist's most benign and innocuous statements were experienced by Elissa as expressions of his sensitivity to her and his undaunted interest in her.

It is common at some point in psychoanalytic psychotherapy for patients to form transferences in which they distort the statements and actions of the therapist in a negative direction. Many patients have had a long-standing relationship with a parent whom they experienced as critical or misattuned, and therefore they are prone in the transference to feel easily misunderstood or hurt. At such times they react with resentment, and a devaluing attitude toward the therapist ensues. In the course of psychotherapy such negative transference is to be welcomed, since with a skilled therapist it affords the patient the opportunity to work out core interpersonal problems in new ways. In Elissa's therapy this did not happen. Her need to idealize her therapist prevailed, even when he made errors such as confusing the content of her previous session with that of another patient. She had assigned to her therapist the role of the perfect therapist, and his lapses were ignored or misperceived in a positive direction.

Elissa gradually made some progress in being able to view other people more realistically and to reduce her expectations of perfection in others as well as in herself, but she continued to have transient relationships with men. She was an oedipal winner and was attracted to married men whom she could draw away from their wives. When her lovers became available to her, she would find them flawed in that they did not measure up to her view of her therapist.

He, like her father, had become her standard of perfection. Her ongoing idealization created countertransference problems for the therapist. Although he felt that there was progress achieved in analyzing her oedipal and narcissistic issues, her idealizing attachment to him in which she misperceived his innocuous gestures to reflect his intense interest in her made him increasingly uncomfortable.

One day Elissa came to her session loaded down with packages from her Christmas shopping. At the end of the session, as she prepared to leave, she collected her many packages. Since she was fumbling with them, the therapist, departing from his usual custom of letting patients exit on their own, went to open the door for her. Elissa was thrilled and expressed her gratitude by pointing out how extraordinarily caring and sensitive the therapist's gesture had been. The therapist, uncomfortable with this undeserved adulation, remarked spontaneously, "But Elissa, I would have done that for anyone with so many packages!" Elissa experienced this insensitive remark as a major narcissistic blow that burst her bubble. Subsequently, she could no longer maintain an unblemished view of her therapist, and he was no longer idealized. What followed was remarkable. She did not bolt from therapy as one might expect, as a function of the impact of this narcissistic injury. Instead, she was able to continue the work, while relating to the therapist in a more appropriate and realistic way. Soon thereafter she began a new relationship with a man whom she recognized had flaws along with his desirable qualities. She could accept his imperfections in a way that was new to her, and she was able to sustain this relationship on a long-term basis.

Although this was not a planned technique on the part of the therapist, it seems that his abrupt confrontation of her excessive idealization served to push her along and move her forward in the real world. It is possible that the same outcome might have been achieved, if the therapist had tackled this transferential issue of Elissa's idealization in a more tactful way earlier in the treatment, but that countertransference enactment had interfered. It can also be argued that because of the power of her illusion about her own specialness and the therapist's flawlessness that she would not have been ready to integrate and utilize such interventions in a constructive way.

Certain patients have an uncanny ability to convert blatant technical errors by their therapists into strategies that were planned and designed by the therapist to be helpful to them. This allows the patients to preserve their illusions about the benevolent therapist. Brief examples of this phenomenon include a case in which the therapist neglected to inform her patient that she would be away on vacation, and the patient misinterpreted this error as the therapist's aim of testing his improved ability to withstand frustration and disappointment. In another case the therapist instituted a substantial fee increase at a time when the patient could ill afford to absorb it. The patient misinterpreted this as something motivated by the therapist's belief that she (the patient) was ready to take on more responsibility and to become more ambitious in her profession. It is common in such cases that a fear of expressing aggressive feelings, along with low self-esteem, combine with the need to idealize the actions of the therapist. These dynamics may fuel powerful transferential illusions.

Other therapists have written about abrupt interventions that have punctured the powerful illusions of their patients. Amati-Mehler and Argentieri (1989) have described cases in which "the analyst is invested with the unrealistic task of preserving the illusion that unsatisfied needs or lost objects can be supplied and restituted. This illusion coexists with constant resentment of its lack of fulfillment" (p. 303). After prolonged and profitable treatment the cases discussed by these authors came to a stalemate because of the adhesiveness of the patients' "pathological hope of continuing to claim what is lost, or perhaps has never been really enjoyed in the primary relationship" (p. 301). When the therapists intervened in a way to suggest that they could not participate as a partner in a script designed to fulfill or restore improbable wishes, the bubble burst. Amati-Mehler and Argentieri conclude, "The analyst's statements were an active and sudden rupture of the transference and, therefore, inevitably traumatic. We realized to what extent our patients felt rejected, attacked, accused, refused, and suddenly banished from a containing relationship, and thus inevitably separated from the analyst" (p. 303). While hope is a necessary ingredient in everyday life, excessive hopefulness may lead to unbridled optimism, which persists and flies in the face of reality checks to the contrary. Individuals whose functioning is generated by powerful illusions that lead them to persist in chasing rainbows are operating beyond the optimal margin of illusion.

Freud has been criticized for paying insufficient attention to the role of disharmony in the early mother–child relationship as a forerunner of adult pathology. Indeed, Freud's emphasis was directed more toward the triangular issues of the oedipal configuration as the cornerstone of all psychoneuroses. Nevertheless, he did recognize the importance of illusions early in life and the reluctance in some individuals to give them up in the harsh light of reality. Karl Abraham (1924), a member of Freud's inner circle, noted that oral fixation may lead to character formation that revolves around an ongoing yearning to be taken care of. "Some people are dominated by the belief that there will always be some kind of person—a representative of the mother, of course—to care for them and to give them everything they need. This optimistic belief condemns them to inactivity" (p. 399). In such individuals growth is stunted by the powerful yearnings to be taken care of, and their adult relationships are often woven around passive-dependent and sadomasochistic features.

Even individuals who have successfully climbed further along the ladder of psychosexual development may harbor regressive wishes to recapture past times that have been idealized. Nostalgia is generally fueled by exalted memories. At times of adversity, when love relationships have soured or when other losses or personal failures have occurred, it is normal to yearn for a more blissful era. Illusions of recapturing lost experiences or lost feeling states may predominate at these times. Fenichel (1945) stated,

> The first two years of life, in which external "omnipotent" persons took care of us, protected and provided us with food, shelter, sexual satisfaction, and re-participation in the lost omnipotence, gave us a feeling of being secure in a greater unit, while at the same time losing our own individuality. This memory establishes in every human being a capacity for nostalgia for such a state whenever attempts at active mastery fail. [p. 561]

Pathological nostalgia is seen in those individuals in whom powerful illusions about recapturing the past are predominant in their functioning. Akhtar (1996) describes "if only" fantasies at the heart of nostalgia. The hallmark of "if only" fantasies is the wish to return to the past and undo the loss of a more blissful time. Fantasied reunions with first loves is an example of the wish to recapture a past that has been idealized. It is as if the person is saying, "Something interrupted my ideal state of being, and if only that hadn't happened, my life would be wonderful." According to Akhtar the genesis of such a preoccupation involves the disruption of a harmonious maternal connection during the preoedipal period. The birth of a sibling or the premature loss of availability of the mother during the practicing phase of separation-individuation can be experienced by the preoedipal child as being thrown out of the Garden of Eden. Under usual conditions these early events are experienced as disillusions and are gradually come to terms with under the impact of the reality principle. Mourning the loss of what once was and can now no longer be is part of normal development. Generally, the child gradually accepts his state of lost symbiosis and moves on. Reality prevails upon him to relinquish his infantile omnipotence, and there occurs a corresponding waning of the view of himself as "His Majesty the Baby" (Freud 1914, p. 91) and the world as his oyster.

The capacity to tolerate despair when one is unable to regain appropriate developmental losses is an ego strength, and as such it is a precondition for growth. "The 'if only' fantasy . . . is, at its core, a product of incomplete mourning over the loss of the all-good mother of symbiosis" (Akhtar 1996, p. 736). Akhtar's depiction of persons who strongly harbor "if only" fantasies is similar to Sydney Smith's (1977) delineation of the "golden fantasy" in which illusions about regaining a paradise lost are prevalent.

According to Akhtar, individuals who tenaciously hold on to "if only" fantasies reveal a counterpart of what he calls "someday" fantasies. The latter refers to a pathological optimism based on an idealization of the future. "Someday" fantasies rely on the illusion that what has been lost can be restored. Reality is often sidestepped in order to preserve the belief that someday (in the future) a time of blissfulness and a relationship characterized by perfect harmony will be restored. As in the situation with "if only" fantasies, the "someday" fantasy includes a yearning to reconnect with an idealized lost object and, along with it, a recapturing of a lost self experience. The message of both sets of these fantasies is a striving to turn back or move forward the hands of time in order to undo the loss of, or restore the bliss of, ideal times. Illusions containing excessive hope and unrealistic optimism about the future are the by-product of "someday" fantasies, while idealizing the past as a way of avoiding the mourning of disillusionment is a distinguishing characteristic of individuals with tenacious "If only" fantasies. Severing the tie to pathological hope is required in order for appropriate mourning to take place. The working-through process necessary to deal with disillusionment is truncated when one is enclosed by "if only" fantasies.

For some individuals the power of illusions is substantial and central to their existence. A great deal of thought, fantasy, and energy is invested in pursuing the fulfillment of their illusions. It is sometimes remarkable to observe how tenaciously they hold on to an illusion in spite of repeated experiences that time and again indicate that reality has a different color, shape, and script from the way they wish to see things. It is extremely difficult for such individuals to accept reality instead of continuing to seek out the achievement inherent in the illusion. It is as if to relinquish the illusion is to give up a core part of oneself—a belief system that feels necessary for one's survival and exists as a raison d'être. In such cases the need to maintain the illusion can be so strong that events are misperceived in order to preserve the illusion at all costs.

Psychotherapists sometimes underestimate the power of illusions as a necessary structure in certain patients. When a patient's energies seem guided by a patently unrealistic dream, it may be tempting for the therapist to represent the respectful voice of reality. Common examples include individuals in their twenties, thirties, and beyond who unremittingly persist in the pursuit of their dream of becoming a rock star, movie star, or famous athlete under conditions of minimal probability of fulfillment. While determination and tenaciousness are usually thought of as admirable qualities, after a while, in the light of perpetual rejection, they may become unproductive. The need to hold on to unrealistic aspirations beyond the optimal margin of illusion may be understood as a way of avoiding dealing with unthinkable alternatives. The latter may involve the recognition and acceptance of a lack of talent, a lack of preparedness or training for other types of work, and having to settle for an unglamorous life with feelings of mediocrity or inadequacy. Grandiose illusions serve to cover up these underlying anxieties. In psychotherapy with these people it is fundamental that the therapist does not burst the bubble of the patient too precipitously. In these cases an approach that provides a balance between supporting the patient's wishes and efforts along with gradually facilitating an awareness and acceptance of the painful realities is indicated. As is the case throughout the course of normal development, disillusionment is best processed in a gradual manner.

Individuals with primitive ego organization have a more limited capacity to tolerate and work through the pain of disillusionment. Consequently, they may attempt to hold on to their illusions against all odds. Their ego functions such as reality testing, frustration tolerance, and judgment are significantly compromised, and, as a result, extensive levels of distortion prevail. While higher functioning individuals are more able to correct their distortions about themselves and others under the impact of reality, and thus are capable of mourning the loss of comforting or cherished false beliefs and then shifting to a more realistic position, those with more primitive personalities get locked into their illusions and rely heavily on primitive defenses, such as denial, to perpetuate them. They nullify signals of veracity and, instead, may pursue their illusions with a vise-like grip.

The character of Alex in the film *Fatal Attraction* (Lyne 1987) is an extreme example of a woman who is obsessed with an illusory love relationship and cannot tolerate disillusionment. After a passionate sexual encounter with a married man, she is determined to continue their relationship. When he makes it clear that he is a happily married man, that he feels guilty about his sexual lapse, and that he is not available, she refuses to accept it. Her illusion is that their tryst was a prelude to a sustained relationship, and she pursues him with a frenzied vengeance. He does not lead her on, but rather is firm in his position that their escapade was an unfortunate mistake. When he declines her further overtures, Alex becomes more desperate; she will not take no for an answer, and she will not allow him to burst her bubble. Her judgment is poor, and she justifies such actions as phoning him at home in the middle of the night with rationalizations such as "I won't be ignored!" Her primitive ego organization, inability to tolerate disillusionment, and profound narcissistic injury ultimately lead her to express murderous rage, which culminates in her own death. There are many less extreme cases of people who are driven by unrealistic dreams and goals, where the margin of illusion is substantial, and who nevertheless insist on pouring their energies into trying to make it happen. It is much like repeatedly trying to fit a square peg into a round hole, rather than accepting that it can't be done. For some people the pain of dealing with disillusionment is so great that they must increasingly bend reality in order to sustain their illusions. This is often the situation in people who have primitive ego organization or who have experienced early abrupt or traumatic disillusionment that was overwhelming to their ego development.

A real-life example of the powerful role of illusion as a dominant force in one's functioning is depicted in the film *The Story of Adele H.* (Truffaut 1975), which is based on the experiences of Victor Hugo's second daughter. After a brief love affair with a womanizing British officer, Lieutenant Pinson, Adele erroneously imagines herself to be in a reciprocal love relationship. When he fails to respond to her interest and overtures, she maintains and protects her illusion about his romantic involvement with her by misperceiving his lack of response.

In spite of his rejecting behavior, Adele follows Lieutenant Pinson to Halifax, Nova Scotia, and is determined to get him to marry her. She sends him a love letter in which she states, "Our separation destroyed me. I am desolate since you left. I know you suffer as I do. I never received the letters you sent, and I am sure mine never reached you." He does not respond to her letter, and subsequently he meets her to say, "you must not pursue me. You must leave Halifax!" She cannot accept his rebuff and clings to her illusion that "I shall win him over." She writes to him again saying, "My love, I'm so happy we are reunited. Our misunderstandings are over. I know you couldn't forget me." Her primitive ego organization is revealed in her writing, "I am not me without you." Adele pursues at all costs the illusion that the lover who spurned her is still in love with her. She needs to rationalize his indifference and rejection. The more he continues not to respond to her overtures, the more she needs to bend and distort reality in a direction that allows her to maintain her illusion about a loving connection to him. To do otherwise would been devastating.

Under the power of her illusion about their reciprocal love, she stalks him when he is with other women, and she masochistically continues to pursue him in inappropriate ways. When her father, Victor Hugo, confronts her about deceiving him by announcing her marriage to Lieutenant Pinson, Adele responds with a further distortion of reality. She tells her father that her lover had reneged on the marriage. She claims that she has his many letters of proposal, and thereby she retains the illusion that she can be united with him. Desperately, she seeks out a hypnotist and offers him a stipend to get the lieutenant to agree to marry her. This plan fails when his regiment is transferred to Barbados. Adele once again follows him; she is still determined to connect with him and to win him over!

Ultimately, her need to hold on to her illusion is so great that she has a break with reality, as an alternative to renouncing her false belief that Lieutenant Pinson will reciprocate her love, take an interest in her, make contact with her, or even notice her. For him it had been a brief amorous interlude, while for her it was like finding the love of her life. The power of Adele Hugo's illusion is so great, and her capacity to tolerate disillusionment is so limited, that when the illusion can no longer be sustained she retreats into psychosis. At this point she becomes disoriented, totally withdraws from the world of reality, and wanders aimlessly around Barbados. When she encounters Lieutenant Pinson on the street, she is so absorbed in her psychotic world that she is unable to recognize him. Soon thereafter she returns to France, and her father places her in a mental institution, where she remains as a chronic patient for forty years.

The story of Adele Hugo illustrates how in extreme cases one can be destroyed by a powerful illusion and the limited capacity to tolerate disillusionment. When one stretches reality testing to an extreme limit in order to preserve an illusion, the bubble bursts, reality is experienced as too painful, and the fall can be precipitous. Adele's need to misperceive the essence of her relationship with the lieutenant required her to twist and stretch reality to the point that she became psychotic. In a sense we can say that it was more palatable for her to embrace psychosis than to relinquish her illusion of reciprocal love.

Individuals who are at a higher level of functioning may also be driven by circumscribed illusions. These are powerful pockets of illusion that do not intrude in their general level of functioning, but interfere in one significant area.

Harold was an eminently successful biochemist whose wit, charm, and generosity made him lovable to everybody except his wife. His wife was emotionally distant and unavailable, and showed little interest in his career or in him personally. For Harold this was a repetition of his early family history in which his parents were preoccupied with the demands of supporting seven children and gave him the message that he should not need too much from them. In spite of this early emotional deprivation, Harold developed ways to win the approval and admiration of those around him. He had many successful relationships, but he received only crumbs from his wife. His illusion was that he could get her to love him, and he set about trying to please her in every way possible. In the face of repeated failure he would find ways to minimize and distort her overtly rejecting behavior. His illusion that someday she would come around overrode his ability to accept the reality that she was never going to be genuinely interested in him, nor emotionally available to him. Through psychotherapy, Harold gradually came to see that he had inadvertently re-created his early relationship with his parents, who were inaccessible.

His wife was not capable of loving him, and their marriage ended in divorce. He was helped to tolerate disillusionment and to mourn the loss of his unfulfillable dream. Unlike many people who repeat the same self-defeating patterns in serial relationships, Harold was able to utilize the insights acquired in his therapy and to enter a second marriage with a woman who was very nurturing and emotionally available.

Another vignette illustrates the movement from illusion to disillusion during the course of psychoanalysis.

Roger, an analysand, was studying to become a psychoanalyst. After several years of training, he had started his private practice, but he received very few referrals. He had believed that once he completed the rigors of professional training, enduring financial and personal sacrifices, he would be positioned to embark on a successful career of treating patients.

Roger became increasingly anxious about the lack of progress in developing his practice. Although he had sent out letters announcing the opening of his office, had made phone calls to colleagues and former supervisors, had developed a specialty in working with adolescents, had sent out announcement flyers, and had pursued many other forms of networking, referrals were not forthcoming. He was told by his current supervisor that times were bad and that he himself, although a prominent figure in the field of psychoanalysis, had not made or received a referral in the last five months. What emerged in Roger's analysis was the fantasy that the people with whom he was professionally involved would come through for him, because they care about him and would want to help him launch his practice. There was a reality aspect to this fantasy in that analytic students often do acquire a mentor, but it was also somewhat of an illusion in the context of the prevailing conditions in the

profession at a time in which many practitioners were hurting for patients and did not have a surplus of referrals.

In the transference Roger expressed that he was "not
feeling protected, mentored, or shielded in these ways." He
added, "I'm disappointed that you are not taking care of
me! The feeling is like I should be your son or something
like that so you would come and help me out in a crisis."
The analyst understood these statements, not only as an expression of Roger's current anxieties, which were largely
based on reality considerations, but also in terms of unresolved conflicts in the separation-individuation process that
were being reactivated. More specifically, the analyst was
aware of how Roger's rapprochement crisis, in which he had
exhibited many fears around fending for himself while at
the same time his mother had resented his clinging behavior, was being reactivated by current concerns in the real
world.

In addition to being empathically responsive to Roger's
reality disappointments, the analyst took an interpretive
stance. He said, "Your anxieties also correspond to that
point in your life when you realized that you were ultimately
out there on your own, when you felt like a small individual
in a large and potentially unsafe world, and your anxiety was
about 'How am I going to negotiate this?' "

> *Roger:* It feels familiar. I keep wishing if only you would
> rescue me—send me referrals.
>
> *Analyst:* That would feel good and also make you feel
> safe.
>
> *Roger:* Then I wouldn't have to deal with the fantasy
> being shattered.
>
> *Analyst:* And with the true nature of things—that the
> world does not protect you from feeling vulner-
> able.
>
> *Roger:* I feel like I could really be angry with you—for
> not taking care of me, and for not helping me out.

>But if I start to get really angry, it might destroy
>our good connection. I like feeling that you are
>concerned about me and care about what happens
>to me.

This theme became a primary area in the working-through phase of Roger's analysis. He gradually came to accept the disillusionment that accompanied the realization that he could not count on his analyst to "carry him," to save the day, to make it all right. Dealing extensively with Roger's anger and mourning were central aspects of this process. This represented a reactivation of rapprochement issues in which disillusion is a primary affect to be contended with when an appreciation of reality bursts the bubble of omnipotence and invulnerability, and one comes to view the world as a big, scary, difficult place that one must negotiate as a separate organism.

The case of Roger represents an example of a higher level functioning individual who has the capacity to tolerate the loss of a core illusion and to work through the pain of disillusionment.

THE ILLUSIONLESS MAN

In contrast to those individuals whose functioning is fueled by powerful illusions, there are those who function as if they have no illusions at all. This latter group is characterized by a conspicuous absence of hopes, wishes, and expectations. This state is usually based on a need to ward off the experience of disillusionment, and a conscious decision is made to limit one's dreams and desires. For these individuals the "I want" system is shut down and tightly closed off.

The work of D. W. Winnicott has shown us that the early formation of illusions serves an important developmental function, and adverse or pathological consequences may follow if the conditions for the growth of illusion, followed by optimal disillusionment, are not sufficiently present. Premature disillusionment may preclude the production of subsequent illusions about the self or others. Thus, the illusionless state becomes the ultimate form of protection against further emotional wounds that accompany disillusionment. Their margin of illusion is eroded and becomes very narrow, and, therefore, to risk having illusions is perceived as risking the exposure to too much pain. Daniel Levinson (1978) states, "The best way to avoid illusions is not to want anything very much. And that is hardly a prescription for a full life" (p. 193). In these people there is generally a pervasive emotional constriction that is intrinsic to their functioning. They may harbor deep-seated illusions, but these are vigorously defended against and may emerge only after many years of psychotherapy. Such individuals may seek treatment because the illusionless state has led them to feel empty or depressed. In these cases the course of psychotherapy often involves the activation of an "I want" system in which needs, wishes, dreams, and goals are gradually acknowledged and pursued.

A precocious grasp of reality can lead to a premature shutting down of illusions that are part of normal development. The existential psychoanalyst Allen Wheelis (1966) describes this type of situation in his fictional portrayal of Henry, the exterminator. Henry is depicted as an illusionless adult who too early in life recognized the true nature of things:

> Once upon a time there was a man who had no illusions about anything. While still in the crib he had learned that his mother was not always kind; at two he had given up fairies; witches and hobgoblins disappeared from his world at three; at four he knew that rabbits at Easter lay no eggs; and at five on a cold night in December, with a bitter little smile, he said goodbye to Santa Claus. At six he discovered that his father was not always brave or even honest, that presidents are little men, that the Queen of England goes to the bathroom like everybody else. [p. 1]

Henry, as a representation of those who prematurely have lost their capacity to deal with illusion and disillusionment, grew up taking everything in his stride, was never thrown by adverse events, and led a life bereft of passion and devoid of desire and goals.

The awareness of one's state of vulnerability often triggers disillusion, which may lead gradually to a greater acceptance of reality. Those individuals with substantial ego deficits cannot tolerate the pain of disillusionment, and, instead, they intensify their commitment to their powerful illusions, which may dominate their functioning. It is as if they proceed through life with a frenzied determination that says, "I will not be disillusioned!" A similar type of dynamic is seen in those individuals whose illusions were prematurely lost, and who protect themselves from anticipated further disillusionment by allowing themselves to have no illusions at all.

5

Illusion as an Organizing Principle

With the truth one cannot live. To be able to live, one needs illusions.

Otto Rank
Will Therapy and Truth and Reality

We have seen how core illusions can exert a powerful impact on people's lives. In certain cases a central illusion can become an organizing principle, to the extent that one's ongoing functioning revolves around it. We shall see how such illusions are woven into the very fabric of one's existence, and how energies are relentlessly expended on maintaining these false beliefs. The case of Adele Hugo, described in Chapter 4, is an example of someone who defined herself through the persistent pursuit of an illusion at all costs. No matter how elusive was her goal of winning the interest of the man she loved, she could not let go of it, and she increasingly had to bend reality in order to sustain herself. Unable to force a square peg into a round hole, she was faced with a prodigious emotional dilemma: to give up her central illusion about their love for each other would mean to lose her identity, while to cling to it desperately would involve greater and greater distortions of reality. Less extreme examples abound in which people's lives become organized around the attempt to fulfill an impossible dream, in which the margin of illusion is substantial.

ILLUSION AND GRANDIOSITY

When a separate sense of self is evolving in the first year of life, the child holds the belief that he brings about all the things that happen to him. Thus, as Winnicott points out, the child assumes that the appearance of the mother's breast is brought about by his wish to be fed. Until the ego function of reality testing has taken root, the child's functioning is organized around the pleasure principle, in which a sense of omnipotence and grandiosity prevails. Grandiosity invariably contains an element of invulnerability. To the extent that one's functioning is dominated by fallacious beliefs about oneself and one's abilities, we may speak about the central role of grandiose illusions. Subsequent to the acquisition of firm reality testing, aspects of grandiosity and reality testing coexist throughout the course of life.

Many individuals go through life with an outrageous sense of self-importance. The expectation that one can have the world on one's terms harks back to an earlier phase in normal development, prior to the development of reality testing, in which the child basks in the glow of omnipotence (his own or, later, his parents) and functions as if the world is his oyster. Grandiose illusions often extend into adolescence and beyond. Adolescence is sometimes referred to as the second process of separation-individuation (Blos 1962) in which one emancipates oneself from one's parents on a higher level, as defined by the mores of society. However, the rapprochement crisis, central to the separation-individuation process of the toddler, in which there is an increasing awareness of one's vulnerability in a large and frightening world, is sometimes conspicuously absent in adolescence. Although ambivalence about independence is typical, this is overshadowed by feelings of invulnerability. The parallel that is most pronounced between these two stages of development is the exuberant affective state in which the toddler and the adolescent proceed as if they can have the world on their own terms. Obliviousness to limits or testing them is the norm, and an ex-

pansive view of oneself with endless possibilities prevails along
with a view of the world as conquerable. Pumpian-Mindlin (1969)
has coined the term *omnipotentiality* to describe this regressive
illusion of adolescence characterized by feeling invulnerable and
empowered to be and to do whatever one wants.

In adults grandiose illusions are often fueled by hubris. I
am referring here to the sense of arrogance with which one goes
through life. In the aftermath of the assassination of President
John F. Kennedy, many people felt anger not only toward the
assassin, but also toward the president for allowing himself to
be in a motorcade in a convertible car with the top down. Their
reaction was based on the impression that he displayed a conscious or unconscious arrogance in thinking that he was invulnerable, and that, accordingly, he did not protect himself properly.
Thus, it was perceived that an illusion based on hubris led to
the president's untimely death. In effect his grandiose illusions
about his safety prompted him to be oblivious to the true danger.

The arrogance of youth based on illusions about invincibility and immortality has often been noted. The extension and
persistence of the illusions of infantile omnipotence and grandiosity may continue beyond adolescence into adulthood. These
illusions are generally based on a false perception of safety, when
in fact potential danger exists. An obliviousness prevails, which
may be seen as corresponding to the appropriate mood of the
child during the practicing phase (age 15 to 20 months) of separation-individuation, in which the child is unaware of the true
nature of things and proceeds with a feeling of emotional in-
toxication, as though the world is his oyster. To a certain degree
illusions about oneself and the world, which is the core experience of the practicing phase of normal development, may persist in some way throughout life. In the rapprochement phase
of development, which follows the practicing phase, the task of
the child is to learn to give up his omnipotence and to accept
his limitations. This process is described by Phillips (1998) as

follows: "We are born in turbulent love with the world, which is assumed to be made for us, of a piece with our wishes; then we suffer the humiliation of disillusionment, in which our rage is the last vestige of our hope. And then, if we are lucky—if we have the character, or the right parents, or both—we accommodate to the insufficiencies" (p. 39). However, this is a developmental milestone that many people do not attain.

THE MYTH OF ICARUS

The Greek myth of Icarus highlights the role of grandiose illusions and hubris. Icarus was the son of Daedalus, who was the greatest artist of his era. After being found guilty of murdering his nephew, whose artistic work began to outperform that of his own, Daedalus fled from Athens and was given refuge by King Minos in Crete. After many years Daedalus became increasingly oppressed by his long exile and devised a plan in which he and Icarus would attempt to return to Athens. He fashioned a pair of wings constructed out of bird feathers and wax, fitted them to his body, and then practiced flying up into the sky. He made a smaller pair of wings to fit Icarus, and the two, father and son, prepared to fly to Athens. Upon departing, Daedalus instructed Icarus to fly a middle course between the sea and the sun. He cautioned him lest he fly too low and his wings pull him into the sea, or too high and his wings melt from the heat of the sun. Icarus followed his father into the sky and all went well for a while. However, at some point Icarus, riding the crest of his feelings of invulnerability, decided to soar to higher zones in the sky. Oblivious to the danger he flew too close to the sun, whereupon the wax that held his feathers together melted, and Icarus plunged to his death into the sea below. As this was happening Daedalus looked back helplessly, unable to save his son.

The tale of Icarus illustrates the potential danger of following unbridled grandiose illusions. His urge to soar above the margin of safety, his poor judgment, and his lack of sufficient appreciation of reality testing combined to set the stage for his self-destruction. As the writer Anthony Stevens (1995) observes, "Icarus, having hubristically over-reached himself by flying too close to the sun, plummet[ed] back into his encounter with Nemesis—the sea—the element from which we all spring" (p. 321).

This memorable myth in which Icarus disdainfully overestimated his capabilities and underestimated the dangers around him, corresponds to the practicing phase of separation-individuation, in which the toddler is spurred on by his excitement over his newfound abilities and is oblivious to reality limitations and the obstacles in his path as he explores the world on his terms. The intoxicated-like state of the toddler is akin to the hubristic attitude of Icarus. When the toddler comes to recognize the reality of limitations in his path, his grandiosity is deflated and he enters the rapprochement phase with the accompanying mood of disillusionment and renewed attachment to the caregiver. We may adopt Freud's metaphor of the troops in an advancing army in which he attempts to describe the concepts of regression and fixation. In Freud's account a victorious army will leave a certain number of troops behind to protect its newly won territory while sending the majority of troops forward to undertake the challenge of the next battle. The advancing troops may fall back to their earlier position if they encounter a major struggle. Freud utilized this metaphor to explain the child's progression through the psychosexual stages of development. Thus, for example, in moving forward from the anal stage to the oedipal stage, the majority of troops are available to deal with the issues at hand in the oedipal conflict. If the conflicts at this stage are overwhelming or not smoothly facilitated, then the child may regress to the more familiar territory of the anal stage. An alternative scenario occurs when the issues of the anal stage persist and are unresolved, and in this situation the child remains fixated at the anal stage and has only a limited number of troops available to send forward to the oedipal arena.

In a similar way we can envision the child moving from the practicing phase to the rapprochement phase. For some children the pathology in the available emotional atmosphere promotes a fixation in the practicing phase, while for some others the difficulties in successfully negotiating the rapprochement crisis prompts a regression to the unrealistic glory of the practicing phase. Under these conditions characterological problems evolve in which such features as an excessive sense of entitlement, grandiosity, a poor appraisal of reality, omnipotence, and an outrageous sense of self-importance are prominent. They grow up unprepared for the challenges of the real world. Their interpersonal relationships are severely compromised by their characterological difficulties. For these individuals the normal process of taming their grandiose illusions has not taken place.

Thus, unresolved issues from the practicing phase of development in which grandiose illusions prevail may be seen in the light of what might be called Icarus-like conflicts. Adult pathology that stems from this era of preoedipal development might be viewed in terms of an "Icarus complex." What the child requires during this period is to have the best of both worlds—the freedom to explore the outside world on his own from the vantage point of grandiose illusions, and the emotional availability of the mother when he returns for refueling (Mahler et al. 1975). When the mother at this junction is either overprotective or prematurely abandons her toddler, pathological outcomes eventuate.

THE ICARUS COMPLEX

The Icarus complex can be distinguished from the Oedipus complex in that it originates from an earlier point in development. Moreover, it is different from the Oedipus complex in that it is not about sexual and aggressive drives related to the family tri angle, but rather reflects a pathological view of the self in relation to the world.

Hence, the term *Icarus complex* might be used to describe the source of difficulty in those individuals whose problems revolve around the wish and/or fear of ambitious overreaching. This syndrome may be expressed in a variety of ways. One type can be seen in those individuals whose functioning is organized around a sense of arrogance based on grandiose illusions about one's capabilities and immunity to vulnerability. These people act as though they can have the world on their terms without regard for limitations or the need to consider other people's needs and priorities. Another type is seen in those individuals who operate with a state of anxiety in relation to their powerful wishes to challenge the fates—metaphorically to fly too close to the sun. It may be experienced as "If I follow my desires to take risks with reality, I will be shot down!" In this type it is the fear of one's own hubristic strivings that is most prominent and needs to be defended against.

I am proposing applying the term *Icarus complex* to those disorders that are characterized by grandiose illusions fueled by hubris, along with a fear of the consequences of exposing these strivings. It used to be believed that certain types of disturbances directly correlated with specific stages of development. Thus, problems around competition were invariably viewed as emanating from oedipal psychodynamics, issues around control and power stemmed from unresolved anal conflicts, dependency problems coalesced around oral fixations, and so on. Currently, psychoanalysts have come to appreciate that there are some problems that may originate from either oedipal or preoedipal conflicts, and it may require a long period of analytic work before the locus of origin can be determined. For example, in those patients who experience apprehension about the consequences of being too assertive or successful, it was formerly assumed that such symptomatology was an expression of oedipal dynamics, that is, the fear of incurring the retaliating wrath of an oedipal rival. However, it is just as likely that such concerns reflect a preoedipal conflict around fear of retaliation or abandonment for separating from overattached parents, or for pursuing one's own inner dictates rather than honoring the wishes of parents whose love was conditional on the child's adherence to their value system. In psychoanalytic work, features of impotence and unassertiveness are often prominent symptoms, and it is crucial to determine whether these symptoms spring from oedipal or pre-oedipal layers. Thus, for example, impotence can represent a defense against the exposure of omnipotent illusions, or it can be a defense against castration anxiety. A thorough exploration and understanding of the vicissitudes of the patient's preoedipal and oedipal experience will highlight the central source of the conflict.

Metaphorically speaking, many individuals defend themselves against their anxiety about flying too close to the sun by underreaching, underachieving, and underplaying their attributes. Their Icarus complex, so to speak, takes the form of presenting themselves as incompetent and ineffective, and they hold themselves back in order to ward off the unconsciously anticipated dangers associated with being or appearing to be successful.

> Pamela, a well-trained psychologist, experienced herself as incompetent in her work with patients. Her father had been a very outspoken, assertive, and successful businessman, and his dictates were treated as gospel within the family. Pamela was groomed to follow his lead rather than to trust her own thoughts and feelings. Her mother established a powerful attachment to Pamela, and subtly undermined her autonomous functioning. When the father was traveling on business, the mother relied upon Pamela for companionship. Together they waited by the window for the father to come home and revitalize the family, much like Madame Butterfly standing at the shore waiting for her sailor to return or like Penelope waiting endlessly for Odysseus.
>
> During her formative latency and adolescent years, Pamela felt the pressure of the burden of providing emo-

tional sustenance for her mother. When she became involved in peer relationships, she felt rejected by her mother. Pamela grew up feeling guilty about following her own feelings in her outside relationships. Nevertheless, she was determined to find her own voice, and she overruled the career plans suggested by her parents and decided to become a psychologist. During her training she sought out psychoanalysis because she repeatedly felt that she didn't know what she was doing in her work with her patients. Although her superiors praised her and attempted to reinforce her strengths, she persistently felt like a fraud.

In her personal analysis she presented herself as somewhat scattered and at times disorganized. She frequently could not remember what was discussed in the previous session and she would leave things behind when she left, such as scarves, eyeglasses, and appointment books. Her transference expectation was that the analyst would be a parental figure who would guide her and help her to be more centered through his input. In this way she was attempting to repeat her early history with her father. She would seek out help on her work with her difficult cases, and although she felt overwhelmed and lost, she always seemed to be doing things right and was helpful to her patients. Thus, while her supervisors and analyst viewed her as doing productive work, she viewed herself as an impostor.

Gradually, over a long period of time, her analyst came to recognize that Pamela's fraudulent, incompetent view of herself was a defense. Underlying this portrayal of herself were secret fantasies about unlimited success and invitations from around the world for her to present her treatment approach. As she increasingly got in touch with these underlying wishes, she became increasingly apprehensive. Her anxiety was expressed in such statements as "It's risky and dangerous to try to fly too high! I could get shot down!" When she submitted a paper for publication, she expressed concern: "I shouldn't be doing this. I'm not supposed to be having my own ideas. There will be dangerous consequences." Although these anxieties contained oedipal dynamics, the deeper roots that were being reactivated pertained to her fear that if she became too much of her own person, with her own voice and her own set of beliefs, such assertiveness and independence would be destructive to her overly attached mother, and she would lose her connection to both parents. The ebb and flow of allowing her successful side to emerge alongside of her self-defeating, holding herself back persona became the core arena in the working-through phase of Pamela's personal journey in psychoanalysis.

At the other end of the spectrum are those cases in which grandiose illusions prompt behavior in which an individual hubristically ignores reality considerations and self-destructive consequences ensue. We can cite many examples from everyday life, such as not wearing seat belts, drinking and driving, practicing unsafe sex in the era of AIDS, doing drugs, smoking, and excessive sunbathing (literally getting one's body too close to the sun). In the psychoanalytic literature self-destructive behavior has often been understood as being motivated by masochistic trends, for example, a need for punishment for unconscious guilt. In this view individuals might unconsciously seek out relationships in which they will be abused, or inappropriately be aggressive or demanding with a boss to the point of being fired, in order to fulfill the need to bring about the punishment that they feel they deserve for their unacceptable underlying sexual and aggressive feelings.

From an object relations theoretical perspective, masochistic relationships are seen not as stemming from a need for punishment triggered by unconscious guilt, but rather as a way of repeating that which is familiar. Individuals who were neglected, rejected, or otherwise mistreated as a child may unconsciously be drawn to relationships in which they will be abused. Such individuals have internalized a view of relationships in which mistreatment is a major component. In a sense an abusive relationship has become their internal definition of a loving relationship, and they seek to repeat, in new relationships, that which is known and familiar. The organizing principle in such cases is that a bad mother is better than no mother, and to be in a nonmasochistic position is tantamount to not knowing how to be in a relationship. Self-defeating masochistic patterns prevail as a way of playing out a known habitual role.

An alternative point of view, consistent with the material presented here, is that individuals whose functioning is punctuated by self-defeating patterns are being driven by grandiose illusions and a primitive defensive structure that prompts them to be oblivious to the potential dangerous implications of their behavior. Like Icarus, they tend to overestimate their powers and their invulnerability. They suffer from illusions that risky behavior is safe, and illusions about their invincibility prevail. Their need is not to be self-destructive, but self-destructive consequences may result from their need to disregard reality considerations. In such cases the central theme is that their self-destructive way of functioning may be organized around narcissistic issues rather than masochistic issues. For such individuals their unhappy love affairs or their difficulties in work relationships are often fueled less by a need for punishment, a need to suffer, or a need to repeat familiar unproductive relational patterns, than from ego lacunae that prompt them to view situations from a somewhat skewed and tinted vantage point. Thus, it is common for these individuals to have successive failures in love and/or work because of the blind spots with which they proceed. They may go full steam ahead in pursuing a love relationship without giving due consideration to the indications of unavailability in their partners. They insist on seeing what they want to see and tuning out the rest of the picture. These individuals frequently suffer disappointments and pain in their love relationships because they overestimate their position in the relationship. They are prone to disillusionment when their unrealistic expectations and illusions about the relationship are unfulfilled.

Claudette sought psychotherapy at age 40 because of a series of unhappy love affairs and her inability to find a permanent partner. Although she was attractive and intelligent, she significantly overestimated these qualities and the effect she would have on men. Her parents had treated her as an especially gifted and beautiful child, and she came to expect others to treat her in a similar way in her adult life. Her relationships had failed primarily because she wanted more than these men could supply. When she got involved in a new relationship, she required that the man be intensely devoted to her and exclusively available. In several instances she had pressured men to propose marriage after a relatively short interval of dating. In fact she frequently had selected men who were emotionally or physically unavailable, but her sense of her own specialness and self-importance overshadowed her ability to recognize their limitations. One suitor wined and dined her in fancy restaurants, but he was never able to see her on a Saturday night. For several months she basked in the glow of these special outings, while de-emphasizing the meaning of his limited availability. Another beau was handsome, attentive, and generous, but earned his living in a mysterious way that he would not disclose. After tuning out on many clues that he was involved in an illegal operation, Claudette belatedly came to recognize that his man was a prominent drug dealer, and that it was dangerous for her to be connected to him.

Claudette's pattern of getting involved in destructive or dead-end relationships was not based on masochistic dynamics. Consciously her goal was to find a man with whom she would share a good life in the style to which she had been accustomed. However, her exaggerated sense of specialness, and her blind spots regarding the limitations of the men she chose, severely compromised her ability to fulfill her goal. Her need to maintain her illusions about herself and her entitlement prompted her to continue to experience serial relationships through a distorted prism. As a result, her journey in psychotherapy was a difficult one. Her patterns were entrenched. Consequently, it took several years before she was able to acquire a more realistic view of herself and to develop the ability to better evaluate her relationships. She left treatment at a point when she was fortified with an ego structure that enabled her to be involved in a more genuinely satisfying relationship.

For many individuals a sense of well-being is organized around the maintenance of a central illusion. Taylor (1989) describes the value of positive illusions in adapting to the stresses of life. These positive illusions are normal, according to Taylor, and cluster around self-enhancing beliefs about one's abilities, overconfident expectations of the future, and a feeling of control over events in one's life.

Illusions become maladaptive when they seriously interfere with one's functioning in the real world. False beliefs that are damaging to mental health may be difficult to relinquish, especially if one's sense of security has been built around them. Marital therapists see couples repeatedly reconcile after breaking up in spite of the therapist's attempts to help their patients recognize the futility of expecting to have their unrealistic expectations met. It is common in such instances that the illusion of attaining greater harmony outstrips the therapeutic work, because of the difficulty in accepting a painful reality. This pattern is most prevalent in those people who are loath to tolerate the disillusionment of a failed marriage and whose sense of self is based on their connection with their spouse. Such anxieties lead them to cling to illusions about marital harmony, when, in fact, they are unable to meet each other's needs.

The yearning for all of one's needs to be fulfilled in a perfect relationship is described as the "golden fantasy" (Smith 1977). Although these yearnings are ubiquitous, they often become a core dimension in the personalities of those individuals with more primitive ego functions. As Smith notes, "To give up the fantasy is to give up everything, to lose the primary source of comfort.... It is as if the fantasy provided a self-definition: without it there is no existence and the world becomes a place without hope" (p. 311).

Thus, to a certain extent, maintaining illusions might be seen as a necessary organizing principle. We all need illusions, dreams, and fantasies in order to feel hopeful about our lives and our future. For some individuals the need for illusions remains especially central to their ongoing functioning. While they are able to relinquish an illusion in response to a shattering reality, they quickly move on and replace the lost illusion by forming the next one. It is as if possessing some illusion is a central and necessary component to their adjustment. It is not only the fear of the pain that accompanies the process of dealing with disillusionment that propels these people, but also the powerful investment in illusion itself as a central component of life and existence. While we all do this to some extent inasmuch as it is valuable to have hopes and dreams, and the illusion about them may often provide us with the courage to attempt to fulfill them, these people carry this out to an extreme degree.

The pattern in which an individual has serial monogamous relationships that break up at the point that disillusionment makes its presence felt may illustrate the need to preserve one's illusion about finding the perfect relationship. Instead of attempting to work through the feelings of disillusionment and revising their expectations, these individuals tend to respond to the rupture in their relationship by moving away and pursuing perceived greener pastures in which the hope of fulfillment of their illusions can be rejuvenated. It is as if the need to fulfill the illusion is so central to one's existence and sense of well-being that it must be pursued, and it overrides the capacity to work through the feelings of disillusionment. In these relationships sometimes we see a sequence of idealization followed by vicious devaluation, which reflects the intensity of the upset over the intrusions of reality that interfere with the sustaining of one's illusions.

REINFORCEMENT OF ILLUSIONS

People unconsciously may seek out partners who will collude with them in maintaining an illusion. When a false belief is shared, one is further protected from the truth and is that much more able to avoid the experience of disillusionment. As long as the collusion continues, the illusion is reinforced. Such shared illusions between couples is a common occurrence (Person 1995), and the fabric of these illusions is frequently an organizing principle within these relationships. A relationship may become organized around a central illusion that is shared by the participants. Sometimes these illusions have a positive impact and are perpetuated by another family member. An example would be a tennis enthusiast who holds the belief that if he practices enough, he will become good enough to be a professional player. If this long-shot dream is shared and reinforced by his wife, it may serve to intensify this man's determination, as well as provide an ongoing central focus to their relationship. In other instances shared illusions may be maladaptive and serve a pathological function.

When a partner in a shared illusion withdraws his or her collusive participation, the illusion often collapses, and the relationship may disintegrate as well. The disappointment in the partner who no longer continues to perpetuate and reinforce a central illusion can be severe and intense. It is often experienced as a devastating abandonment and narcissistic injury. This sequence of events may precipitate devaluation and excessively hurtful actions toward the partner who is now perceived as abandoning. Such overreactions correspond to the severity of the perceived injury that occurs when central illusions are no longer supported and reinforced.

The role of a shared illusion that operates as a central dimension in an ongoing relationship is vividly portrayed in Edward Albee's (1963) play *Who's Afraid of Virginia Woolf?* The main characters, George and Martha, have a profoundly sadomasochistic relationship that is held together by their joint illusion about an imaginary son. Illusions may be conscious or unconscious, and there are many gradations of awareness along this continuum. George and Martha have entered a conscious collusion in the formation of their shared illusion. They each have a powerful investment in perpetuating this illusion, which serves to keep them intact both individually and as a couple. At the same time they are dependent on one another to perpetuate the illusion, and to honor their mutual commitment that it remain their shared secret. At one point George states, "Truth and illusion, who knows the difference!" (p. 201).

During an alcohol-frenzied evening with another couple, George and Martha alternate in their sadistic and masochistic roles with each other. Throughout the early part of the encounter Martha repeatedly verbally abuses George with vicious castrating remarks, and she humiliates him in front of the other couple. They also engage in banter and contradictions about their son. It appears that George is the masochistic container for her sadistic aggression, but ultimately he registers the last and most devastating assault. In a fit of vengeful desperation, George announces that while Martha was upstairs having sex with the other woman's husband, a messenger had delivered a telegram stating that their son had been killed in a car crash. Martha is instantly devastated by the realization that they could no longer sustain their shared illusion about their imaginary son as a living being. George has shattered the illusion and Martha along with it. In despair and horror she cries out, "No! No! You cannot do that! You can't decide that for yourself! I will not let you do that! . . . You can't do this! . . . You can't have him die! . . . You have no right!. . . Why?" (pp. 232, 233, 236). To which George triumphantly replies, "You broke our rule, baby. . . . You mentioned him to someone else!" (p. 236).

It is the abrupt crashing of the illusion about the fictitious son that is most remembered about Albee's play. Indeed, there was a crescendo of sadomasochistic interactions during the evening between George and Martha that paved the way for this most dramatic event. Upon closer examination, however, we can see that a more chronic breakdown in the illusion-disillusionment cycle had previously occurred. It is revealed, at least from Martha's perspective, that her earlier disillusionment about George's lack of success was fueling her vitriolic and taunting put-downs of George. She had nurtured the illusion that George would become chairman of the history department at his college, and that when her father, who was the college president, retired, George would take over his position. When it gradually became apparent that this was not going to happen, her disillusionment was profound. She railed at George for his ineffectiveness, and exclaimed, "George didn't have the stuff, didn't have much push, wasn't particularly aggressive. In fact, he was a flop!" Thus, Martha experienced ongoing chronic rage and disappointment over her husband's lack of fulfillment of her illusion. Like many women of her generation, Martha's status needs were inextricably linked with the success of her husband. When he failed, her illusion about their successful life together could not be sustained. As a result she experienced a sense of failure around herself, and her wrath toward George was ignited.

AVOIDING THE PAIN OF DISILLUSIONMENT

Safeguarding oneself against the anticipated pain of disillusionment can be a central motivating force in the decision-making process of certain people. This is particularly evident in individuals who have anguished over prior disillusions. One such patient, in musing over his three failed marriages, stated, "After my first wife, I was determined only to marry women that I didn't love, because I didn't want to be disillusioned and brokenhearted again!"

Burton, age 33, sought psychotherapy in order to resolve his ambivalent relationship with his girlfriend and to work on his problems with authority figures in his work world. He was being seen in a low-cost mental health clinic in which patients were assigned to work with therapists who were receiving psychoanalytic training. Burton was assigned to a newly entering psychologist. During the previous two years Burton had been in treatment with four different therapists at the same clinic. In each situation he had fairly quickly found something objectionable in the therapist's way of doing therapy. He was not open to repairing the therapeutic relationship, and so in each instance he prematurely terminated and requested a new therapist.

The psychologist was alerted in supervision to anticipate a repetition of this patient's pattern of finding a flaw in the therapist and using this to extricate himself from the treatment. It was hypothesized that this behavior reflected Burton's fears about getting involved in exploring his problems and getting involved in the therapeutic relationship. Fortunately, the supervisor's prediction did not come true, and Burton worked effectively in treatment with this, his fifth therapist. The psychologist noted that Burton had become fully engaged in the therapy, had married his girlfriend, and was making slow but steady progress in addressing his problems with authority figures.

After four years the psychologist had completed his training program and was going to be leaving the clinic. The policy of the clinic was to allow their graduating therapists to take their patients with them on a private basis, if this was in the best interests of the patients. The alternative was for the patients to continue in the clinic with a new therapist. When the psychologist presented this choice to Burton, he expected that because of the work that they had accomplished, as well as their positive therapeutic relationship, which was in sharp contrast to the patient's previous experiences, Burton would surely opt to continue their work together in the psychologist's private practice. The psychologist was totally surprised when after several sessions Burton indicated that while he still felt he needed more therapy, he had decided to continue at the clinic rather than leaving along with the therapist. In exploring the patient's decision what emerged was that Burton had had a maternal transference to the clinic. He felt safe and secure there, and, although he valued the work he had accomplished with this psychologist, he needed to count on the reliability provided by the clinic. He did not want to risk something happening to disrupt his therapy if he went into the psychologist's private practice. He feared that the therapist might develop an incapacitating health problem or that a substantial fee increase would make it unaffordable, and that he might wind up stranded. These anticipated events, although farfetched, were very real possibilities to Burton, and the potential for overwhelming disillusionment was great. It was more comforting to assume that no matter what happened with a particular therapist, his needs for treatment would be taken care of by the clinic.

In effect this patient had harbored a nondiscernible illusion about the clinic-mother as a ubiquitous provider, which influenced his decision to continue within the safe confines of the clinic. The therapist had not elicited this illusion during the course of their work together, and he had overestimated Burton's capacity for object constancy. They continued to explore these issues in their remaining sessions, and ultimately Burton requested that he be transferred to a new therapist so that he could continue to remain at the clinic.

There are many ways in which Burton's choice can be understood. On one level he was once again defying the position of an authority figure. This could be seen as an acting out of his long-standing presenting problem. On another level his decision served to bypass having to deal with the hurt and anger he may have felt about the therapist's disrupting a stable arrangement. A third possibility is that Burton's fantasies about what it meant to be seeing his therapist in private practice provoked too much anxiety. Other interpretations may apply, but I believe that on some level his need to safeguard himself against anticipated disillusionment was a prominent factor in the patient's decision to terminate this therapy.

In the first two years of life the child is reliant upon the mother to mediate the external world, and to provide signals to the child about safety and danger in the ways he navigates in the world. The mother stands between her child and the real world and her construction of reality is pivotal in the child's emerging development. The mother's worldview is generally conveyed to the child and utilized by him as a barometer in his perception of himself and the world. If the mother's construction of reality is highly idiosyncratic as a function of her being excessively anxious, depressed, narcissistic, or detached, the child is presented with a skewed construction of reality. For a while the child may adapt to this distorted reality and adopt it as his own, but gradually, with the solidification of further ego functions, there occurs a divergence in his construction of reality from that of his mother's. As his own ability to synthesize cues from the environment increases, he is able to consider alternative forms of reality and to sense the caregiver's inappropriateness. One patient described how she came to realize when she was 9 years old that her mother was inappropriate. A classmate had invited her to come over to watch a television special at seven in the evening. This was at first quite puzzling to this patient, since in her household her mother gave her dinner at 5:30 and then immediately put her to bed. The friend's invitation and further inquiry made her realize that 9-year-old children are not usually sent to bed at six o'clock, and that it was an inappropriate reality being imposed on her by her depressed and overwhelmed mother.

Thus, some children gradually become aware that their caregivers' construction of reality is aberrant, and that they cannot count on them to provide an accurate worldview. At a time when it is still phase appropriate to be able to view one's parents as omniscient and omnipotent, these children recognize that their parents are off target in some fundamental way. As a result a premature disillusionment in the parents sets in, and a defensive armor is established in order to prevent future disillusionment in their relationships. Modell (1991a) speaks to this when he points out that some children learn that their parents'

> judgments of the real world [are] eccentric and, in a sense, crazy . . . that a parent's view of reality is off . . . that his mother's judgment was unreliable and could not assure his safety in the world. . . . These children learn that their world view is apt to be more dependable than that of their parents. The loss of their parents as protective objects induces a precocious yet fragile maturation supported by grandiose illusions regarding the self, illusions that prove to be necessary for the child's psychic survival. [pp. 236–237]

Many patients in psychotherapy find it necessary to ride the crest of the wave of idealization of the therapist for an extended period of time. When the need is to repair a damaging parental introject through a new object experience with the therapist, as, for example, when a patient who had a very critical parent basks in the glow of feeling accepted by his therapist, there is a tendency to glorify the wisdom and healing powers of the therapist. In such circumstances the therapist has become the embodiment of the parent as the patient had wished him to be. Some patients make substantial improvements based on this type of connection, and a transference cure takes place. In the course of deeper psychodynamic treatment, it is usually desirable for the patient to go beyond this level, and to be able to modify his illusions about the all-perfect therapist in accordance with reality. It is often a goal of treatment for the patient to gain a fuller appreciation of the therapist's imperfections, without this destroying the positive, helpful, curative aspects of their work together. Toward the end of treatment it is hoped that a more realistic view of the therapist prevails, in which his strengths and flaws have been more accurately perceived and integrated by the patient. Some patients who have grown up in an atmosphere of rejection and criticism are reluctant to acknowledge flaws in their therapist out of fear that to do so would jeopardize their positive connection.

> Mark was the oldest of five children in a dysfunctional family. His mother was overwhelmed with having to raise her children, and his father was a workaholic who was largely absent from the home and highly critical and devaluing toward Mark when he interacted with him. Mark experienced both parents as emotionally rejecting, and his connection with each of them was quite limited. He sought psychotherapy at age 35 because of his difficulties in sustaining relationships with women. He was distressed over still being single and yearned for an attachment in which he felt appreciated, understood, and accepted. Mark was superficially very personable, but he did not know how to talk about feelings. In the course of therapy he was helped to enter the realm of emotional communication, and he was able to discover and explore many feelings that had been bottled up inside of himself. Eventually, he was able to bring this new dimension of emotionality into his relationships with women.
>
> Mark was hungry for a positive emotional attachment, and he quickly came to idealize his male therapist. He felt supported by their connection and able to grow from it. He

had found the perfect parent substitute who made him feel appreciated, understood, and accepted. On a conscious level he was determined to retain his much-needed idealized connection to his therapist. As the treatment moved forward, his underlying oedipal rivalry emerged in the therapy material, and these feelings were explored. Toward the end of his therapy he had the following dream, which depicted his struggle over needing to retain his idealization of the therapist versus allowing himself to perceive his therapist as flawed:

> I had a dream in which I had a cushion from the couch in your office. I need to return it, so I go in to put the cushion in your waiting room. It's early in the morning, but you're already there. I hasten to explain what I'm doing here, and I worry if it's okay to enter your place at this unusual time without knocking. You joke, "Looking for an exit?" or something like that, and I worry it might be a snide barb, and then you come out and I recognize it's you.

His associations to the dream were as follows:

> Our relationship is important. The dream makes me realize that I'm gathering courage to look at you emotionally and deal with you more directly. I'm afraid to see you as an imperfect human being. I want to maintain the illusion that you are perfectly trustworthy and perfectly giving. It's difficult to let myself think about you as imperfect, and that's why it's hard to be angry with you. I fear that this dream might be the precursor to my seeing you with human faults. You might use my emotional vulnerability to hurt me. A big issue in the dream is whether it's okay to enter your place, your domain without knocking, whether it's okay to be in your personal domain. I'm also curious about who you are as a person.

In the context of ongoing clinical material, Mark's dream reflected his oedipal guilt about the wish to transgress on his therapist's territory. His associations go in the direction of the therapist's being hostile and aggressive toward him, which would then burst his bubble in which he views his therapist as an idealized all-perfect being. His transference illusion is challenged, and he responds with a readiness as well as a fear about relinquishing his idealization and tolerating a more imperfect image of his therapist.

This vignette demonstrates how an idealized view of the therapist is defensively utilized by the patient as an organizing principle. Maintaining the transference illusion was central to this patient's sense of well-being for an extended period of time, until his dream signaled a readiness to begin to dismantle it.

It is not uncommon for psychotherapists to underestimate the organizing function of illusion. We all need illusions, dreams, and goals in order to feel purposeful and hopeful about life and the future. Levinson (1978) has pointed out that "some men make the pursuit of the dream the central element in the life structure and build everything else around it" (p. 245). Since the early days of Freud, mental health was equated with the acceptance of reality and pathology was equated with the adhesiveness of illusions. However, it also needs to be recognized that illusions can serve a sustaining and even an organizing function.

Yalom (1989) presents a therapy case in which the therapist's agenda of facilitating the relinquishing of a powerful illusion is overridden by the patient's underlying agenda of fortifying and restoring her illusion. The patient was a 70-year-old depressed and lovesick woman who eight years earlier had had a twenty-seven–day love affair with her former therapist. She was obsessed with thinking about him, and she had glorified the brief period of the affair as the high point in her life. She revealed that 90 percent of her life was spent musing about their relationship, and how she could regain from him a modicum of interest in her. Although he had abruptly and permanently severed their relationship without explanation, her sense of well-being was organized around the illusion that she could recapture the blissful period of paradise when she felt exquisitely connected to her lover. She was preoccupied with "someday" fantasies (Akhtar 1996) in which her lover would initiate occasional contact with her and express his interest and concern about her; this would enable her to feel sustained and to live out her time happily.

In the initial consultation the patient and the therapist determined that this woman's masochistic attachment to a lost love and her illusion of regaining a loving connection severely compromised her capacity to lead a satisfying life. The goal of treatment was to eradicate the obsession. Yalom set about the task of disillusioning her and helping her to accept and cope with the prevailing reality in which eight years had passed without any indication of reciprocal interest on the part of her former lover. His therapeutic technique was to repeatedly point out the unrealistic nature of her unattainable dream as well as her self-defeating expenditure of psychic energy. Although he was aware of powerful resistances to change in this patient, Yalom overestimated his ability to help her to eradicate her obsession and relinquish her illusion. He had mistakenly assumed that her obsession was draining her ability to have a richer life experience, when in fact it was her tenacious clinging to the obsession that provided some meaning to her otherwise empty life.

After a three-way session had been arranged in which the patient was able to confront her ex-lover, and experienced him as callous, she lost her hope in reigniting their relationship. The illusion was shattered! She became regressed, despondent, and despairing, and soon thereafter she terminated the therapy. In retrospect the therapist sanguinely explored his countertransference in which his grandiosity and hubris had prompted him to strip this patient of her illusions without her having other adaptive structures to fall back upon. In his well-meaning efforts to help her to abide by the reality principle, he was the disillusioner. Her existence had become organized around the central illusion that she had a 1 percent chance of reconciliation, and she felt bereft when this illusion had been pierced and taken away from her.

Unfortunately, in this case the therapeutic alliance was not strong enough to enable the patient to continue the treatment and work through the necessary mourning of her loss. In an ironic postscript, the patient improved dramatically when, subsequent to their three-way session, her former lover contacted her, and they arranged to meet and chat over coffee on a once-a-month basis. Her original agenda of fortifying her 1 percent chance of reconciliation had now come to fruition. Ultimately, this patient's need to hold on to a fragile and threadbare connection, even though she might lose it again in the future, was stronger than the impact of the therapeutic interventions that were aimed at freeing her from the crippling effects and bondage of her obsession.

6

Depression

Litost is a state of torment caused by a sudden insight into one's own miserable self.

Milan Kundera
The Book of Laughter and Forgetting

Depression can be understood as being intricately related to illusion and disillusionment. The point of view espoused here is that depression often emanates from the loss of core illusions and the concomitant disillusionment that is experienced. This is in contrast to the traditional view about depression as resulting from unexpressed aggression that is turned inward upon the self. An alternative proposition is that clinical depression frequently is a function of the loss of an exalted, idealized, and illusory view of oneself, one's specialness, or the painful awareness of the true nature of our vulnerability in the world. To put it differently, depression emerges from being forced to relinquish certain illusions about oneself in relation to the world.

Thus, depression is characterized by the absence or lack of sustaining illusions, and a preponderance of disillusionment. Hope counteracts depression, and hope is fueled by illusions. Sometimes people try to hold on to their illusions at all costs in order to ward off an underlying depression. This may occur either at a conscious or unconscious level. In the biography of Marlene Dietrich, the actress is reported to have said, "You can't live without illusions even if you must fight for them." When there is an overwhelming sense of loss, a feeling of hopelessness and helplessness prevails and paves the way for the affective experience of depression. Gaylin (1968) describes the depression syndrome as one in which the ego is unable to meet life's dangers, its adaptational function shuts down, and there is a breakdown in the reparative function of symptom formation. If depression is viewed as a reaction to loss, we might pose the question, What kind of loss do we mean? Are we referring to loss of a significant object relationship, or loss of an aspect of one's self image, or loss of an illusion? I believe that depression can be triggered by any of the above. According to Gaylin, "Depression can be precipitated by the loss or removal of anything that the individual overvalues in terms of his security" (p. 390).

Freud originally viewed depressive symptomatology as a manifestation of aggression turned inward upon the self. The drive theory framework of classical psychoanalysis stated that the inability to express aggressive feelings outwardly results in the rechanneling of these feelings inwardly, which leads to depression. Clinical experience has shown us that this formulation is oversimplified, because depression can spring from various sources.

Psychoanalytic theorists have increasingly come to understand that setbacks in self-esteem regulation is a central predisposing factor to depression in certain cases. The man who is depressed because he has lost his job, the man who is depressed because his marriage is ending in divorce, and the woman who is depressed over her inability to find a suitable relationship are all reacting to the feeling of loss or failure and the impact this has upon their self-esteem. In cases in which a feeling of well-being is primarily derived from external supplies the individual's sense of worth may rise or fall according to the availability of these supplies. When nurturing supplies such as approval, affection, and affirmation are absent or withdrawn, the person who is reliant on these supplies may become depressed. Hence, what we are mourning in depression is not essentially the loss of the love object, but the loss of self-esteem. It is the loss of the illusion of well-being derived through the connection with the love object that is central in certain depressions.

Fenichel (1945), an early follower of Freud, was one of the first psychoanalytic theorists to acknowledge the connection between self-esteem and depression: "Experiences that precipitate depressions represent either a loss of self-esteem or a loss of supplies which the patient had hoped would secure or even enhance his self-esteem" (p. 390). While the connection between loss and depression had long been acknowledged, Fenichel's position reflects the beginning of a basic theoretical shift from a primary emphasis on the role of the loss of a love object to an emphasis on the loss of self-esteem. It is interesting to note that a hundred years earlier, the existential philosopher Kierkegaard (1849) came to a similar conclusion. In his essay, "The Sickness Unto Death," he stated:

> Despair is never ultimately over the external object, but always over ourselves. A girl loses her sweetheart and she despairs. It is not over the lost sweetheart, but over herself-without-the-sweetheart. And so it is with all cases of loss, whether it be money, power, or social rank. The unbearable loss is not really in itself unbearable. What we cannot bear is in being stripped of the external object. We stand denuded and see the intolerable abyss of ourselves. [cited in Gaylin 1968, p. 15]

Kierkegaard's statement highlights the connection between depression and loss of self-esteem. It is the loss of an illusion and the accompanying existential emptiness that defines "the intolerable abyss of ourselves," when we are faced by truth and without the comfort of illusions. Gaylin (1968), known for his work on depression, proposes a view similar to Fenichel and Kierkegaard:

> It is not essentially the loss of the love object or its symbolic counterparts that causes depression. Indeed, only when a

loved object is invested with our self-esteem does its loss
produce a depression. What we are mourning is our lost self-
esteem, the love object merely being symbolic of it. . . . The
loss of the loved object is then the instrument for depression in those dependent people who perceive (even if inac-
curately) that particular loved object as the essential instrument for survival. [p. 17]

Palombo (1985) approaches the understanding of depression from a self psychological perspective in which the awareness of the absence of selfobject functions is paramount. This
constellation in many cases leads to what Palombo terms a
"depletion depression," which is experienced as "a deficit in the
self or as resulting from an irreconcilable yearning within the
self for a missing selfobject function" (p. 33). Thus, this type of
depression emanates from a missing aspect of self experience,
and without this aspect of internal psychic structure a sense of
emptiness, that is, depletion, occurs. In this framework the treatment approach involves the facilitation of an idealized transference in which the illusion of the analyst as a magical healer is
cultivated and uninterrupted. Repair of the self deficit occurs via
the experiencing of the selfobject function of the analyst. Eventually, through gradual disillusion and the transmuting internalization of the analyst's function, the patient acquires a more
cohesive sense of self. This in turn enables him to explore new
opportunities to further replenish the missing selfobject functions or to establish compensatory structures.

Unsustainable illusions about one's abilities, powers, and invincibility lead to a heightened sense of disparity between the
ideal self and the experienced self, and the awareness of this
disparity may be a precipitating factor in depression. Phillips
(1998) speculates, "What are variously described in the psychoanalytic literature as disillusionment, narcissistic rage, the depressive position, are all versions of a familiar story—that the visible
self is a diminished self" (p. 56). It is the realization of one's
difficulty or inability to measure up to the standards of the ideal

self that provides the soil for the blooming of depression. Thus, conflicting self representations in which the ideal self, bolstered by illusions about one's unlimited capacities, is significantly dissonant from the experienced self, which recognizes one's feelings of vulnerability and dependency, bring about a feeling of deflation, which in more extreme form becomes depression. Mahler draws attention to this in her separation-individuation theory when she points out that the core affective experience of the rapprochement stage is disillusionment. She describes the experience of deflation that typically occurs in normal development when the reality principle has taken root and the child recognizes that his world is a place with limitations. The child's increased awareness of his vulnerability is deflating, especially since it follows upon the elation of the practicing phase with its grandiose illusions. Under the impact of disillusionment the child retreats back to the mother for support and restabilization before proceeding with further development. If the mother is not emotionally available for her child's need to step backward before proceeding forward, the child experiences profound disappointment, which Mahler maintains leads to depression.

Jacobson adopts a similar position in highlighting her belief that an unsatisfying maternal attunement during this crucial rapprochement phase of development leads to a weakening of self-esteem and predisposes the child toward depression. Jacobson also maintains that the source of depression originates in the discrepancy between wishful self-images of the ideal self and the image of a failing self. It is the gulf between the real self and the wished-for or ideal self that sets the stage for depression. Thus, both Mahler and Jacobson assert that the key factors that cause depression involve a reduction in self-esteem brought about by a painful awareness of reality, that is, the loss of illusion, and a lack of maternal attunement, which promotes disillusionment. Jacobson emphasizes that premature and excessive disappointment in the first years of life leads to a premature devaluation of the love objects, the parents. This disrupts the normal building up of self-esteem, which is based on identification with the love object, and the perceived loving attitude emanating from the love object. Thus, this early disappointment, occurring at a time prior to the development of solid ego structures, results in the devaluation of the love object, and simultaneously a devaluation of the self. Illusions of parental perfection and self-omnipotence are shattered. Jacobson believes that this profile characterizes the early life of many depressed patients.

In a seminal paper Joffe and Sandler (1965) explore the relationship between psychic pain, mourning, and depression. They echo the view of Fenichel and Gaylin in highlighting that what is really lost when object loss occurs is the state of well-being derived from the relationship. In the human craving for an "ideal state of well-being," Joffe and Sandler see the role of the love object as merely a "vehicle." Again, it is the loss of the satisfying feelings derived from the connection, over and above the love object in itself, that results in psychic pain. "Although clinically we may deal with states of object loss, we would stress again that what is lost in object loss is ultimately a state of the self for which the object is the vehicle" (p. 421).

When idealization of the love object falters, with its inherent illusions about the object's magnificence, the devaluation of the object may occur. What was previously overvalued is now undervalued. To the extent that the love object represented a vehicle for the ideal state of well-being, a sense of self-devaluation also takes place. It is this discrepancy between the wished-for state of the self and the actual self representation that leads to psychic pain. According to Joffe and Sandler (1965), the most adaptive response to these circumstances "involves 'working through' in a manner analogous to mourning. It involves the adaptive abandoning of the pursuit of lost ideal states and their replacement by new ideals which are both ego and reality syntonic" (p. 421). This mourning process, when it occurs, enables the individual to resolve the situation that brought about mental pain. A more maladaptive response to this type of psychic pain is that of helpless resignation. For Joffe and Sandler it is not so much the discrepancy between actual self representations and the wished-for state of self that defines depression, but rather the state of helpless resignation in the face of this type of psychic pain that defines the depressive reaction. Thus, Joffe and Sandler's position goes beyond that of Gaylin, Fenichel, and Kierkegaard, and lies closer to that presented by Mahler and Jacobson.

Gedo (1989) describes cases in which depressive crises prompt patients to seek psychotherapy. According to Gedo the basis for these crises "usually involves collapse of illusions, either about the perfection of another or about the absence of personal limitations" (p. 1). Here, again, depression is conceptualized in terms of loss of unsustainable illusions.

As life expectancy increases, older people have more years in which to struggle with their feelings of disillusionment. An increasing number of patients now seek psychotherapy in order to deal with their life's disillusions. They mourn the loss of hopes and dreams from earlier times, which are no longer sustainable. Unfulfilled dreams and illusions tamed by the realities of life often trigger longings for past relationships and past times, which are retrospectively idealized. Although the adolescent years are generally described as a stormy period of development filled with turmoil, midlife and senior adults often reveal a nostalgia for adolescence when hopes for the future were boundless and ran high. The onset of physical infirmities and the realization of the finiteness of time and unreachable goals reinforce these yearnings for the feeling state of years past. External life events may also serve to undermine precarious illusions about oneself and cast a depressive pall over one's outlook. In reacting to the news of a major earthquake in Japan, one patient commented, "The awareness of total powerlessness in a world in which we want to think we have some control is terrifying!"

George, a midlife adult, sought psychotherapy because he was depressed over his lack of success in life. His career as an advertising executive was floundering, and he had recently been bypassed when a promotion opportunity arose. His wife was increasingly dismayed by his emotional inaccessibility and was threatening to divorce him. George mused repeatedly about the carefree years of his adolescence and young adulthood when he was full of ambition and dreams about the future. He lamented and protested about the reality that "things can't be what I once had!" He ultimately found a new career and another wife, but he never felt happy, and he perpetually longed for the halcyon days of an earlier era. From a psychodynamic point of view it became clear that George's plight was overdetermined insofar as he was repeating an unresolved conflict from his past. Although he consciously yearned for his carefree years as an adolescent, further analysis revealed that the deeper roots of his depression revolved around the loss of the blissful harmonious relationship he had with his mother as a very young boy. His father had died soon after his birth, and his mother subsequently bonded with him in a way in which she anticipated his every need and responded with excessive gratification. Consequently, George's early protracted experience of the world was of a place where all of his needs were quickly met. His bubble was abruptly burst at age 5 when his mother remarried and a limit-setting stepfather entered his world. Thus, George had to contend with an excessively indulgent preoedipal period that was traumatically interrupted by the arrival of a harsh oedipal rival. It was only the working through of this early conflict that allowed George, as a 50-year-old, to come to terms with life's limitations and to find a greater degree of satisfaction in his marriage and career.

Illusions provide protection against depression, while disillusionment breeds depression. It is disillusionment pertaining to the loss of life dreams, ambitions, and goals that leads to depression. When illusions are unsustainable and break down, disillusionment follows. Without illusions we come face to face with despair. The popularity of Prozac and other so-called mood brighteners is based on the ability of these drugs to distance patients from their legitimate despair (Kramer 1993). In *Listening to Prozac*, Peter Kramer states, "Studies show that depressed people tend to be more accurate in predicting probabilities than 'normal' people, who are too optimistic; it is the 'normal' whose view of reality is distorted, however adaptively. Giving an antidepressant to a depressed patient thus disconnects him or her from (bleak) reality" (p. 253).

Taylor (1989) comes to the same conclusion, and refers to the state in which illusions are lost or absent as "depressive realism." Taylor concludes that mildly depressed people "appear to have more accurate views of themselves, the world, and the future than do normal people" (p. 213). She maintains that it is the lack of forming or sustaining the normal positive illusions that buffer most people against the painful side of reality that paves the way for depression. In contrast "depressive realism" may be a precipitating factor in causing depression. It is the loss or absence of illusions that occurs when depressive realism is strong that promotes the development of depression.

The sequence of illusion and disillusionment traverses different roads. While it is natural and even necessary for us to harbor illusions that enable us to proceed through life with hope, it is also considered normal for illusions to be disrupted by the stark picture of reality. When disillusionment occurs, prompted by the forces of reality, there are a variety of possible outcomes that may follow. Five characteristic patterns or sequences can be discerned:

> Type A: Illusion-disillusionment, followed by the acceptance of reality. The individual mourns the loss of the illusion, makes an appropriate adaptation to reality, and moves on. This sequence is generally considered to be the most healthy route. For example, the young boy's

dream of becoming a major league baseball player gives way to the reality that he may not possess the talent required, and he ultimately pursues a more attainable career.

Type B: Illusion-disillusionment, followed by distortion and denial. The individual fights against the impact of reality, and continues to cling to the illusion to an extreme degree. The need to bend reality may take on pathological proportions. For example, a woman sees a man at a party whom she had been dating, but he hasn't called her in a month. She is infatuated with him, but he socializes with others and avoids her. She deceives herself into thinking that he is networking for his business, rather than to accept the obvious fact that he has lost interest in their relationship. This allows her to maintain the belief that she is desired and to ward off the pain of rejection. In this way her illusion allows her to minimize the discrepancy between actual and ideal self representations. It is transparent to an objective observer that reality is being excessively stretched in order to avoid dealing with the unacceptable.

Type C: Illusion-disillusionment, followed by a replacement or compensating illusion. A synthetic adaptiveness is prominent. One avoids the pain of dealing with the loss of an illusion by quickly developing a new illusion. In this way the mourning process is truncated and new hope abounds. An example would be a man who comes to recognize that he cannot fulfill his life dream of becoming an acclaimed actor, and now transfers his energy in the direction of becoming a rock and roll star.

Type D: Illusion-disillusionment, followed by a defensive armor that precludes future illusions. Hypervigilance is prominent and is needed to protect the ego from further loss and pain. There is a determined shutting down of fantasies, dreams, and hopes in order to ensure against additional hurt, disappointment, and shame, which is anticipated if one allows room for illusion. There is also a fear in these cases of feeling overwhelmed by disillusionment. An example would be a man who is jilted by his fiancée and does not allow himself to ever again have a romantic relationship. In this pattern it is paramount that one has no expectations.

Type E: Illusion-disillusionment followed by despair. The experience of disillusionment results in an outcome in which the individual feels depleted and shot down. The loss of an illusion is profound and a lack of resiliency is characteristic. An attitude of resignation is prominent and is experienced as "life has lost its meaning" or "things will never be the same again." An example is the Willy Loman character in Arthur Miller's *Death of a Salesman*, who, when confronted with failure and inadequacy, drowns in self-pity, sorrow, and feelings of hopelessness and unlovableness.

These five common patterns are outlined in Table 6–1. The outcomes are not presented as mutually exclusive entities. In some individuals there is a sustained preference for one of these patterns, while in other cases there are considerable overlap and combination. Depression can involve the lack of replacement illusions (type C), and defensive hypervigilance (type D), but is most intricately related to despair (type E).

Table 6–1
Response Patterns to Illusion and Disillusionment

Type	Outcome
A	Illusion ➜ Disillusionment ➜ Acceptance of reality
B	Illusion ➜ Disillusionment ➜ Denial, distortion of reality
C	Illusion ➜ Disillusionment ➜ Replacement illusions
D	Illusion ➜ Disillusionment ➜ Defensive hypervigilance
E	Illusion ➜ Disillusionment ➜ Despair

Several vignettes, drawn from theater and literature, present the themes of illusion, disillusionment, and depression:

The theme of Eugene O'Neill's play *The Iceman Cometh*, which opened on Broadway in 1946, is that people cannot live without their illusions. To maintain a sense of hope as well as an interest in life, one must have cherished illusions. O'Neill's message throughout the play is that life is tolerable only when men deceive themselves in not looking at or dealing with the truth.

The play takes place in a New York saloon and involves a dozen or so alcoholic characters who follow and cling to their respective pipe dreams, that is, illusions, as a form of survival oxygen. For each character the sequence is reiterated in which he is persuaded to give up a core illusion, he cannot tolerate the despair that is engendered by the ensuing disillusionment, and he ultimately needs to find a way to recapture his illusion. To lose one's hopes, even if they are based on pipe dreams, is unendurable for these people, and they rely on alcohol to anesthetize themselves from the realities of life and to bolster their illusions.

The plot of *The Iceman Cometh* centers around the annual visit of Hickey, the main character, to the saloon run by Harry Hope. It is Harry's birthday and all the regulars are assailed by a reformed Hickey, who departs from his customary role of inciting a drunken encounter, and instead cajoles them to give up their alcoholic pipe dreams and face reality. Hickey has come to save his cronies from their dysfunctional pipe dreams, and yet it is these very pipe dreams that keep them from facing their hopeless inadequacy and profound underlying depression. For O'Neill, the *iceman* represents death, and the symbolic meaning of *The Iceman Cometh* lies in the characters' recognition that their pipe dreams are illusions that keep them alive. When they are forced to let go of their illusions and face reality, they become depressed and face a life without hope, which is tantamount to death.

Throughout the play each of the characters is portrayed as embracing a central illusion that keeps them going. These range from Jimmy Tomorrow, whose central illusion is that he is a dysfunctional alcoholic because the woman he loved has left him, to Willie Oban's self-deceptive beliefs about his dropping out of law school, to Hickey, who maintained the illusion that he loved his wife and killed her as a way of protecting her from misery, when in truth it was his underlying hatred toward her that led him to become murderously violent.

At the opening of the play Hickey arrives at the bar in an uncharacteristic state of sobriety and seriousness. He declares to the others that he is a changed man, because he has found peace through facing the truth about himself. He confronts each of the others with their foolish pipe dreams, shames them, and gradually persuades them that their salvation lies in relinquishing their pathetic illusions and facing themselves as they really are. In the denouement they each venture forth into the harsh light of reality outside the bar, they attempt to resume their former occupations, only to return in a despairing state to the safety and security of the saloon. They are unable to function effectively in the real world, and they come back defeated and demoralized, hoping to recapture their lost illusions. Hickey's efforts have freed them from their pipe dreams, but they cannot live with disillusionment. For these derelicts life has lost its interest and its savor once their illusions are destroyed. They require self-deception in order to survive. They turn against Hickey as the grand disillusioner. The moral of the story is that the greatest illusion of all is the belief that coming to terms with disillusion is the road to peace and happiness. For some people, represented by the characters in this play, the process of dismantling illusions and accepting truth is intolerable. The inability to deal productively with disillusionment is summed up by the character Larry Slade, who proclaims, "To hell with the truth! As the history of the world proves, the truth has no bearing on anything. . . . The lie of a pipe dream is what gives life to the whole misbegotten mad lot of us, drunk or sober" (cited in Carpenter 1979, p. 152). Thus, the play implies that truth is equated with the iceman and death. It doesn't set you free, but rather robs you of the illusions that provide hope and make life bearable.

The conflict between the soothing comfort of illusion versus the painful acceptance of reality has been written about since the time of Plato. In *The Republic*, written circa 388 B.C., he addressed this theme via a metaphor of a group of prisoners chained to a wall in a cave that is dimly lit by a fire. They can only barely perceive the silhouettes of themselves and the others as they are reflected on the wall. They assign names to things, but they are constantly in error, for all they are able to really see are shadowy figures. Plato describes how reality exists outside of the cave in the bright light of the sun. He argues that it would be a painful experience for these prisoners to be set free, to climb out of the cave and face the harsh light of the sun as a representation of reality. Their inclination would be to fight against the reality that what they had experienced in the cave was based on shadowy errors of perception. Their beliefs had been formed via illusions and not reality. Plato concludes, "Would he not be perplexed and believe the objects now shown him to be not as real as what he formerly saw?" (cited in Cornford 1945, p. 229).

Disillusionment is frequently a precipitating factor in the onset of depression. This is especially true in situations in which unrequited love prevails, as in the case of Adele H. (see Chapter 4), or in relationships in which a lover's expectations are unfulfilled. There are many pathways that may emerge from disillusionment. One may react by developing a protective hard shell and a cynical approach to the world based on the realization that life is full of disappointments and that other people often do not respond as we would wish them to. Under optimal conditions disillusionment may lead to the acceptance of reality and the capacity to move on. In other situations disillusionment may be a prelude to the formation of new replacement illusions. In certain cases when a disillusioning experience is not metabolized, it may usher in a period of depression. If a certain kind of relationship is needed in order to feel whole, complete, or good about oneself, then the loss of that relationship may leave one feeling lost, depleted, empty, and depressed. Sometimes the depression is counteracted by revenge fantasies or enactments.

An example of the latter is portrayed in *The Heiress*, the theater (Goetz and Goetz 1948) and film (Wyler 1949) adaptations of Henry James's (1881) novel *Washington Square*. The main character, Catherine Sloper, is the oppressed daughter of the patriarch, Dr. Austin Sloper. Her mother died one week after her birth. Catherine is a plain and dull young woman who has always been a disappointment to her aristocratic, wealthy, and domineering father. Her very ordinariness made her unacceptable to him, and he never was able to provide her with the love, approval, and affection that she craved. She assumed the role of the dutiful daughter as her only way to garner some measure of attention and approval from her father. Ultimately, she is pursued and falls in love with a handsome, rakish young man named Morris Townsend, who is accurately assessed by Dr. Sloper as a fortune hunter.

Catherine accepts Morris's marriage proposal and misperceives the underlying mercenary motives that propel his interest in her. Against her father's wishes she is determined to marry Townsend and pursue her own dreams and fantasies about a new life, free of her father's tyranny. Catherine agrees to meet Morris in order to go off together and to get married, but when Morris learns of Dr. Sloper's plan to financially cut off his daughter, he fails to show up for their appointed rendezvous and abandons her. Catherine is humiliated, devastated, and disillusioned by the betrayal of the man she trusted and loved. She withdraws into depression, is unreceptive to other subsequent suitors, and over the years she settles into an identity of a cynical old maid. Her disillusionment is so profound that she can never again allow

herself to be vulnerable in a relationship. Many years later, after her father dies, Morris Townsend reappears and indicates his
desire to renew their lost love. Catherine, still experiencing the
wounds of the earlier abandonment, seizes upon Morris's interest as an opportunity for revenge. She once again agrees to receive him at her home so that they may go off together. At the
denouement he arrives as planned, only to be barred from her
home. In the final scene Morris is hopelessly knocking on an
unanswered door, while Catherine sits smiling in her living room.
By turning the tables on Morris she has finally softened the blow
of her disillusionment. It is interesting to note that in James's
novel, in contrast to the play, this aspect of Catherine's character development, in which her final rejection of Morris is driven
by revenge, is understated.

In Cervantes's *Don Quixote*, (1605) the hero relies on powerful illusions in order to tolerate the ordinariness of his mun-
dane life. In his world of illusions he transforms himself into "a
knight of La Mancha, Don Quixote by name, and [that] it is my
office and profession to go over the world, righting wrongs and
redressing grievances" (p. 86). This transformation, based on
illusion, allows him to avoid his inner feelings of shame, humiliation, and ineffectualness. When others observe his strange way
of talking and his dilapidated appearance and inquire about who
this odd-looking person is, one of his supporter's replies, "Who
should he be but the famous Don Quixote de La Mancha, the
redresser of injuries, the righter of wrongs, the protector of
maidens, the dread of giants, and the conqueror of battles?" (p.
283). This is the way Don Quixote has presented himself, and
he succeeds in deceiving others as well as himself. When the
stories of his escapades are challenged and questioned, he relies on defenses of externalization and projection. He attacks his
accusers and thereby preserves his grandiose illusions. His sense
of well-being is also fueled by his amorous connection with his
imaginary lover, Dulcinea del Toboso, whom he idealizes and
places on a pedestal.

On his deathbed Don Quixote suddenly becomes lucid, grounded, and realistic: "Look not for this year's birds in last year's nest. I was mad; I am now sane. I was Don Quixote de La Mancha; I am now, as formerly, styled Alonzo Quixano the Good" (p. 625). Thus, at the final moment of reckoning, he is able to let go of his illusions and make peace with reality.

A typical transition during the middle phase of psychotherapy frequently involves the patient's realization that s/he has embraced certain needed illusions as a means of warding off anxiety or depression. Psychoanalytic theorists such as Winnicott and Klein view the capacity to tolerate depression as a developmental milestone. According to Winnicott (1954), the ability to deal with depression is contingent on the child's attainment of a sense of identity and a sufficient degree of ego strength to tolerate uncomfortable tensions and feelings such as hatred.

While many patients seek psychotherapy because they are depressed, many others are cut off from their underlying depression and as part of the treatment process they get in touch with their feelings of depression. Thus, to experience previously warded-off feelings of depression may be a sign of therapeutic progress.

Chip was a college student who came to psychotherapy because of academic problems. He was personable and intelligent, and had many friends and girlfriends. On the surface he appeared to be an all-American young man who everyone wanted to be seen with. The problem was that he was a high-level people pleaser who constantly did things for others at the expense of his own needs. He was strongly invested in his "nice guy" image, which made him feel worthwhile and lovable. This was his compensatory defense, which dated back to the stormy environment surrounding his parents' divorce when he was 8. He had experienced both parents as totally caught up in their own personal crisis, with the result that Chip felt neglected and rejected. He feared further abandonment and developed a happy-go-lucky false self in order not to add stress and strain to a chaotic family situation. In one session after a year of therapy the following illuminating exchange took place:

> *Patient:* I see that I've been feeding myself an illusion.
> *Therapist:* How do you mean?
> *Patient:* That I'm together. I realize now that I'm not, because of what went on at home around the divorce.
> *Therapist:* Where does that take you in your feelings?
> *Patient:* I can feel my sadness now, which I couldn't do before.
> *Therapist:* Is there more?
> *Patient:* It has messed me up. I felt like it would have been a burden on my parents to express my needs and my feelings at that time.
> *Therapist:* You are allowing your pain to come in and that's progress.

The writings of Alice Miller are essential to our modern understanding of depression and mourning. Miller (1981) postulates that depression involves a giving up of one's real self as a condition for preserving the love object and the tie to that object. It is this loss of the self that gives rise to feelings of emptiness, futility, loneliness, hopelessness, and other correlates of depression. In a sense Miller sees depression as a defense against the real pain over the loss or alienation from the self. In the early life of depressed patients there was a need to relinquish the real self in order to accommodate to the parents' need for them to be a certain way. In essence they are loved, but for their inauthentic self, not for their own unique qualities. Such patients often present themselves in psychoanalysis with the illusion of having had a happy childhood.

Miller maintains that the goal of psychoanalytic treatment in these cases is to help the patient get in touch with his true feelings as well as to facilitate the mourning for what was missed in childhood and can never be regained in its original form. "This ability to mourn, that is, to give up the illusions of his 'happy' childhood, can restore the depressive's vitality and creativity" (1981, p. 57). It is the freedom to experience spontaneous feelings that counteracts depression. To reach this desired state these patients must relinquish their illusions about their early childhood as an era in which they were appropriately nurtured in an emotional sense, and face the mourning process that accompanies their ensuing disillusionment. In Miller's schema the need to repeatedly develop new illusions in order to avoid dealing with the pain of the true situation subsides when the reality has been faced and experienced as such. Miller argues that through treatment we find a way

> to give up the most flagrant of our illusions. This means tolerating the knowledge that, to avoid losing the object-love . . . we were compelled to gratify our parents' unconscious needs at the cost of our own self-realization. It also means being able to experience the rebellion and mourning aroused by the fact that our parents were not available to fulfill our primary narcissistic needs. [pp. 22–23]

Through the treatment process patients are helped to further develop their capacity to mourn the loss of their illusions and to tolerate disillusion, disappointment, and pain. Along with this comes the freedom to experience spontaneous feelings, in place of the feelings generated by the false self's need to maintain an accommodating facade.

The following vignette describes a sequence during the working-through phase of analysis in which the patient dismantled her illusion about her "happy" childhood, and came to terms with the inappropriate mothering she had received.

Eunice was an accomplished young professional who had difficulty in establishing and maintaining limits and boundaries in her relationships. She readily experienced sexual feelings, but was unable to experience a whole host of other human feelings including anger, sadness, loneliness, envy, and resentment. She had experienced an exquisitely blissful closeness with her mother in her earliest years, in which she was treated as an extension of the mother. A highly charged sexual atmosphere pervaded their relationship. They would take baths together until Eunice was an adolescent, and Eunice would be brought along when the mother engaged in numerous sexual affairs. Accompanying her mother on these escapades made Eunice feel very special and important. She was treated as her mother's confidante and met all of her boyfriends, and a powerful collusion was formed in which she kept her mother's secret life away from her father. Eunice assumed the role of her mother's china doll, and never expressed needs and feelings of her own. In fact she was never aware of having her own set of needs and feelings, and she was enthralled by the special attachment she experienced with mother. She recognized at an early age that her mother was quite unstable. At times when her mother had threatened to cut herself with a knife or jump out of a window, Eunice assumed the responsibility of defusing her mother's destructive behavior by injecting her soothing, calming, and nurturing presence into the stormy family climate.

During the course of her psychoanalysis Eunice came to realize that this seemingly close relationship with her mother had also been very damaging to her growth. At the same time she fought against relinquishing her illusion about her happy childhood. Gradually, as she began to experience new feelings of anger, rage, and sadness, she was increasingly able to mourn the loss of her illusion that she was loved for her true self, rather than for her false self. The realization that one is loved not for one's self but as an extension of the mother, that is, as a selfobject rather

than in the way needed by the child, is a very painful awareness. As she dealt with these feelings over a series of sessions, the following exchange took place between Eunice
and her analyst:

> *Patient:* You've taken away my relationship with my
> mother, who was my best friend. It feels like a
> huge loss. I had the most wonderful thing going.
> Such closeness, it was magical. I was beyond ordi-
> nary kids. I didn't do what ordinary people do.
> Somehow I was involved in this thing with my
> mother that was sexually charged, secretive, adven-
> turous, fun, and had an element of danger.... I
> was in a league of my own. It was so special! No
> one else could hold a candle to it.
>
> *Analyst:* Those were powerful and exciting feelings.
>
> *Patient:* The image that comes to mind is when we
> would drive out to the shore in the summer and
> stop on the way to watch birds. On the way to an
> adventure. To meet a man. It was very exciting.
>
> *Analyst:* What was it like when you were watching the
> birds together?
>
> *Patient:* It was fun. It was close. It was my mother at
> her most normal, to stop with enthusiasm to watch
> the birds.
>
> *Analyst:* So you are mourning the loss of that special
> time with your mother when you had that magi-
> cal feeling of closeness and you only recognized
> the wonderful side of it and didn't realize that
> being brought into your mother's sexual adven-
> tures was also damaging to you.
>
> *Patient:* Yes, I see it now and it makes me angry. At
> the time I only felt how special it was.
>
> *Analyst:* You are connecting your feelings of hurt and
> pain to the feeling of loss of an earlier special

closeness that you had with your mother as a child.
It's something that you feel that I and analysis have
taken away from you.

Patient: Yes. I never used to understand what you
meant, when you said I was dealing with the loss,
because I came to see that I wasn't cared about
in the right way, and that I was being neglected—
and neglect is about something you never had,
something you missed, rather than something you
lost.

Analyst: That's right. It seems that you were neglected
in that your emotional and psychological growth
was not considered by your mother, and as a child
you misinterpreted, misperceived, and misunderstood her inappropriate involvement with you only
as a form of love. But, in addition to your own set
of needs being neglected, the exquisite feeling you
got from the closeness is something that you
struggle to hold onto even as you see things more
clearly as they really were.

Several sessions later, as the working-through process
continues, Eunice deals further with the loss of the illusion
about being special and her disillusionment.

Patient: I was so deceived. What I thought of in my
childhood, in my growing up with my mother, as
being loved and special, was inappropriate, bad,
and kind of abusive.

Analyst: How does it make you feel?

Patient: When I think about it as I now see it, it fills
me with sadness. I feel like I'm bleeding inside.

Analyst: That's from the wound that you feel. That's
your way of mourning the loss of your belief about
your loving wonderful childhood.

Patient: I get knocked out from this stuff, and then I can figure out how to pick myself up and put myself together.

Analyst: Yes. I understand what you mean.

7

Narcissism

Life is a very sad piece of buffoonery because we have . . . the need to fool ourselves continuously by the spontaneous creation of a reality . . . which from time to time reveals itself to be vain and illusory.

Luigi Pirandello
Autobiographical Sketch in La Lettere, Rome

Nowhere is the theme of illusion-disillusionment more prominent than it is in narcissism. The need to preserve and sustain illusions about oneself in relation to the world is most prevalent in the narcissistic personality.

The term *narcissism* has been used in many different ways in psychoanalytic parlance, and there is a startling and confusing absence of conceptual clarity in the way in which the term is used to describe human interaction.

A person who is self-absorbed and oblivious to the presence, needs, and feelings of others is described as a narcissistic personality. At the same time, a person who craves acknowledgment and admiration from others and engages others in a way designed to extract their approval or interest is also described as narcissistic. In terms of relatedness the first person, Mr. A., seems totally uninterested in others, while the second person, Mr. B., is interested in others in order to win their affirmation of himself. Mr. B. is adept at sensing the needs of others and he accommodates himself to them in an attempt to feel loved. We might distinguish between these two styles of narcissism by designating Mr. A. as the self-absorbed or oblivious type of narcissist, type A, and Mr. B. as the vigilant or accommodating type of narcissist, type B. The myth of Narcissus, in which the Greek boy falls in love with his own reflection in a spring and is oblivious to the world, would be an example of type A (the self-absorbed or oblivious type), while the performer who needs constant applause as a form of emotional sustenance would exemplify type B (the vigilant or accommodating type). Sometimes we see an admixture of both types in varying degrees. The message sent out by type A is "I am wonderful and special and don't need anyone for anything." The contrasting message sent out by type B is "I need you to be impressed by how wonderful I am, so that I can feel special." Thus, the agent of the reflection of specialness in type A is the self, while in type B it is the other. The common denominator linking these seemingly different types of narcissism is a basic withdrawal into self needs and a lack of genuine connectedness with others. This pattern is obvious in the inaccessibility of the self-absorbed narcissistic person described as type A. However, the type B narcissistic person is invested in a similar withdrawal from the world of objects, despite his facade of charm, vitality, and a pseudo-interest in others. These individuals often specialize in pseudo-relationships that lack depth and mutuality.

While the concept of narcissism has received considerable interest in current psychoanalytic theory and practice, there has been little attention given to the question of why and how Narcissus became narcissistic. Ovid (n.d.), who first described the myth of Narcissus in his *Metamorphoses*, did not address how Narcissus weathered the universal developmental experiences of childhood. We are told only that he had little interest in those around him, even though they admired his beauty and pursued him, and that he fell in love with his own image. Thus, he appeared to have no illusions about his place in the world and how he might receive gratification from others. He was impervious to disillusionment because he harbored no interpersonal illusions. This degree of self-absorption and obliviousness to others is the hallmark of the type A narcissistic personality described above. Freud (1914) viewed this as a state in which libidinal cathexis is withdrawn from the object and redirected toward the ego. How did this come about?

We might speculate that Narcissus's preoedipal developmental needs for maternal attunement, such as a phase-appropriate mirroring selfobject in Kohut's terms, or a mother sufficiently responsive to his needs for refueling in the practicing and rapprochement subphases of separation-individuation in Mahler's terms, were severely thwarted or neglected. When the preoedipal mother does not fulfill the normal expectations and needs of the child, that is, when there is a significant degree of misattunement and/or emotional neglect, or the balance of frustration and gratification is significantly tilted toward the pole of frustration, a state of disillusionment occurs in which the child's expectation of receiving good supplies from the world is shut down. Ultimately, insofar as the world is perceived as an unfriendly and ungiving place, the foundation for positive self-esteem has not been fortified, and basic trust is undeveloped. Under these conditions a personality formation is likely to evolve in which narcissistic, depressive, avoidant, and paranoid features are prominent. There may exist an underlying narcissistic hunger, fraught with illusions about gratification and fulfillment from others, but this is vigorously defended against via the building up of an exaggerated lack of expectation that narcissistic supplies will be available or provided by others. What is important here is that there be no further experience of disillusionment. This is in sharp contrast to the type B narcissistic personality in which the cycle of illusion and disillusionment is repeated over and over again with a limited capacity to modify this pattern in accordance with advances in reality testing.

Hence, we might view the plight of Narcissus as a constellation in which he became totally self-absorbed with his own beautiful image and could not allow himself to risk emotional involvement with others as a result of the early damage that emerged within the early mother–child relationship. In this scenario the exposure of residual narcissistic hunger was too threatening, allowing for emotional involvement with others was perceived to be too dangerous, and the fear of further disillusion was too great. Thus, the overdetermined route of survival for Narcissus was to ward off others and to stroke himself.

Freud (1914), drawing from Greek mythology, described narcissism as the earliest developmental stage. In the libido theory, the state in which objects do not yet exist for the child is called primary narcissism. Freud also delineated what he called secondary narcissism, which involves the withdrawal of libidinal cathexis away from the object and the redirecting of it toward the ego. In secondary narcissism the capacity for differentiation between self and object has been attained, and objects are valued in terms of the gratification they provide. Hartmann (1939) utilized these principles in outlining a progression of object relatedness in normal development. The initial stage of primary narcissism, characterized by a lack of differentiation, is followed by the stage of what Hartmann called need gratification or need satisfaction. In this stage the object is related to essentially as a provider of supplies or services. Ultimately, this gives way to the stage of object constancy, which is characterized by the ability to value the object for his or her own qualities, over and above the services rendered. With the attainment of object constancy, usually by the age of 3, object relatedness involves the capacity for sustained cathexis of the object representation independent of the state of need. Following Hartmann, Mahler (1968) viewed object constancy as a relative rather than a discrete developmental accomplishment by age 3, and she preferred the concept of "on the way to object constancy" as the final step in her theory of separation-individuation.

Stolorow and Lachmann (1980) attempt to provide greater conceptual clarity in examining narcissism. They suggest that the view of narcissism as simply the libidinal investment in the self needs to be replaced by a functional definition in which narcissism serves the purpose of maintaining the cohesion, stability, and positive regard of one's self representation. These authors hold that the Freudian position on narcissism is based on the economic model prevalent in the early 1900s in which narcissism is understood in terms of the direction and degree of investment of libidinal cathexis. The implication from drive theory, that narcissism and object relationships cannot coexist, is not substantiated in clinical practice. One can be intensely connected with an object based on the need for that object to provide supplies for the enhancement and reinforcement of one's positive self-regard. This is what is meant by a narcissistic object choice. The functional definition proposed by Stolorow and Lachmann emphasizes that narcissistic activity fuels self-esteem, but is not synonymous with it. In this vein they state, "Narcissism embodies those mental operations whose function is to regulate self-esteem (the affective coloring of the self representation) and to maintain the cohesion and stability of the self representation (the structural foundation upon which self-esteem rests)" (pp. 20–21). Utilizing this functional definition Stolorow and Lachmann seek to clarify the way in which the term *narcissism* can be understood as it applies to such dimensions as sexual perversion, modes of relating to objects, a developmental stage, self-esteem regulation, and diagnostic classification. Narcissism can be normal insofar as we all require routes to bolster and maintain the cohesion and stability of our self representations. Pathological narcissism is indicated from barometers such as the degree of structural impairment of the self representation, a franticness in the reparative activity in the face of damage to self-esteem, and the reliance upon primitive selfobjects rather than consolidated internal structure to reaffirm a positive sense of self.

Pathological narcissism can be thought of as an overestimation of oneself or an excessive inflation of the self. Under normal circumstances the child initially experiences himself as the center of the universe, and his level of functioning is dominated by the pleasure principle. Illusions of omnipotence prevail and are reinforced by the gratifications provided by loving caregivers. In his treatise on narcissism, Freud (1914) coined the term *His Majesty the Baby* to describe this earliest sense of self. Robert Bly (1990), in his book *Iron John*, echoes this view: "When we are tiny we have the feeling that we are God" (p. 33). Along these lines, the existentialist Milan Kundera (1996) notes,

> Perhaps it is as an infant that one first experiences the illusion of being elect, because of the maternal attentions one receives without meriting them and demands with all the more determination. Upbringing should get rid of that illusion and make clear that everything in life has a price. But it is often too late. [p. 50]

Narcissistic pathology can be expressed in many directions. Self-absorption and obliviousness and insensitivity toward others may be one form. Seeking acknowledgment and validation from others to an excessive degree in order to bolster self-esteem is another pattern. Relating to others on the level of need gratification without reciprocity is yet another prototype. In assessing the different types of narcissistic engagement, it is useful to consider the experience of self in relation to an object. In narcissism the self appears to be characteristically overvalued while the object is undervalued in his/her own right. Narcissistic individuals tend to be fixated at the need gratification stage of development, either as a function of deprivation or overindulgence, and therefore, their object relatedness is tinged with a lack of mutuality. They operate under the illusion that "the world owes me a loving," and they may search perpetually for a primary caregiver who will serve their needs in an all-giving way and require nothing in return. This pattern of relating is a carryover from the early era of narcissistic bliss when the child got his needs met by an object who is not as yet perceived as a separate being, and the child believes that he has brought about these good feelings for himself, that is, that he controls the ministrations provided by the object who is perceived as a part of oneself. Alternatively, the carryover may have its repetitive roots from the era of secondary narcissism, when there is greater awareness of separation between self and object, but the prevailing experience is one in which one's needs are taken care of in an atmosphere in which no demands are placed upon the child. Gradually, in the course of normal development the caregiver incrementally exerts restrictions on the child's unbridled narcissism, and the child comes to adapt to the boundaries and limitations set in place by the caregiver.

The parental challenging of the child's omnipotent fantasies of controlling the object facilitates the child's capacity for adaptation to reality. This is set in place via the restrictions, frustrations, and limitations gradually imposed by the parent. In this way the dethronement of the illusion of His Majesty, the Baby (Freud 1914) occurs.

To summarize this developmental perspective, the earliest experience of the child reflects an omnipotent sense of self in which he is at the center of the universe. Initially, he maintains the illusion that he brings about the good feelings associated with contact with the mother's breast. With the increased awareness of separateness, the child comes to realize that good things, nurturance, safety, soothing, and other blissful feelings come from the outside, that is, from the primary caregiver. Along with the awareness of the reality of his loss of omnipotence the child now utilizes the caregiver, as a partially separate object, as the source of his much-needed sense of omnipotence. Phillips (1998) maintains: "Ultimately, the child needs to abrogate his omnipotence—abjure his magic—and learn to wait. Accepting his dependence, and bearing the fact of his parents' independence of him, he makes good his survival and his pleasure by relinquishing his fantasies of self-sufficiency (his omnipotent self-strivings)" (p. xv). Thus, idealized objects now become the refuge of the child's lost omnipotence. Winnicott's notion of how the parent is used by the child is pertinent here, and we see the transferential repetition of this type of relating in the treatment of certain types of narcissistic patients.

As ego development proceeds, there evolves an increase in the child's autonomous functioning and the recognition of increased limitations imposed upon the child by his love objects. At this point the child must begin to reckon with the realization that the expectation of uninterrupted narcissistic bliss must be dismantled. Subsequently, developmental progression continues and the stage of need gratification is replaced by object constancy in which the object comes to be valued as a separate being in her own right, over and above the state of need in the child. This is not to suggest that narcissistic expectations are fully relinquished. In varying degrees one must contend with feelings of disillusionment when the primary caregiver does not fulfill one's expectations and needs. Alongside of maturational advances there coexists a yearning to recapture the feelings of having one's needs blissfully attended to. Some move on to higher levels of relatedness, while those who have received too much gratification or too much frustration maintain a powerful residual force designed to refind the lost or missing supplies and a relationship in which their entitlement needs are met. This reflects a kind of narcissistic hunger that is fueled by narcissistic illusions in which the perfect object will come into their lives and be available to meet all of their needs.

Let us return to the issue of the lack of conceptual clarity in our understanding of narcissism. This problem has been addressed by Plakum (1993): "At times that which has been written about narcissism has suffered from imprecision, since the term has been used variously to describe a) a line of development in all individuals, b) a particular domain of psychopathology, and c) a specific personality disorder" (p. 804). It is clear that to some degree unresolved narcissistic issues are ubiquitous. However, for some individuals narcissistic problems are especially prominent. Various psychoanalytic writers have focused on different dimensions of narcissism. For example, Morrison (1986) emphasizes shame and the related affects of humiliation, embarrassment, despair, and mortification as central ingredients in the experience of narcissism. Blanck and Blanck (1986) highlight the distinction between normal and pathological narcissism insofar as the latter reflects "a pathology of object relations resulting from an imbalance in cathexis of self and object representations" (p. 19). Bergmann (1979) accentuates the prevalence of the (defense) mechanism of splitting in individuals with narcissistic pathology in which there is a seesawing between idealization and devaluation of the self and/or others. Such narcissistic splitting reflects "the need to project the bad feelings in order to keep the narcissistic self image intact or to masochistically phantasize all bad feelings as belonging to the self in order to preserve the object, whose hostile behavior needs to be rationalized" (p. 72). In this formulation, narcissism not only is seen as a self-inflated view of the self, but is extended to encompass the wide pendulum-like swings in overevaluation and underevaluation of self as well as object.

A great deal of debate among psychoanalysts has revolved around the respective views of Kernberg and Kohut and their contrasting approaches to the understanding and treatment of narcissistic disorders. Kernberg (1975), in line with classical theory, regards narcissistic pathology as stemming from conflict centering around the management of the aggressive drive in the oral stage of development. These individuals cannot tolerate their feelings of envy and rage toward their primary objects, and as a result they build powerful narcissistic defenses such as primitive idealization, splitting, devaluation, grandiosity, and projective identification, which predispose them to narcissistic functioning. Kohut (1977), in contrast, conceptualized narcissism as a normal and separate line of development, parallel to the development of the drives and object relatedness, and narcissistic pathology occurs as a result of developmental arrest in which the child's normal narcissistic needs were not adequately responded to by the maternal environment.

Rothstein (1980) argues for a definition of narcissism as a fantasy of perfection in which omnipotence and omniscience are cornerstones. According to Rothstein (1991), "Fantasies of perfection are a ubiquitous aspect of human experience that facilitates distortion of one's sense of reality, particularly as this relates to one's sense of vulnerability and finiteness. These fantasies differ from person to person in their elaboration and integration by the ego" (p. 317). It is the lack of recoverability from the loss of blissful feelings of perfect harmony between self and primary object that stands out in pathological narcissism.

Moore (1975) defines narcissism broadly as one's "positive libidinal feelings toward the self" (p. 271) and he attempts to further clarify the concept by drawing from Kernberg in describing narcissism as seen in those individuals who display "an unusual degree of self-reference in their interactions with other people, a great need to be loved and admired by others, and a curious apparent contradiction between a very inflated concept of themselves, and an inordinate need for tribute from others" (p. 265). These features are further elaborated in the fourth edition of the *Diagnostic and Statistical Manual of Mental Disorders* (*DSM-IV*; American Psychiatric Association 1994) (Table 7-1).

Table 7-1
Diagnostic Criteria for Narcissistic Personality Disorder

A pervasive pattern of grandiosity (in fantasy or behavior), need for admiration, and lack of empathy, beginning by early adulthood and present in a variety of contexts, as indicated by five (or more) of the following:

1. has a grandiose sense of self-importance (e.g., exaggerates achievements and talents, expects to be recognized as superior without commensurate achievements)
2. is preoccupied with fantasies of unlimited success, power, bril liance, beauty, or ideal love
3. believes that he or she is "special" and unique and can only be

understood by, or should associate with, other special or high-status people (or institutions)

4. requires excessive admiration
5. has a sense of entitlement, i.e., unreasonable expectations of especially favorable treatment or automatic compliance with his or her expectations
6. is interpersonally exploitative, i.e., takes advantage of others to achieve his or her own ends
7. lacks empathy: is unwilling to recognize or identify with the feelings and needs of others
8. is often envious of others or believes that others are envious of him or her
9. shows arrogant, haughty behaviors or attitudes

Such classification, although useful for diagnostic considerations, does not address the etiology of narcissistic pathology. In different ways, Kohut, Kernberg, Modell, Mitchell, Johnson, and others have attempted to explicate the developmental origins of pathological narcissism. In Johnson's view the normal grandiosity, omnipotence, and self-involvement that occur in the practicing phase of separation-individuation persist and are insufficiently replaced by accommodation to reality, which is the hallmark of the subsequent phase of rapprochement. Thus, the illusions pertaining to "the world is my oyster" are not sufficiently attenuated and continue to play a central role in the functioning of the child. Johnson (1987) states:

> Because this grandiosity usually is to be neutralized in the next, rapprochement phase, I believe that the developmental arrest of narcissism usually occurs in rapprochement. [p. 25]. . . . The narcissistic character derives primarily from a failure to accommodate around the issue of grandiosity and limitation. Due to one kind of environmental frustration or

another, the narcissist is arrested around the neutralization of grandiosity. His grandiose view of himself has been walled off from the necessary repeated exposure to limitation. [p. 29]. . . . The evolution of the child's consciousness demands that he face limitation and separateness just as the natural desire for comfort and the vicissitudes of grandiosity and symbiotic illusion press for non-awareness. [p. 30]

Mitchell has pointed out that the way in which the concept of narcissism currently is used revolves around self-regard. This reflects a significant departure from Freud's original definition in which narcissism was explained as libido directed inward. Mitchell goes so far as to say that the key issue in pathological narcissism has to do with illusion. While it is phase appropriate for the infant or toddler to maintain grandiose illusions about his omnipotence and perfection, when these features are prominent in adulthood they reflect pathological narcissism. Mitchell (1985) contrasts the traditional classical approach to narcissism, as a defense against dealing with the world of reality, with the relational conflict position, in which both the defensive as well as the growth-enhancing aspects of narcissistic illusions are considered. According to Mitchell, healthy functioning emanates from an effective synthesis of illusion and reality. "Optimal experience emerges from the parent who can participate in the child's world of illusions involving grandiosity and perfection, while also not needing to see the child in this (perfect) way, and can also represent the world of reality." Mitchell's position moves a step further than Johnson's in pointing out that healthy adjustment "involves learning how to negotiate the real world . . . to move back and forth (between reality and illusion), but never to fully give up one's illusions."

Mitchell notes that in the approach of contemporary psychoanalytic theorists such as Winnicott and Kohut, illusion is not viewed essentially as a defense, but rather as a necessary and primary element for the development of a cohesive self. In these approaches grandiose illusions are seen as central to the development of self, and psychoanalytic treatment involves providing and/or reactivating the patient's core illusions temporarily, rather than interpreting them away. This is in sharp contrast to the traditional Freudian view in which narcissistic illusions are seen as stultifying growth and need to be renounced in favor of reality.

With the development of ego functions the pleasure principle gives way to the reality principle as the dominant organizing principle in mental functioning. Under the impact of the reality principle, illusions are tempered and a greater appreciation of one's limitations is acquired. The world and one's place in it are now seen in more realistic terms. However, this transition from pleasure principle to reality principle as the dominant mode of functioning does not always fully occur. Pathological narcissism may result from deprivation in the child's earliest needs to feel affirmed and special. In such situations a hunger to be mirrored emerges and may be present or defended against throughout one's life. While the aspects of deprivation and misattunement to the child's earliest needs have been most emphasized in the roots of narcissistic pathology, excessive narcissism can also be generated by parental overindulgence. When the balance of gratification and frustration is tilted too strongly in the former direction in the early experiences of the child, a tenacious sense of specialness and entitlement often develops. These individuals grow up with an outrageous sense of self-importance, along with deficits in frustration tolerance and impulse control. They continue to be driven by illusions of omnipotence and a sense of entitlement in which the world owes them a loving. This demand to be treated as special has powerful interpersonal consequences. Driven by illusions of specialness, these people frequently and repeatedly suffer from profound experiences of deflation when their expectations are thwarted or unfulfilled.

In most situations the child starts out with experiences that reinforce a feeling of omnipotence and a sense that he is at the center of the universe. This state represents the original narcissistic illusion and is part of normal development. The caregiver provides gratification of his needs and wishes, and frustrations are relatively minor, that is, the moments of gratification far outweigh the moments of frustration. This implants in the child a sense of infantile narcissistic bliss, buttressed by the illusion of oneness or merger with the caregiver. Gradually, there occurs an awareness of separateness, and the capacity to engage in autonomous functioning, in which he explores the world on his own, which provides the child with the next level of narcissistic satisfaction. At the same time the caregiver incrementally reduces her participation in providing for all of his needs, and he experiences rage and disappointment at her failures to respond to his needs and desires as readily and completely as he had expected.

Thus, the child in the midst of the practicing phase of separation-individuation takes great pride in his evolving autonomous independent functioning, and he cherishes the pleasure this furnishes for him. Hence, normal narcissistic gratification is derived from the autonomous achievements accomplished during this period. At one and the same time we can postulate that he resents the loss of the all-giving caregiver whose availability, nurturance, and responsiveness provide him with a feeling of infantile narcissistic bliss in which he is very special and is at the center of the universe. This might be described as the experience of Paradise lost. Bettelheim (1976) captures this aspect of development in stating that "infancy ends when the belief in an unending supply of love and nutriment proves to be an unrealistic [sic] fantasy" (p. 187), that is, an illusion that is unsustainable.

In this phase of development the child becomes increasingly aware that the mother is a separate being who takes care of her own set of needs and interests, and no longer serves him unconditionally, and, furthermore, she imposes limitations and restrictions upon him and makes demands upon him for socialization. On some level this creates in all of us a powerful and prolonged yearning to recapture the period of infantile bliss, that period in which we experienced the caregiver as a constant source of reliable nourishment. Thus, to some degree we all share some variegated form of narcissistic illusion in which we will someday find again an all-giving (maternal) object who takes care of all of our needs and imposes no restrictions upon us. For those individuals whose early experiences of gratification were excessive or significantly absent, these narcissistic illusions, and/or the defenses against them, become a central driving force in their personality organization and in the nature of their interpersonal interactions and expectations.

Developmental progression takes place with varying degrees of intensity. Freud used the metaphor of the movement of troops in an advancing army. When a battle is substantially won, a small number of troops remain behind for cleanup operations, while the vast majority of troops move forward to the next battlefield. If the victory is not secure, then most troops must be left behind to deal with the battle, and fewer troops are available to advance. Freud equated this to what takes place in the stages of psychosexual development. While all individuals move forward from oral, to anal, to phallic conflicts, they do not do so with the same degree of intensity. For those who are fixated on the need to receive oral gratification, the maturational thrust into anal, phallic, and oedipal corridors may be somewhat attenuated. Many individuals are able to weather and accept the loss of infantile bliss and move forcefully forward into anal, phallic, and oedipal territory. Residual issues from these later stages of psychosexual development can be powerful and are played out over and over again throughout the life cycle. In these individuals the yearning to find a new all-giving (maternal) object who will provide for all of one's needs and make no demands, while present in their mental organization, remains peripheral to the unresolved dramas related to these later stages of development. In contrast, for those individuals who are more fixated at an earlier (oral) stage, either as a result of excessive gratification or excessive frustration, the powerful wishes to find an all-giving caregiver in a new object exerts a dominant influence on their interpersonal relationships. Their relationships are colored by a strong residual force designed to refind or discover the lost or missing supplies, and a relationship in which their entitlement wishes are fulfilled. This is fueled by narcissistic illusions in which the perfect object will come into their lives and be available to meet all of their needs. These supplies need not necessarily be provided by a nurturing woman, but by a perfect object who takes care of all of one's needs. The fantasy of "Someday My Prince Will Come," common among young girls, could reflect not only the yearning for the perfect oedipal partner, but also the yearning for the all-giving object who supplies nurturance, safety, and so on.

It should be noted that there are others who share a similar background of early overgratification or deprivation who erect powerful defenses against their underlying yearnings to find an all-giving new object. For them the fear of retraumatization is profound and it propels them to function as if they don't need any supplies from anyone.

For many years the treatment approach in the psychoanalysis of narcissistic personalities was to prevail upon the patient to relinquish his narcissistic strivings associated with the pleasure principle, in favor of the maturity associated with adherence to the reality principle. This has been referred to as the "maturity morality" within psychoanalysis. It is only with recent advances in psychoanalytic theory that narcissism has been understood and approached from different vantage points. For example, there are many ways in which patients with unfulfilled narcissistic needs may attempt to take repeated liberties with the frame of treatment. They may come late and expect the analyst to extend the session beyond the usual ending time. They may linger and continue to engage the analyst at the end of the session, which may represent their unconscious illusion that the analyst will extend the session and thereby prove himself to be the caring, all-giving object they yearn for. They may be chronically late in paying for sessions even though they are realistically able to do so. These are all examples of transference enactments that are unconsciously designed to extract something extra or something special from the analyst in order to fulfill one's entitlement needs. If the analyst recognizes and understands that these behaviors emanate from a need to find an all-giving caregiver who will provide supplies and fulfill narcissistic illusions, the pull toward countertransference feelings of irritation, resentment, and of being manipulated by the patient will be significantly toned down. These patterns and their unconscious meaning can then be constructively interpreted to the patient in a way that makes him feel better understood and not criticized.

In addition to considering different types of narcissism such as the self-absorbed type and the accommodating type, it is useful to think of different aspects of narcissism, such as narcissistic needs, narcissistic wounds, and narcissistic defenses. Essentially narcissistic needs need to be understood and accepted, narcissistic wounds need to be healed, and narcissistic defenses need to be softened.

NARCISSISTIC NEEDS

Everyone requires narcissistic supplies throughout the course of the life cycle. This includes the need to be properly mirrored, affirmed, and validated. The experience of the 8-year-old child who returns home from school eager to share with his caregiver the events of his day reflects an age-appropriate narcissistic need that continues in some form throughout life. In the language of self psychology, we all need a selfobject who provides a mirroring function, that is, someone we can talk to about our day and confide in, and who soothes us at times of heightened stress. These are suitable sources of normal narcissistic gratification.

When these supplies are absent, as, for example, when the primary caregiver is unable to mirror the child's elation, narcissistic needs go unfulfilled. Under these circumstances narcissistic hunger, in which one seeks to compensate for the missing mirroring structures, may prevail. Unhealthy narcissism, in the form of excessive self-absorption, self-references, and self-centeredness, may predominate.

The state of being in love is another example of the fulfillment of a normal narcissistic need. To feel one's loving feelings toward another person provides one with a sense of narcissistic satisfaction. The notion of being in love with love is relevant here. In many love relationships we might question how much it is the love for another that is so gratifying, and how much it is the wonderful feeling that one has as a function of feeling love. This is captured in a Valentine's Day greeting card in which the message reads, "I love what I feel when I'm with you, because when I'm with you I feel love." Freud (1914) went so far as to proclaim that even parental love underneath reflects a form of narcissistic love once removed.

Children's narcissistic needs are fulfilled to the extent that they receive unconditional love and are responded to by caregivers who make them feel special, desirable, understood, and accepted. When the child's illusion about his own omnipotence is shattered by his ineluctable appreciation of reality, he seeks to derive narcissistic feelings of well-being through sharing in the omnipotence he attributes to his caregivers. When the normal narcissistic needs of childhood are thwarted or remain absent, narcissistic pathology usually emerges. One may become a self-absorbed narcissistic personality, intent on serving one's own needs and oblivious to the needs of others, or one may become an accommodating narcissistic personality who is exploitative toward others in his quest to obtain the supplies that enable him to derive a sense of well-being. Narcissists' relationships with others have pronounced colorations of idealization and devaluation. Their energies are directed toward seeking or defending against connectedness with a representation of the primary object, that is, the all-giving mother who provides the perfect fit and supplies the narcissistic needs. Many patients in psychotherapy come to experience the therapeutic environment as a reservoir that supplies their basic narcissistic needs to be understood and accepted, and to interact with a significant figure who is interested in their thoughts and feelings. One patient, when preparing to switch from individual therapy to group therapy, expressed his apprehension and lamented as follows: "Individual therapy is like a narcissistic bath. It's all about me! In the group I will have to relate to everyone and share your attention with them." For this patient the holding environment of individual therapy had fostered his illusion of specialness insofar as he felt he had received a form of blissful attunement that repaired the premature abandonment by his preoedipal mother.

NARCISSISTIC WOUNDS

Freud (1930) proposed that the human race had endured three great narcissistic wounds. The first of these wounds was perpetuated by Copernicus, the Polish astronomer who debunked the belief that Earth was the center of the universe, when he developed the theory that Earth is a moving planet that revolves around the sun. Darwin inflicted the second great wound through his theory of evolution, which demonstrated that man was simply a later descendant of earlier animal species rather than a special entity of creation. Freud's discovery of unconscious drives and instincts, which motivate how human beings function, levied the third wound. With this revelation man could no longer assume that his behavior was simply ruled by conscious determinants that were fully under his control. Through their discoveries, Copernicus, Darwin, and Freud, like Columbus before them, challenged basic illusions that had been central to the belief systems of mankind. As often occurs when cherished illusions are dismantled by reality, these discoveries were at first met with denial and ridicule. Such wounds are not easily accepted. In the words of Jerome Levin (1993), who writes about narcissistic injury, "The essence of narcissistic injury is an affront to our grandiosity" (p. 46). Levin (1993) defines narcissistic wounds as "special kinds of hurts—those that cut to the quick, that assail us where we live, that threaten our identity or our self-image, or our ego-ideal or our self-esteem. They are the hurts that go to the core. The emotional response to narcissistic injury is hurt, shame and rage" (p. xiv).

We are exposed to narcissistic wounds from the very beginning of life. Otto Rank's theory of birth trauma is predicated on the notion of birth being the essential narcissistic wound in which we are thrust out of a safe and secure intrauterine environment into an overwhelming world. The toddler's realization that demands and limitations are being placed upon him by the caregiver's agenda requiring conformity and socialization is experienced as a narcissistic wound that relates to the awareness that love is not always unconditional. Joyce McDougall (1980) goes so far as to suggest that "to be obliged to speak in order to be understood, and to have wishes granted, is a continuing narcissistic wound in everyone's unconscious" (p. 281). A basic narcissistic need of the child is to be mirrored. Misattunement, loss, or abandonment by the mirroring object elicits narcissistic injury and produces narcissistic rage. In a discussion of Shakespeare's *Richard III*, Freud highlighted Richard's physical deformity as a narcissistic wound that produces an attitude of entitlement. Freud (1916) maintained that we all identify with Richard III in seeking reparation for the wrongs and psychological injuries inflicted upon us: "Richard is an enormously magnified representation of something we can all discover in ourselves. We all think we have reason to reproach nature and our destiny for congenital and infantile disadvantages; we all demand reparation for early wounds to our narcissism, our self-love" (p. 322).

NARCISSISTIC DEFENSES

The grandiosity, sense of entitlement, and need to be special are characteristic features of the narcissistic personality, which make him particularly prone to narcissistic injury. The character of the Queen in Disney's *Snow White and the Seven Dwarfs* (Hand 1937) is an excellent example of this pattern. The Queen's sense of well-being is chiefly derived from her beautiful image. She requires repeated reassurance and affirmation about her beauty in order to maintain her narcissistic structure. Thus, she implores the mirror repeatedly with the question, "Mirror, Mirror on the wall, who is the fairest of them all?" As long as the mirror continues to reply that the Queen is the most beautiful woman in the land, she is able to sustain her precarious sense of well-being. However, at the point in which the mirror comes to recognize and identify Snow White as the most beautiful woman, the Queen is narcissistically mortified. Her reaction to her narcissistic injury is unbridled rage toward Snow White. There are obvious oedipal implications that underlie her wrathful reaction to a more youthful competitor, but her deepest wound pertains to the inability to sustain her narcissistic definition of her self. As long as she remains the most beautiful, her sense of self is intact and preserved. But when cracks in the mirror begin to emerge, she is devastated. This is the dilemma of many narcissistic individuals, who rely on their good looks to prop up an inflated sense of self, which is reinforced by the positive responses of others. When their beauty begins to fade, their narcissistic defense crumbles and they are left without sufficient compensatory structures.

The powerful sense of entitlement often seen in narcissistic personalities is in many cases a result of unresolved issues in grandiosity stemming from the practicing phase of separation-individuation. These individuals maintain an outrageous sense of self-importance because they have been unable to appropriately mourn the loss of the early illusion that the world is their oyster. If the child does not sufficiently incorporate his realistic position in the world and work through the disillusionment of his earlier belief, he will build narcissistic defenses to support the remnants of his grandiose illusions about himself and the world. Bach (1985) has noted that dealing with disillusionment is particularly anathema to adult narcissistic patients.

McDougall (1980) addresses the importance of narcissistic defenses in these individuals:

> People who must constantly struggle to maintain their narcissistic homeostasis may do this in two different ways: they may keep a prudent distance from others felt to be a threat to their equilibrium, or on the contrary, they may grasp on to others, displaying unquenchable need of the person chosen to reflect the image that is missing in the inner psychic world. Sometimes the sexual partner is asked to fulfill this function. In both cases it is frequently a question of psychic survival. [p. 303]

Some writers have emphasized aspects of alienation from the true self and a fragile sense of self as core features of the narcissistic personality that require the establishing of narcissistic defensive structures. Lowen (1983) states, "Narcissism denotes an investment in one's image as opposed to one's self. Narcissists love their image, not their real self. They have a poor sense of self; they are not self directed. Instead, their activities are directed toward the enhancement of their image, often at the expense of the self" (p. 25).

McDougall (1991) describes patients who perpetually seek need-satisfying objects in attempting to repair their damaged sense of self:

> Others, with the same basic need to avoid the loss of the sense of self, are compelled to defend themselves ardently against the fusional danger that narcissistic relationships imply. They tend to create an elaborate series of narcissistic

defenses and to maintain a distance from the rest of the world, for fear of losing their self limits and feeling of identity. [p. 222]

McDougall's view speaks again to the self-absorbed and accommodating styles as two contrasting types of narcissism. In the former the presenting picture is one of aloofness and self-sufficiency, which defend against dependency needs. The individual acts like he's absorbed in his own world and is oblivious to the feelings and needs of those around him. His manner of relating is marked by detachment and indifference. In the latter pattern there is a need for others to serve as need-satisfying objects who provide narcissistic supplies, which allow one to feel admired, important, worthwhile, and special.

Modell (1975) stresses that the etiology of narcissistic character disorders is based on environmental failure in which the child accurately perceives the mother's faulty judgment. As a result the child suffers a traumatic disillusionment in the mother's ability to provide a safe environment, and precociously develops an illusion of self-sufficiency. In addition, an affective nonrelatedness evolves that serves as a narcissistic defense against closeness and further disillusionment. In this respect Modell's view of narcissistic defenses is similar to Winnicott's false-self syndrome and Kohut's depiction of narcissistic pathology.

The ultimate narcissistic defense involves a self-imposed state of isolation in which the individual resides in his own impenetrable fortress in which he is immune to the impact of others. In such cases it is imperative that there be no further experience of disillusionment. To ensure against disillusionment, the individual walls himself off and, in effect, disconnects from his feelings and need of others. Fried (1979) has described this as narcissistic inaccessibility, which needs to be viewed as a defensive armor that covers over the wounds inflicted by environmental failure. The haughtiness, self-involvement, and propensity toward self references displayed by the narcissistic personality disorder reflect defenses that can be very off-putting to others. Their self-centeredness is often experienced as obnoxious and malevolent. In working with such patients it is essential to recognize this behavior as a defensive mask and to search for the underlying wounds and unfulfilled narcissistic needs. Beneath their obnoxious veneer there often resides a wish and fear of connectedness. In their contrasting treatment approaches, Kernberg addresses the narcissistic defenses while Kohut addressed the narcissistic needs and wounds of the patient. For Kernberg the technique of choice is to confront and interpret the characterological defenses in order to expose and address the instinctual conflicts around aggression and envy. For Kohut the preferred approach is to facilitate a treatment environment in which the patient's narcissistic needs and injuries can be revived and worked through.

NARCISSISTIC ILLUSIONS

Narcissistic illusions are false beliefs that are embraced or held on to in order to sustain and enhance the sense of self-cohesion. Narcissistic illusions are defensive insofar as they are unconsciously designed to ensure a continued sense of well-being, and to protect the individual from fuller knowledge of the truth, which threatens to arouse the experience of intolerable anxiety. A hallmark of narcissistic personality disorders is the narcissists' overarching attempt to retain the illusion of their own magnificence. Narcissistic illusions often involve situations in which individuals expect and mistakenly assume that others will treat them as special. They are unprepared for disappointments that inevitably occur in relationships and are easily injured or set back when their bubble is burst. Excessive reactions to relatively minor disillusionment may lead them to abruptly end a friendship or love relationship, only to repeat the same pattern in the next relationship. They do not seem to learn from experience, but rather are prone to externalize "the blame" for their interpersonal conflicts. They blame others for not understanding them, not being reliable, not caring enough, and not being trustworthy. They are driven by powerful illusions in which they are adored, desired, and admired as if this is their due, and their capacity to tolerate disillusionment is limited. Disillusionment is so painful to narcissistic personalities that it is something they strive constantly to avoid. They do not perceive that their expectations of the world may be unrealistic, for example, that things sometimes happen to interfere with the good intentions of others, and they thereby leave little margin for the disillusionments that occur in ordinary life. A caring partner or friend may be quickly devalued when a traffic jam makes him twenty minutes late for an appointment. One patient described with indignation how he rejected a lifelong friendship when his friend forgot about a dinner meeting. His outrageous sense of self-importance was shattered if his friend could forget about him. The underlying illusion that he would be perfectly attended to was dashed and his way of repairing the damage to his self-esteem was to extricate himself from their relationship. He winds up in a victimized, masochistic position, but this is spurred not so much by masochistic needs as by his grandiose illusions, which are unfulfilled.

The needs that fuel narcissistic illusions can outstrip an appreciation of reality. Narcissistic personalities harbor narcissistic illusions about their specialness and entitlement, and have a limited development of the ego function that enables them to anticipate the consequences of their behavior. Thus, their distorted, overinflated sense of self makes them prone to exercise poor interpersonal judgment, and they tend to have difficulty in accepting limits. This formulation is supported by Cooper and Maxwell (1995):

> Basic to this narcissistic way of thinking is the belief that it is the infant who creates and controls the good object. This illusion allows them to deny the primal facts of life [which

include that] the chief source of goodness required for an infant's survival resides outside him in the external world [i.e., the acknowledgment of separateness, and] the recognition of the inevitability of time and ultimately of death. This means that all good things have to come to an end, and that access to the breast cannot go on forever. . . . We know that narcissistic resistance will put up strong armor against acknowledging or working through these basic facts of life. [p. 20]

Sexual promiscuity often represents an attempt to fulfill narcissistic illusions through the arena of sex. Many narcissistic persons enter into quick sexual liaisons with people they hardly know, because they do not feel equipped to relate with mutuality on an emotional level. Their need is to feel desirable, important, and special, and they easily overestimate the meaning of a new partner's interest or sexual attention. Certain elements of the singles' scene, in which one-night stands are commonplace, favor the acting out of narcissistic illusions.

This pattern is very prevalent in some homosexual circles, where fast pickups and easy sex are somewhat normative. There are men who report having had a thousand or more partners; they are addicted to their sexual fix, which fortifies their illusion of specialness. In many cases their erotic activity was only superficially about satisfying a sexual need; the underlying need to fortify the narcissistic illusion about being desirable and special is a deeper driving force. The compulsion to feed this illusion frequently leads such individuals to engage in high-risk situations and self-destructive behavior. Under the sway of their need to satisfy their narcissistic illusions, basic ego functions such as judgment, reality testing, and anticipation of the consequences of one's actions may be severely compromised. In many instances these ego functions remain successfully intact when dealing with other spheres of their lives, but break down selectively when their need to pursue reinforcement for a narcissistic illusion is triggered.

In contrast to neurotic patients who struggle with conflicts over the expression of unacceptable drives, those who suffer from narcissistic pathology are excessively involved in attempting to hold on to their aggrandized self-image. Rothstein (1980) emphasizes the intense pursuit in these individuals to restore a quality of narcissistic perfection to their self representations. Due to environmental failures during the separation-individuation phases, these individuals were limited in their ability to overcome the loss of omnipotence in their self and object representations imposed by the growing awareness of the reality of separateness. As adults they lack the flexibility and resiliency required to weather narcissistic injuries, and instead continue in their search for narcissistic perfection. Dealing with the experience of vulnerability is anathema to them, and they resist the mourning process involved in revising their perceptions in accordance with reality. The wish is to regain the sense of blissful narcissistic perfection that was once experienced during the "love affair with the world" characteristic of the toddler's practicing phase of development (Mahler et al. 1975). Psychotherapy with narcissistic individuals entails getting them to recognize and work through the issue that they pay a high cost for retaining the illusion that they are invulnerable, immortal, and entitled to special treatment. While there is disagreement among psychoanalytic schools of thought regarding the optimal approach to narcissistic pathology (cf. the Kohut model vs. the Kernberg model), the advent of object relations theory and self psychology has promulgated a greater interest in treating patients with this type of personality disturbance, who previously had been considered to be untreatable. As a result more successful treatment outcomes now occur.

Lydia, a very pretty 35-year-old, sought group psychotherapy because of her difficulties in getting along with people. She was engaging and charming, but seemed to relate to others primarily from a self-referential vantage point. She was assertive and displayed a powerful sense of entitlement, which prompted her to seek the lion's share of attention in many of the group sessions. In her childhood she had been neglected by a mother who seemed always to be busy attending to Lydia's four younger siblings, and a working-class father who was seldom home. Her outstanding early memory was about an incident in which she had been taken in her stroller by her mother to shop at the supermarket. After spending some time in selecting her groceries, her mother paid the cashier and went home. She had forgotten about Lydia and left her behind in the store. It was only when she returned home that she realized what had happened, and she went back to retrieve her daughter. Lydia recalled this memory with considerable hurt and sadness. This event, which seemed to be a microcosm of her experience of maternal misattunement, inflicted an indelible wound within her in which she felt unwanted, unloved, and abandoned. Early environmental failure of this sort sets the stage for the development of narcissistic hunger, in which one subsequently yearns to satisfy these unmet early needs.

When she was 18, Lydia left her home and family in the Midwest, and moved to New York, where she took a job as a cosmetic salesperson in a department store. She married a physician, substantially older than herself, who was attracted to her beauty and her charm, and treated her in a nurturing and indulgent fashion. He became the representation of a composite mother-father figure who adored her and required little in the way of reciprocity. In due course they had two daughters with whom Lydia established a secure and satisfying maternal environment. She identified with her children and vicariously enjoyed the good mothering they were receiving. It is striking to see how some narcissistic people can become good parents, as an indirect way of providing for themselves (through identification) what they had needed and missed. In her other relationships Lydia felt easily slighted by friends and co-workers, could not feel love toward her husband, and was perennially disappointed when her excessive expectations of others were not met. Her relationships, other than with her children, also reflected a lack of empathy and insensitivity toward other people's feelings, as well as a lack of awareness of her impact on others.

These interpersonal characteristics evolved in her interactions with other group members. Over a period of time Lydia established a pattern in which she would regularly come to the group session about ten minutes late. Group business was usually in full force when Lydia would sweep into the room with a Loretta Young-type of flourish. Her nonverbal statement seemed to be, "I'm here, I'm special, notice me!" She seemed to be impervious to the fact that her late and flamboyant entrance was disruptive to the group. There were a number of very passive members of the group who were upset, but reluctant to confront Lydia about her disquieting entrance. Gradually, as this pattern continued, the group members began to more openly react to Lydia's disruptiveness and questioned the meaning of her lateness. She would apologize for her lateness and explain it away as being due to traffic, bad weather, or difficulty in getting a baby-sitter, with the expectation that the group would be understanding and accepting.

Ultimately the group members felt increasingly provoked by Lydia's disruptive pattern, and this came to a climax in one session when one member deliberately took Lydia's usual seat in the circle of chairs prior to her later arrival. The other members colluded in wishing to convey the message to Lydia that she could not expect to be treated as special, and that if she wanted her familiar chair, she would have to arrive on time to claim it. When Lydia walked in she was horrified to see that her usual chair was taken. She vehemently expressed her outrage at the group for being so cruel and insensitive to her. After all, she said, they all knew how she had always sat in that particular place. The members responded by way of pointing out the reality that there were no reserved seats, that the group members could sit wherever they chose within the circle. Lydia would not accept their argument and continued to express how hurt she felt by their mean-spiritedness. As the group leader I felt that the other members were technically correct in their position, but that it was important for me to support Lydia in the midst of this narcissistic injury and to try to understand the deeper source of her pain. Consequently, I highlighted how much hurt and pain I sensed beneath Lydia's rage toward the group. This served to calm her down, and we could now look more into what was being triggered. It seemed to me that although she had provoked it, Lydia was reacting to feeling dismissed by the group. I recalled her early memory of being abandoned in the supermarket, and I linked this up by saying that the group's reaction to Lydia, while understandable on some level, had reactivated this old trauma for her. The group members still needed to press their point about how disruptive her behavior had been, but they were able to better understand her need to be special and the scope of the current narcissistic injury. Lydia, in turn, felt more deeply understood by the group. As a result she was then able to examine and acknowledge her provocative impact on the group.

This vignette is intended to highlight a two-step approach to dealing with narcissistic injury. The first part is to provide understanding of the patient's point of view, even if it does not appear to make logical sense. By conveying such understanding from the vantage point of the patient's psychic reality, the patient feels accepted and connected with. Once this is accomplished, we can then shore up the patient's sensitivity to the impact s/he has on others. Invariably in narcissistic injuries of this type, there is a core illusion, conscious or unconscious, around entitlement, specialness, and unconditional love that is being assaulted; this produces reactions of rage, withdrawal, or other narcissistic defensive maneuvers. This approach could be conceptualized as providing empathic attunement followed by clarification of distortions.

For many psychotherapists one of the most rewarding aspects of the work occurs when we help patients understand some behavior or reaction that makes no rational sense on the surface of things, but is relevant to some earlier situation. To achieve this it is useful to employ a developmental model in which the current reaction might be understood as appropriate to an earlier in life set of circumstances. The following clinical vignette is illustrative.

> Bart, a 50-year-old computer programmer, was recently divorced after fifteen years of marriage. He came to therapy to deal with his depression over the failure of the marriage. As a child he had been overly gratified by his mother, who had raised him as a single parent after her husband had died of a sudden aneurysm during the first year of Bart's life. In the marriage he had expected unconditional love, and he could not tolerate his wife's reluctance to be available on his terms. She increasingly felt resentful that her needs were not being met, and after several separations she eventually asked for a divorce. Most of the first year of Bart's treatment involved mourning the loss of the relationship. It was not only the loss of his wife that was painful, but also the loss of the connection that he needed in order to feel whole as well as the loss of the dream that he could be blissfully nurtured.

> Bart was terrified of living alone. He had difficulty sleeping, had frequent nightmares, and he had to soothe himself nightly with several glasses of wine in order to fall asleep. He woke up exhausted and was barely able to func-

tion in his high-pressure job. He was very isolated in that he had no friends and did not socialize with people at work. He was convinced that the solution to his depression was to quickly establish a relationship with a new woman. Consequently, he placed a personal ad in a local magazine, and received numerous responses from women who were eager to meet him. After several unsuccessful blind dates, he found a woman toward whom he felt a powerful attraction. She listened to his problems and was attentive to him, but after four dates she distanced herself from him. Bart felt devastated and could not accept nor understand her loss of interest in him. This pattern was repeated over the next six months during which he alienated several other women by bypassing the "getting to know each other" stage of a new relationship and pressuring them to make a quick commitment to him. He felt the pain of rejection, and he was continually puzzled as to why these women did not want to be involved with him.

Throughout this period in the treatment I made numerous interventions that were designed to strengthen Bart's ego functioning. These included such strategies as building his frustration tolerance and capacity to delay gratification, developing his utilization of better reality testing, and enhancing his ability to anticipate the consequences of his premature demands for nurturing involvement. He was partially bolstered by this approach, but the pressure of his desperate need to connect prevented him from implementing good judgment in the way he proceeded. On another level he experienced these interventions as a command to relinquish his infantile narcissistic striving and to grow up.

I came to recognize that although Bart functioned at a high level in the corporate world, in terms of object relatedness he had only attained the level of need satisfaction (Blanck and Blanck 1986). Moreover, in this approach to finding a woman who could serve his need to be nurtured, he had regressed to the level of primary narcissism (Blanck and Blanck 1974). His situation was analogous to that of the normal infant who maintains the illusion that positive things happen (like a good feeding) because he brings them about. I drew from Winnicott's (1965) work on illusion to try to give meaning to Bart's desperate way of being in the world. My train of thought was as follows: The infant indicates that he is hungry, and the mother provides a good feeding. Prior to the awareness of differentiation between self and other, the infant develops the belief that *he* brings this about. This is an illusion. The mother is there for the needs of the child and not to serve her own needs, although she does receive some maternal satisfaction from her ministrations. In this way the mother promotes the infant's illusion. This process in the early mother–child relationship is also purported to be the precursor for the development of self-esteem. It is postulated that positive self-regard develops initially from a nurturing maternal presence. As differentiation progresses, the baby gradually discerns aspects of the gleam in the mother's eye, and he internalizes this view of himself and comes to feel lovable.

Bart was functioning at an early level of object relatedness. He wanted a woman who would be available to provide unconditional love, and he was blinded to the reality that an adult woman also brings her own agenda to a relationship. In sessions he would protest, "I have this romantic fantasy that if I like a woman, she should like me, and we should have a relationship in which she takes care of me." Bart felt overwhelmed, anxious, and depressed over his inability to establish a new relationship on his terms. The power of his urgency to connect in this way outstripped his judgment about how to proceed in a way that could make it possible for it to happen. What ultimately was helpful to Bart was a developmental approach that addressed the role of the earliest illusion. I pointed out to him over a period of time, and in different ways, that his actions with women could be understandable from the perspective of the young child's belief that he has the power to bring about desired responses from the environment. Gradually, this approach, which allowed us to make sense out of his seemingly irrational behavior, made him feel understood and less frantic. It took several additional years of psychotherapy before Bart could enter and maintain a reciprocal relationship, but this had given him a much needed handle to hold on to.

It is poignant to see how frequently primitive illusions guide the course of a relationship, even among people who achieve a high level of functioning in other aspects of their lives.

NARCISSISTIC DISILLUSIONMENT

All disillusionment could be viewed as a narcissistic injury insofar as it disrupts a needed way of perceiving oneself, others, or the world. In pathological narcissism such disillusionment is undermining to one's basic cohesiveness of self.

Narcissistic people often live in a world of unreality, not in a psychotic sense, but in that their expectations of themselves and others are significantly warped. They are prone to view others as they need them to be, rather than as they really are, and profound disillusionment sets in when their idealized expectations are unmet. They can ill afford to grasp the true nature of things, because this would force them to give up their cherished false beliefs. Self-knowledge is perceived as dangerous and something to avoid, because it threatens the continuation of these illusions. Narcissists strive to preserve the illusion of their own grandeur. With fuller knowledge of reality, the myths related to one's sense of perfection or of finding the perfect fit with another person are shattered. Thus, the needs that fuel narcissistic illusions (of perfection, grandeur, entitlement) can outstrip an appreciation of reality, and when this system breaks down, one's basic self and object representations are demolished.

Disillusionment in early childhood can be metabolized and lead to a productive restructuring and revision of one's expectations of oneself and others, or it can leave a lasting traumatic imprint. Under optimal circumstances the child comes to tolerate the realization that at some point his parents can no longer protect him from the dangers of the world. If solid parental introjects have been established, the child is able to take over for himself the functions previously managed by the lost omnipotent parent. When this type of disillusionment occurs in a gradual fashion, it solidifies further psychic structure of self and object representations. In the view of Jacobson and Winnicott, such disillusionment serves to further self-other differentiation. In contrast, when it occurs in an abrupt way it cannot be effectively integrated into the ego, which is not yet completely anchored, and the child is predisposed to have repeated overreactions to disappointment.

In narcissistic adults, when the bubble bursts and they can no longer sustain their illusions, the sense of vulnerability can be intense. Disillusion for these individuals is often a precursor of narcissistic depression. Depression in narcissism emerges from being forced to relinquish certain illusions about oneself in relation to the world. Thus, narcissistic depression has to do with the loss of an exalted, idealized, illusory view of one's self, one's specialness, or one's immortality, or the awareness of the true nature of our vulnerability in the world. It is not the loss of a mature object relationship that brings about depression in narcissistic individuals, but rather the loss of illusions about the self or others. In some cases a narcissistic style masks a preexisting depression that erupts when the narcissistic defenses crumble.

The lack of a firm sense of self is characteristic of narcissistic personalities. It is likely, therefore, that narcissistic individuals are especially prone to harbor many illusions about themselves, such as how special or important they are, or illusions of arrogance, which lead them to break the rules of society or take risks. These illusions serve to bolster their self-esteem and shaky self-image. In some cases a depressive core based on early misattunement may underlie a narcissistic facade. This notion is elaborated on by Goodman (1989), who has developed the concept of the depression of the narcissistic personality: "This depression is based on the withdrawal and rejection by the mother of the emotional needs and affective expression of the infant which were threatening to the mother's sense of self" (p. 77). He further relates this depression to the difficulties in processing disillusionment. Goodman observes that in the narcissistic patient "there has not been a successful transition from the use of illusion to the acknowledgment of disillusionment. The narcissistic personality clings to illusion in a defensive manner to protect the self from experiencing emptiness and a loss of self esteem" (p. 80).

8

Politics, Sports, Movies, Theater, and Songs

We all need our fantasies in order to live. Sometimes relin-
quishing them can be extraordinarily painful, not a rebirth
into something exciting and new, but a kind of death.
                                                    P. D. James
                                                Innocent Blood

There are many arenas in everyday life that are enveloped by
the themes of illusion and disillusionment. These themes are pervasive in our involvement in the world of politics, sports, movies, theater, and songs.

POLITICS

Under the impact of intensified media scrutiny over the last forty
years, our illusions about the omniscience and perfection of our
national leaders have been repeatedly demolished. People need
heroes whom they can idealize and with whom they can identify. The increased media attention in which the flaws in the
leader's character and personal life are exposed and highlighted
undermines the illusions that people are ready to develop toward
their leaders, and creates a built-in atmosphere for disillusionment. A prime example is the sex scandal involving Bill Clinton.
In misleading the people for many months about his relationship with Monica Lewinsky, he fed them an illusion. By so do-

ing he delayed the time before the American people would learn the truth, and become disillusioned about his character flaws reflected in his poor judgment and reckless behavior. As noted by the journalist Frank Rich (1997), "What has changed in our faster paced media age is the lag time between the idealization and the debunking of our icons. What used to take years, even decades, now takes days" (p. A21).

American presidents are authority figures about whom we form illusions, and then become disillusioned. Expectations that our hopes for better times will be somehow fulfilled through political pledges is often followed by disappointment and devaluation of the president. The journalist Anthony Lewis (1994) states, "At least since the New Deal, we have had this romantic notion of what presidents ought to do for us. Asking for the impossible, we are bound to be disappointed. And as in a failed romance, we turn bitterly on the one who has failed us" (p. A35).

Frequently, a fatal flaw in judgment, grandiosity, or hubris has contributed to the downfall of a president. Lyndon Johnson's miscalculations about the war in Vietnam (see below), and Richard Nixon's attempts at stonewalling in the Watergate scandal are prime examples. As a result the American public has become increasingly cynical and mistrusting toward their presidents and are quicker to devalue them and thereby protect and insulate themselves from subsequent disillusionment.

The golden era of illusion in twentieth century America occurred during the Kennedy administration. His reign in the White House was frequently alluded to as "Camelot," a reference to the legendary King Arthur's court, which was characterized by enchantment and glamour. The appeal of the Kennedy image, more so than his accomplishments during his abbreviated term, accounts for the fact that in a 1975 Gallup poll Americans considered Kennedy to be their greatest president (Kifner 1997). Most historians would agree that illusions about his greatness far outweigh the reality of his achievements. The national atmosphere of optimism and sense of affiliation with Camelot was destroyed when President Kennedy was assassinated in 1963. A feeling of disillusionment swept across the country, and high hopes were smashed in reaction to the loss of this president and what he represented to the people. In addition, many people felt angry and disillusioned at Kennedy himself for what they perceived as his hubris in traveling in a motorcade in an open-roofed car. Their thought is that he would not have been murdered and their dream would not have died with him if he had been more cautious.

Lyndon Johnson had a vision of creating a "Great Society," and, indeed, his programs achieved substantial advances in race relations and social welfare. However, his presidency was brought down by his illusory commitment to winning a land war in Vietnam, and the term *credibility gap* was coined to describe his administration's misrepresentations to the increasingly disillusioned American electorate. Johnson was succeeded by Richard Nixon and his part in the cover-up of the Watergate burglary ultimately led to his forced resignation. Once again the American public was severely disillusioned about the integrity of a president, and many political observers maintain that this mood of disillusionment in regard to our leaders has persisted to the present. Throughout the course of history there have been national leaders whose downfall has come about as a result of their own illusions about the magnitude of their power. As one historian put it, the problem with Napoleon was that he thought he was Napoleon.

Many a war has been waged based on illusory miscalculations about the strength of one's forces as compared to those of a foe. For example, in the American Civil War, a brutal confrontation that took more American lives than any other war, Southern pride and grandiosity led the leaders of the South to provoke a war it could not win. A belief in the righteousness of their cause led them to secede from the Union with the arrogant belief that they could defeat the North in an ensuing war. The superior resources of the Northern forces tilted the probability of an ultimate victory in their direction.

Other types of illusions have played a significant role in major wars. One of the most infamous political miscalculations, which escalated the beginning of World War II, was British Prime Minister Neville Chamberlain's illusory belief that he could barter with Hitler for peace in Europe. His need to view Hitler as a reasonable man, despite considerable evidence to the contrary, allowed Chamberlain to emerge from their Munich conference with the false belief that Hitler would have no further territorial aspirations in Europe. He returned to England and reassured the populace that he had achieved "peace for our time." Within a year Chamberlain and the world were disillusioned when Germany invaded Poland, which was the formal beginning of World War II. As an experienced statesman, Chamberlain was in a position to recognize that Germany, under Hitler's ruthless leadership, was bent on a program of aggressive expansionism that threatened the sovereignty of nations and the balance of power throughout Europe. Nevertheless, in conferring with Hitler, his judgment and reality testing failed him, and he was swayed by the grandiose and fateful illusion that he could effectively stop Hitler through negotiation. In the light of subsequent events, Chamberlain was roundly vilified for taking a position of appeasement, which merely fueled Hitler's megalomanic illusion that he could conquer the world.

In the face of the increasing persecution of Jews in the early years of the Hitler regime, preceding the Holocaust, an aura of denial and illusion permeated the public reaction to the implications of Hitler's programs. In the wake of the 1935 Nuremburg Laws, which decreed that citizenship in Germany was limited to Aryans, Jews were now designated as subjects of the state. The writing was on the wall that the persecution of Jews was indeed a menacing reality. Nevertheless, perhaps under the impact of unthinkable anxiety, relatively few Jews opted to emigrate from Germany during this precious window of time prior to World War II. As historian Saul Friedlander (1997) points out, "The Jews themselves were only partly aware of the increasingly shaky ground on which they stood because like so many others, they did not perceive the depth of liberal democracy's crisis" (p. 214). In retrospect it is understandable that the horror of confronting the reality of the Nazi pogrom, which would result in the annihilation of six million Jews, created an environment in which people clung to sustaining illusions about how conditions would get better.

It was also widely believed that the illusion that the Japanese would not dare to assault the United States led to a state of unpreparedness resulting in the attack on Pearl Harbor. Subsequent tribunals within the armed forces determined that there were substantial indications of Japan's intentions that were disregarded by commanding officers, whose judgments were clouded by their illusory beliefs. Gordon Prange (1981), the eminent historian of the inchoate events surrounding the Pearl Harbor attack, highlights the role of false assumptions on the part of the U.S. government in the months preceding the surprise attack. In his comprehensive account of this era, he points out that the U.S. commanding general in Hawaii was erroneously preoccupied with the threat of Japanese sabotage in the area of Pearl Harbor rather than preparing for a possible air attack. Prange writes, "Thus, Short focused much of his thinking, his plans, and his efforts in chasing an illusion" (p. 155). It is likely that a grandiose misbelief about invulnerability also contributed to the United States's lack of readiness to properly anticipate Japan's aggression. Prange concludes, "Leadership in Washington proceeded from a false premise at the very outset: that the U.S. Pacific Fleet located in Hawaii could act as a brake on Japan. On the contrary, the stronger the Fleet, the more [Japanese Admiral] Yamamoto would have wanted to strike it a surprise blow to keep it from threatening the Japanese flank in Southeast Asia" (p. 134).

Another military illusion is reflected in the strategy of General Douglas MacArthur in the early days of the war with Japan. At the beginning of World War II, the U.S. government and General MacArthur could not accept that the Philippine Islands, which lie much closer to Japan than to the U.S. mainland, could not be defensible against a Japanese attack. Accordingly, after the Japanese invasion of the Philippines, MacArthur assured Philippine President Quezon that "he could hold Bataan and Corregidor for several months; the morale of our forces was high, and there was no reason for immediate worry" (Spector 1985, p. 112). Historical accounts indicate that there was no factual basis for this statement; it was based on a totally erroneous assessment of military realities. As viewed by the historian Ronald Spector, MacArthur was an inspiring leader, but the "vainglorious and ambitious" dimensions of his personality colored his judgment in making crucial decisions about the defense of the Philippines. Moreover, staking this position of defensibility served to feed the illusions of U.S. Secretary of War Henry Stimson and Army Chief of Staff George Marshall. Although it was unfounded, MacArthur was telling these high-ranking officials what they wanted to believe.

In the Vietnam War a different kind of illusion prevailed. The United States leaders were convinced that their country's overwhelming military superiority would enable them to win a land war 10,000 miles away against a foe that was determined to resist submission through guerilla warfare.

There is evidence that when President Johnson first came to power, he viewed the war as pointless, but that he would be destroyed by Congress if he attempted to pull out. The American people, indoctrinated by the fear of the spread of Communism, were initially in support of military involvement. However, as the war continued with unsuccessful results and a mounting death toll of American soldiers, public opinion eventually turned against the war. As suggested by Johnson's biographer Robert Caro (1990), "A mood of disillusionment, disillusionment and rage, spread through America, a mood symbolized by that horrible song, 'Hey, hey, LBJ, how many kids did you kill today?' " (p. xxv). In truth it was a war that the United States could not win, and the deepening involvement resulted in the most unpopular conflict and humiliating defeat in the history of the country. In addition, the presumption that the nation's economy could supply both "guns and butter," that is, sustain a distant war operation and simultaneously build a "Great Society" at home, was an unrealistic and unreachable goal, which ultimately led to disillusionment in the populace and the downfall of the presidency of Lyndon Johnson, a presidency that represents a case of negative illusion.

In the first year of his presidency, Johnson was at the height of his popularity but preoccupied with negative illusions and plagued by narcissistic disillusionment. He had grave doubts and pessimism at a time when his chances to be elected were realistically excellent. During the 1964 Democratic convention, Johnson seemed to have seriously considered withdrawing himself from nomination. The record of his interactions with confidants indicates that he was in the throes of a narcissistic depression characterized by a substantial gap between the reality of his popularity and his perception of how unacceptable he was to the American people. He bristled over his perceived unpopularity in the North, in the South, among blacks, and with the press, which frequently maligned him. He craved acceptance and approval and became despondent over what he felt were distortions about him reported by the press. In thinking about not running for president, he lamented, "I just want to be away from it. And I know that a man ought to have the hide of a rhinoceros to be in this job. But I don't. . . . And I'm not seeking happiness. I'm just seeking a little comfort once in a while" (Beschloss 1997, pp. 529–530).

Ultimately his dream about creating a "Great Society" prevailed, and he went on to win a landslide victory in the election. His belief that bad press meant that he would not be wanted by the American populace was an illusion. However, four years later, in 1968, in the wake of the growing anti–Vietnam War sentiment throughout the country, he decided that he could not risk the humiliation of a reelection defeat. In March 1968, he announced that he would not seek or accept his party's nomination for president. In part his disillusionment over being increasingly unaccepted and unloved by the electorate had worn him down, and he withdrew in despair.

With the approach of the twenty-first century there is concern that China as an emerging power will fall into a collision course with the United States in terms of the vital interests of these respective nations. The ability to realistically evaluate each other's power, position, and priorities will go a long way toward influencing the outcome of this potential conflict. This political dilemma has led Steven Goldstein (1992), a Sinophile, to write, "A future in which the U.S. and China view each other as they are and not as they wish each other to be would be a significant change from the past. While a relationship without illusions, built out of conflict, would lack the equilibrium or even the stability of the past, it might be less volatile" (p. 123).

SPORTS

As a young boy growing up in Brooklyn, New York, my life centered around the travails of the Brooklyn Dodgers. Like many kids, my feelings of well-being rose and fell in conjunction with my team's won-and-lost record. Through baseball I felt a sense of affiliation, purposefulness, and aspiration to achieve. I identified with my heroes, viewed them as role models, and wanted to become like them. Fortunately, in that era of the late 1940s and 1950s my beloved Dodgers were perennial winners in their league. Unfortunately, the first five times in which they faced the enemy New York Yankees in the World Series, they came away as losers. Inasmuch as involvement with baseball was a way of life among the residents of Brooklyn, our spirits would sink to a low ebb in October, when the rival Yankees prevailed. In suffering defeat at the hands of the Yankees our belief that we were the best team was repeatedly debunked, and we felt disillusioned. For us to feel like a winner, our team had to be a winner, and we were deprived of that reality. We handled our disillusionment with resiliency and with the banner cry of the borough, "Wait Till Next Year!" When the Dodgers finally won the World Championship of baseball in 1955 by forging to victory over the Yankees, the natives of Brooklyn were on top of the world.

A scant two years later the owner of the Dodgers decided to relocate the team to Los Angeles. Shockwaves of disbelief, anger, and disillusionment about the loss of the Dodgers vibrated throughout the community, and the image of Brooklyn as an underdog sports town that could take on the behemoth teams of other cities, much like David and Goliath, had been tarnished forever. How was this disillusionment handled? With the defection of the team many Brooklyn fans lost their interest in baseball and turned to other sports and heroes with whom to identify. Others became involved with the Mets a few years later when that expansion team established new roots in New York. Still others have never accepted the loss and they continue to hope for the day when major league baseball will return to Brooklyn. Periodically, we see newspaper reports of businessmen who are trying to put together a deal that will bring baseball back to Brooklyn, and plans are now afoot to move a minor league team from Pittsfield, Massachusetts, to Brooklyn. Thus, repair of this disillusionment continues to be the goal of those who have never recovered from the blow of the departure of the Dodgers. While the margin of illusion appears to be considerable, given the realities of the powers that rule baseball, it is not beyond the realm of possibility that Brooklyn will someday field another baseball team.

Many people get very involved with their city's team in professional sports, and passions run very high when a franchise attempts to relocate to another city. In 1995, the owners of the Cleveland Browns football team threatened to move to Baltimore. There was an uproar among the disillusioned fans, and, on behalf of their constituents, legislators from Ohio introduced the Fans' Rights Act to Congress, which attempts to provide professional sports leagues with a limited exemption to antitrust laws if a league has voted to block a move. Ultimately, the franchise moved and the fans were left to deal with their loss.

The quest to find sports heroes is essentially related to the need to provide oneself with a feeling of well-being. Heroes are embellished and they are assigned qualities of perfection with which we identify. When the performance of the hero is outstanding, we soar along with him in a glow of heightened self-worth. But when the hero topples off his pedestal we may experience it like a personal blow, and our self-esteem plunges.

The infamous Black Sox scandal of 1919, when several players on the Chicago White Sox were found guilty of conspiring to lose World Series games, was a crushing blow to the disillusioned believers in the purity of baseball. Shoeless Joe Jackson was the hero of many a Chicago youth who found it hard to accept that their star had taken a bribe to lose games. In spite of conclusive evidence that underscored Jackson's culpability, his fans struggled to maintain their belief in his innocence. A legendary incident involved the plea of a young boy, who cried out, "Say it ain't so, Joe!" as Jackson was about to appear in court. Many baseball fans felt devastated when Jackson and his coconspiratorial teammates were banned from baseball for life.

Hero worship promotes the illusion of specialness, and disillusionment can be profound, especially in children, when heroes abruptly become fallen idols. While this is a normal experience during childhood, latency, and adolescence, many adults do not have a firm sense of self; it continues to rise and fall with the performance of their heroes. This has been described by self psychologists as an idealizing selfobject relationship. According to Bacal and Newman (1990), this type of relationship "denotes the experience of feeling linked to the admired other: the self, in effect, walking proudly in the shadow of his admired object" (p. 232). I have conceptualized this as a satellite relationship in which one attempts to feel whole, powerful, special, and secure through hitching one's wagon to a star.

In a similar vein Post (1997) delineates the psychopathology of what he calls the ideal-hungry personality:

> These individuals can experience themselves as worthwhile only so long as they can relate to individuals whom they can admire for their power, prestige, beauty, intelligence. . . . They forever search for such idealized figures. Again, the inner void cannot be filled. Inevitably, the ideal-hungry finds that his God is merely human, that his hero has feet of clay. Disappointed by discovery of defects in his previously idealized object, he casts him aside and searches for a new hero, to whom he attaches himself in the hope that he will not be disappointed again. [p. 207]

Whether we speak of idealizing selfobject relationships, satellite relationships, or ideal-hungry personalities, the central element for these individuals is their need to define themselves via their connection to an exalted other. The connection often becomes precarious when the human flaws, the chinks in the armor of the admired other, become too real to be ignored. At this point, under the impact of profound disappointment, the object may be discarded and the search for a replacement object who can fill the bill will begin. Many adults' development has been truncated, and they function at this level of adjustment. In such cases the conditions are ripe for idealization and devaluation to occur, and the opportunities for illusion and disillusionment will proliferate.

MOVIES

The movie *Cocoon* (Howard 1983) deals with the irresistible appeal of reversing the aging process. The story focuses on a group of elders at a senior residence home who are struggling with the vicissitudes of getting old. Cancer, failing eyesight, dementia, and depression are among the many problems encountered by their residents. Inadvertently, a small group of extraterrestrials from Antera, an outer-space planet, take up residence next door. It seems that 100 centuries ago they had had an outpost at this location on Earth, and they are returning in order to evacuate those that previously had been left behind. The latter had been placed in huge cocoons made of rocks, and these cocoons had survived in the bottom of the ocean for all these centuries. To bring these aliens back to life, their cocoons were transferred from the ocean to a large pool, which the senior residents had been using. The presence of the cocoons energizes the water, and when the three central male characters from the senior residence subsequently use the pool they are completely rejuvenated. They become vigorous, sexual, and excited to be alive. It is as if they have fortuitously stumbled onto the Fountain of Youth, which is an unconscious illusion shared by many people as the aging process takes its toll. The magical power of the pool to reverse the afflictions of old age is symbolized by one of the men, whose cancer goes into total remission.

When news of this magical water spreads throughout the senior residence, everyone rushes to swim in the pool in an attempt to fulfill the illusion that they can regain the lost vitality of their youth. In doing so they disrupt and dislodge the cocoons, and, as a result the life force is completely drained from the water. Despair follows in both groups: among the aliens, who recognize that they will now not be able to revive and bring their long lost brethren back to Antera, and among the seniors, who are no longer able to reap the benefits of bathing in the fountain of youth. The seniors must now contemplate returning to the depressing conditions of old age and their impending mortality. However, they are once again rescued from that plight.

As the extraterrestrials prepare to return to Antera, their leader offers to take thirty of the senior residents with them. It is an opportunity to attain immortality, but it means giving up their connections to their loved ones on Earth. In a touching scene, a grandfather confides in his grandson about the imminent departure to outer space. When questioned by the alarmed and saddened young grandson, the older man says, "What's important is that when we get where we're going, we'll never be sick, we won't get any older, and we won't ever die." Ultimately, the wish for immortality prevails, and the aliens are joined by the group of seniors in taking off for outer space.

The wish for not only immortality but also a perfect state of bliss resides on some level in all of us. Some people are more consciously aware of such yearnings, while others defend against them, and they remain to a greater degree in the realm of the unconscious.

This motif is portrayed in the film *Lost Horizon* (Capra 1937), which is an adaptation of James Hilton's (1933) novel about an illusory paradise on Earth, a hidden valley that he called Shangri-La.

The story revolves around the hero, Robert Conway, who was a highly regarded British diplomat. Conway was sent to the Chinese city of Bashul, on the border of Tibet, to rescue Western citizens who were in danger of being slaughtered in the midst of a local revolution. After barely escaping the violence surrounding them, their plane crashes in a desolate blizzard-ridden wilderness some 8,000 miles from civilization. Conway and the other survivors are found by a group of local natives, who escort them through hazardous mountains to their nearby community called Shangri-La. Shangri-La is a garden-spot valley in Tibet that is sheltered by mountains on every side, and has no communication with the outside world. In sharp contrast to the barren Arctic and dismal area outside, the enclave of Shangri-La, like Camelot, has perfect climate and living conditions. Moreover, the inhabitants live to a ripe old age there, as much as two hundred years, and "a perfect body in perfect health is the rule here." When one enters Shangri-La the aging process is immediately arrested, and people maintain the appearance and vigor of 20-year-olds, even when in reality they are old. However, to maintain this state of well-being they must remain permanently in Shangri-La. If they leave, their appearance and functioning automatically reverts back to that of their actual age.

Conway finds love and a spiritual blissfulness in Shangri-La, but he is persuaded to leave by his brother, who had been on the plane with him. They were encouraged to attempt the journey back to civilization by the brother's lover, who deceived them into thinking she was a vigorous 20-year-old, when in fact she was nearly 70. Against his better judgment, Conway agreed to leave with them. The journey through the blizzard-filled mountains was most hazardous, and was too rigorous for the woman, who soon reverted to her true age and died. The brother was killed in an avalanche of snow, and Conway continued to wander in the wilderness until he was miraculously found by a Chinese mission. He returned to England, where he was despondent and longing for his lost Shangri-La. The story ends with Conway once again trekking through the desolate wilderness outside of Tibet, until, with great determination, he finds his way back to Shangri-La.

There is a wish for Shangri-La in everyone's heart. Indeed, the appeal of Shangri-La resonates so profoundly within us that this term, taken from Hilton's novel, has attained widespread usage in the English language. Appropriately, the film, *Lost Horizon*, begins with the following caption:

> In these days of wars and rumors of wars—haven't you ever dreamed of a place where there was peace and security, where living was not a struggle, but a lasting delight? Of course you have. So has every man since time began. Always the same dream. Sometimes he calls it Utopia. Sometimes the fountain of youth. Sometimes merely "that little chicken farm."

Star 80 (Fosse 1983) is a film that illustrates how in disturbed personalities the magnitude of disillusionment can lead to violent consequences. The movie is a partially fictionalized story about Dorothy Stratton, a model who became a Playboy centerfold and actress, and her husband, Paul Snider, who murdered her. Dorothy is portrayed as a naive, innocent, and masochistic young woman who is caught up in the web of Paul's psychopathic, narcissistic, and paranoid pathology. Paul discovers her, charms her, courts her, and marries her. He places Dorothy on a pedestal, and through his idealization of her he is able to elevate his self-esteem to greater heights. Through fantasies of merger and connection to his idealized object, he derives a sense of power, success, and specialness. In promoting her career he is driven by the belief that "together we could be somebody." Thus, his identity is excessively overlapping with hers. As Dorothy gradually becomes more of her own person, she distances herself from Paul in an effort to gain more freedom, and their relationship, which had been based on symbiotic attachment, is destroyed. The destruction of their relationship is disillusioning and narcissistically devastating to Paul, who cannot bear the thought of losing her. For Paul losing the relationship with Dorothy is tantamount to losing a core part of himself. He tells her, "I don't think I want to go on living without you." When she pursues divorce, he kills her and then kills himself with a shotgun. This theme of destruction and demonization of love objects when necessary illusions have been shattered is developed by Michael Vincent Miller in his book *Intimate Terrorism: The Deterioration of Erotic Life* (1985).

The potential for violence in understructured personalities when illusions in loving are shattered is further exemplified in the film *Fatal Attraction*, introduced in Chapter 4 (Lyne 1987). After seizing the opportunity to have a weekend sexual escapade while his wife is away, Dan Gallagher decides that he cannot handle an ongoing relationship with Alex Forrest, who is a single woman. Alex is quickly enamored of Dan and cannot let go. She makes further overtures toward him and is humiliated when he politely declines her invitations and ignores her phone calls. Despite the rejection, Alex continues to pine away for Dan, clinging to the illusion that they can have an affair. She presses for a meeting in which he confronts her by saying, "Is this what you want to talk about, our imaginary love affair?" Her perspective is captured in her statement, "You thought that you could just walk into my life and turn it upside down, without a thought for anyone but yourself." Alex's narcissistic mortification in response to her unfulfilled expectations leads her to pursue an escalating path of predatory vindictive retaliation toward Dan. Alex's functioning is dominated by a powerful illusion and an inability to deal with disillusionment (see Chapter 4).

The movie *Belle Epoque* (Trueba 1992) portrays the need for illusion as central to the completion of heterosexual intercourse. In this story a young lesbian is able to actively pursue a heterosexual liaison, when she and her young man attend a costume party dressed in opposite-sex clothing. In addition, she wears a mustache, and he wears lipstick to accentuate the masquerade. Assuming the traditional male role the young woman proceeds to seduce her partner, carried by the illusion that she is pursuing a woman (i.e., a man dressed as a woman). Demasculinizing her man and pretending that he is a woman, aided by visual stimuli consistent with this illusion, are necessary conditions for copulation to take place. The combination of her being able to act like a man *and* to connect with a man who appears to be a woman paves the way for the overcoming of the sexual inhibition, and makes it safe for this woman to engage in heterosexual intercourse.

Subsequently, when the young man, carried away by his passion of the previous evening, declares his love for her and his wish to marry her, she rejects him saying, "Last night was nothing, you idiot!" Hence, once the costume party was over, and they had returned to the reality of their true gender roles, she could not sustain her interest in him as a sexual partner. Without the aid of illusion she was unable to function as a sexual woman.

The popularity of movies that deal with the underlying theme of illusion or disillusionment is attributable in part, I believe, to the readiness with which people identify with these issues. Examples include *Titanic*, *Grease*, and *Quiz Show*. The story of *Titanic* (Cameron 1997), with its tragedy based on blind arrogance of invincibility, touches a deep-seated chord within all of us. It speaks to our grandiose illusions that, if unheeded, can lead to dire consequences à la Icarus. *Grease* (Kleiser 1982) captures the adolescent high school years as a time when one can embrace both the experience of increased autonomy and the illusion that time and life will be forever. Although this age is typically filled with considerable Sturm and Drang and insecurity about oneself, there is also often a sense of enthusiasm, adventurousness, and obliviousness to danger that is reminiscent of the practicing phase of normal development; these are feelings that on some level we all yearn to recapture. In *Quiz Show* (Redford 1994), which depicts the true story of the 1950s' scandal in which an esteemed college professor is discovered to be colluding with a television quiz show that provides him with answers in advance of the show, we identify with the disillusionment related to the loss of innocence. To acknowledge the evidence that our heroes are significantly flawed and that the system is corrupt is to accept the true essence of things and to abandon comforting, but false, beliefs.

THEATER

In earlier sections of this book I have drawn from such venerable works of theater as *The Iceman Cometh*, *The Heiress*, and *Who's Afraid of Virginia Woolf?* to illustrate powerful themes of illusion and disillusionment in the lives of the central characters in these plays. In this section I focus on two musicals, *Gypsy* and *Sunset Boulevard*.

Gypsy (Laurents et al. 1960) is based on the memoirs of Gypsy Rose Lee, a legendary American striptease artist. The story centers around the character of Gypsy's mother, Rose Hovick.

Mama Rose, as she is referred to, is the quintessential ambitious stage mother who is determined to fulfill her own dreams of success in show business through her two daughters, June and Louise. When she is rebuffed in her plans to make stars of her daughters and advised by her father to face reality and settle for a simple life, she displays her fierce ambition and determination to rise above her roots. In the song "Some People," she declares her intent to pursue her dream.

The theatrical act orchestrated by Rose is built around June, the more talented daughter, with Louise being overshadowed, neglected, and content to remain in the background. Rose is passionate in her pursuit of making June a star in vaudeville. Unfortunately, this occurred in an era when vaudeville was dying, and therefore her dream became illusory. When June, as a young teenager, elopes in rebellion against Rose's need to keep her performing as a child in a mediocre act in a failing area of show business, Rose is devastated. Through identification, June has represented Rose's second chance to become a star, and now her illusion is shattered. In Kohutian terms, June had been cast in the role of a selfobject for Rose. Furthermore, Rose's illusory dream is what kept her going and allowed her to maintain her sense of purpose. Her disillusionment over June is quickly transformed into a compensatory illusion, in which she would now devote all of her efforts into making the less talented Louise into a star. As she attempts to recover from June's abandonment, Rose turns to Louise in a powerful rendition of "Everything's Coming Up Roses," in which she utilizes the mechanism of denial in support of her compensatory illusion.

Rose's aspirations for Louise become increasingly unrealistic as interest in vaudeville acts continues to decline. Eventually, through a mistake, their act is unwittingly booked into a burlesque house. At this point Rose finally begins to accept reality. She comments, "What they say in this business is when a vaudeville act plays burlesque it means it's all washed up" (p. 103). It appears that she is getting ready to mourn the loss of her illu-

sion, when a dramatic development occurs. The headliner burlesque queen is suddenly arrested, and Rose seizes upon this
event to prevail upon Louise to perform as a stripper. Rose re-
gresses to her dream of having a daughter who makes it as a
star, even if it is only as a stripper. Ultimately, Louise, known as
Gypsy Rose Lee, becomes the biggest burlesque star of them all.

The role of Rose in *Gypsy* illustrates how illusions can be
pivotal in protecting us from awareness of our vulnerability.
When we recognize the ineluctable true essence of things, our
illusions break down, and we are left to deal with feelings of loss,
despair, and emptiness. When the bubble burst, Rose needed
to sustain herself via a compensatory illusion rather than experience the pain of her disillusionment.

The film *Sunset Boulevard* (Wilder 1950) is replete with
themes of illusion and disillusionment. When it was converted
into a Broadway musical in 1993, the script and the lyrics highlighted these themes even more poignantly. Composer Andrew
Lloyd Webber, working with a variety of lyricists, displays a unique
grasp of illusion and disillusionment as pivotal themes in his
musicals (e.g., *Evita* and *Phantom of the Opera*).

The functioning of each of the major characters in *Sunset
Boulevard* powerfully resonates and revolves around these
themes. Norma Desmond, somewhat analogously to the character of Miss Haversham in Charles Dickens's (1860–1861) *Great
Expectations*, is a caricature of a disillusioned middle-aged
woman. Norma had once enjoyed enormous fame and admiration as an actress in the era of silent films. Twenty years have
passed and she lives in a world of illusion in which she regains
her life of grandeur as a star. In truth she is a relic, hardly remembered as a once-famous silent screen movie star, and viewed
as a has-been by the Hollywood studios. Norma has never accepted her loss of stature, and she nurtures the grand illusion
of regaining her lost fame. She declares that she will return to
her millions of fans who have not forgiven her for abandoning
them. In this position she is putting a spin on reality. To ap-

pease her narcissistic vulnerability she twists the truth. Therefore, she must proclaim that she left filmmaking, rather than that she is perceived as a relic from an earlier period. Along with her difficulty in accepting reality she is determined to cling to her lost grandeur, and she develops a compensatory illusion about making a comeback. Actually, she rails at the word *comeback*, because that implies a loss of stardom, and she insists upon viewing her efforts as "a return." She is consumed with this compensatory illusion and her ongoing functioning is organized around it. She has written a new script for the movies and this is to be the vehicle for her return. Her script needs some work, and through an accidental meeting she hires Joe Gillis to work on it with her.

Joe is a disillusioned young writer who is hitting on hard times trying to make a living in Hollywood. He accurately recognizes that Norma has written a horrible script and that she is pursuing an unfulfillable illusion. He reflects, "I didn't argue, why hurt her. You don't yell at a sleepwalker or she could fall and break her neck. She smelled of faded roses. It made me sad to watch her as she relived her glory. Poor Norma, so happy, lost in her silver heaven" (Perry 1993, p. 149). Joe could plainly see that time was the enemy of her illusion about her ongoing grandeur. Nevertheless, he is in desperate straits, and so he accepts Norma's offer to work on her hopeless script. He comes to live in her home and soon becomes a kept man as the object of her affections.

Max Mayerling serves as Norma's butler and general houseman. Max has his own investment in Norma's illusion of grandeur. His support of and collusion with Norma's grand illusion allows him to sustain a central role in her life and an identity of importance. We eventually learn that many years ago Max had been Norma's first husband and the director of her early films, and he continues to need to be enmeshed in her life. Hence, although Max knows that Norma's dreams are illusory, he consciously colludes with her as the keeper of the flame. He recognizes her fragility and keeps her going by sending her fan mail and pandering to her as a star. Their shared commitment is based on the belief that Norma has fulfilled the need for illusion in her audiences. This is captured throughout the play in the repeated refrain that "Everyone Needs New Ways to Dream," in which lyricists Don Black and Christopher Hampton adeptly capture the appeal of providing dreams, fantasies, and illusions to the mass audience of filmgoers.

Ironically, it was their own new ways to dream, based on a bypassing of reality, that possessed Norma and Max. For Norma there is a thin line between reality and illusion, while for Max it is a conscious choice, generated by his own needs, to perpetuate the illusion. When confronted by Joe about his collusive actions, Max acknowledges his role in perpetuating Norma's illusion.

Ultimately, the studio is not receptive to Norma's efforts, Joe develops a romantic interest of his own, and he experiences anger and guilt in allowing himself to be in the role of a kept man who is also colluding in her illusion. When Norma realizes that Joe is leaving her, she panics. She cannot bear to be abandoned and she threatens to kill herself. In the denouement he attempts to get her to face reality, confronting her with the truths that her fan mail is written by Max and that the studio is interested only in her antique car. The abrupt assault on her illusions is overwhelming to Norma. In horror she turns to Max for clarification, and he continues to feed her illusion that she is the greatest star of them all! As Joe walks out on her, she flies into a psychotic rage, unable to tolerate being abandoned, and she shoots and kills him. When the police arrive to investigate the murder, Max stays faithful to his role of colluding in her illusion of grandeur, and leads her to believe that these people are here to assist her in the shooting of a scene. In her psychotic state, unable to adaptively deal with disillusionment, she allows Max to direct her in a scene. Her final words to her imagined stagehands are, "I can't tell you how wonderful it is to be back in the studio making a picture. I promise you I'll never desert you again . . . and now, Mr. DeMille, I'm ready for my close-up" (Perry 1993, p. 165).

The story of *Sunset Boulevard* depicts how maladaptive illusions may be reinforced or punctured by interacting participants. Max feeds Norma's illusion like a codependent spouse feeds an alcoholic, and thereby attempts to protect her from the pain of reality and disillusionment. It is at the point when Joe punctures her illusion that Norma's fragile personality structure unravels and she violently kills the man who so forcefully shattered the illusory dream that had held her together. For Norma, a retreat into psychosis is a preferable alternative to dealing with the pain and despair of disillusionment. This is similar to the outcome in *The Story of Adele H.* In contrast, we see a different outcome in *Whose Afraid of Virginia Woolf?* and in *Gypsy.* In the former play Martha is initially decimated by George's puncturing her illusion about their fictitious child. She is depleted, but then she reconstitutes. At the final curtain they are able to take solace from each other in dealing with the loss of their shared illusion. There is an acceptance and a capacity to move on. Having someone with whom to share the pain and to provide support may, in some cases, serve as protection against greater decompensation. In *Gypsy* we see yet another alternative outcome following the shattering of a core illusion. Mama Rose bypasses the pain of disillusionment by moving on to a replacement figure, her second daughter, who then becomes the focus of her continuing illusion.

SONGS

From childhood our views about ourselves, our world, and our relationships are significantly reinforced and even shaped by what we see and what we hear on television, radio, in the movies, and in popular songs.

In World War II after the shattering of the illusion that Japan would never dare to make war with the United States, the American people went forward with a tremendous surge of nationalism. This spirit of nationalism, punctuated by the theme of "one for all and all for one," was reinforced by songs with lyrics like "Let's remember Pearl Harbor," which served to impassion the people with a sense of righteousness, determination, and a common destiny in the face of devastating anxiety over the surprise attack.

The ubiquitous wish for nirvana is captured in "Over the Rainbow" (Arlen and Harburg 1939), from the classic film *The Wizard of Oz*. Don't we all share the common illusion of finding that perfect place where we will live in perfect bliss? The lyrics compel us to rise above the human condition, to the land where dreams come true.

The song "Camelot" (Lerner and Loewe 1960), from the Broadway musical of the same name, follows a similar path. The lyrics represent a metaphor for the yearning to find a utopian atmosphere, a place where living conditions are optimal. By royal decree summers are cool, winters are mild, snow is limited, and it cannot rain during the daytime. The description of such ideal conditions of climate in Camelot symbolizes the fantasy of finding (or refinding) a blissful emotional and interpersonal environment. The illusion of everlasting happiness and absence of psychic pain is thereby guaranteed.

Many people are buoyed by songs whose lyrics resonate with their pain. Sometimes they feel better understood by the words of a treasured song than by other people.

Margaret, an attractive single woman in her mid-thirties, felt beaten down by life, and found solace in escaping to a safe and nurturing fantasyland. She had had a series of relationships in which she was abruptly rejected after relatively minor provocations on her part. Her father was characterized as being prone toward "explosive psychotic rages," and unconsciously she sought out men who could be easily triggered toward abusive behavior. Her primary identification was with her mother, who was described chiefly as a martyr. The unfolding of these themes, of course, became a central component of Margaret's therapy, along with her wish and fear about trusting me as a male therapist. She desperately wanted my help, but also feared that she would be hurt and not understood. Her transferential anxiety about retraumatization emerged through concerns such as that I would reject and abandon her if she took a vacation. She feared that I, like her father, would never accept her for herself, but only as I needed her to be. Her gradual progress in treatment was reflected through a dream in which, "I went to Bob, the guy who cuts my hair, and I explained to him that I wanted my hair styled differently. He said it couldn't be cut that way. I was angry and told him that it could be done, and if he didn't do it, I'd find someone else to do it!" In this thinly disguised displacement from myself, as the one who works on her head, she was expressing her need and determination to pursue things her own way rather than by compliantly fitting in with her perception of my agenda for her.

Her growing ability to trust me was indicated by her bringing me a record of a song that captured her fantasies about finding her safe and nurturing haven. This was her way of letting me into her inner life, in which she was absorbed with an imaginary place similar to Camelot. The song was called "The Land of Make Believe" (Mangione 1973), and the lyrics depict an environment in which acceptance, love, immortality, serenity, and happiness prevail.

In her frequent moments of despair, Margaret turned to her illusion about "the land of make believe" as a source of comfort.

The awareness of the interplay between the themes of illusion and disillusionment is embraced in the popular standard "I'm Always Chasing Rainbows" (Carroll and McCarthy 1918). As they come to grips with the unrealistic nature of their dreams and the pain of giving them up, some individuals relate to the lyrics in which pursuing far-reaching dreams and fantasies lead to chronic disillusionment.

Songs of disillusionment also hit the mark for those who suffer intense disappointments in love. A prominent example is "I Dreamed a Dream" (Boubil et al. 1986), from the musical *Les Misérables*, which is based on the novel by Victor Hugo. In this song Fantine, scarred by the abuses of her life, laments the realization that her life can never be as she had wished it. Her words describe her early illusions about love and her disillusioned hopes and dreams. The lyrics highlight the ebb and flow of Fantine's conflict between forming a compensatory illusion about reunited love and accepting the reality of her loss and the emptiness of her life.

9

Psychoanalytic Psychotherapy

*The demand to give up the illusions about its condition is
the demand to give up a condition which needs illusions.*
                                                Karl Marx
          [cited in Fromm, *Beyond the Chains of Illusion*]

Chasseguet-Smirgel and Grunberger (1986) have noted that "human beings have an insatiable longing to regain the perfection
experienced at the outset of life, before the differentiation between subject and outside world. In the Freudian system, the
belief that a return to this primary plenitude is possible would
be categorized as 'Illusion' " (p. 13).

     The ubiquitous wish to recapture the sense of infantile om-
nipotence in which perfect attunement is available is often reactivated in the treatment situation. On some level, consciously
or unconsciously, all patients, whether well-structured individuals with intact ego functions or understructured individuals with
preoedipal pathology, share a common wish. That wish is to be
able to experience psychotherapy and the therapist as the embodiment of the vehicle that will restore the oceanic powerful
feelings of those earlier times. For those who have suffered significant early deprivation in caregiving, the pull toward such idealization of the psychotherapeutic process and the therapist may
be especially pronounced and/or defended against.

     Freud (1916–1917) foresaw the danger of unrealistic expec-
tations about the psychoanalytic process, and he proposed that

psychoanalysis be pursued as an investigative process and not to bring about a cure. Nevertheless, expectations about cure and personality reconstruction have become major sources of illusion and disillusionment for patients as well as their analysts. This is particularly poignant for those patients whose unresolved problems center around issues in developmental arrest. These people frequently seek psychotherapy with a built-in transference expectation that the therapist will be the all-understanding parental figure and provider of nurturing supplies that were missing or inconsistently available during their early developmental years. Thus, in such cases we see prominent illusions about therapy and the role of the therapist as magical healer, rescuer, provider of answers to make one's life better, and the reincarnation of the all-perfect, all-understanding, gratifying caregiver of the symbiotic phase of development (Blanck and Blanck 1974). Later on, with the realization that psychotherapy has not fully healed one's wounds, taken one's pain away, or restored one's sense of perfection, the theme of disillusionment takes center stage in the therapeutic process.

PATIENTS' ILLUSIONS ABOUT PSYCHOTHERAPY

Psychoanalytic psychotherapy may be viewed as a method that gradually challenges the patient's misconceptions and erroneous assumptions, and facilitates the growth and development of tools that enable one to come to terms with the true essence of things. Many patients enter treatment with illusions about how psychotherapy will be of help to them. A major step in the formation of the treatment alliance occurs when the patient recognizes that it is not the therapist that brings about progress and change, but rather the mutual work done together by patient and therapist. This may seem to be patently obvious, but for those individuals who are not initially psychoanalytically sophisticated there is often the expectation that one will be healed by presenting one's problems to the omniscient doctor. Such illusions are often at the root of early treatment resistances. One masochistic man, when asked about his motivation to change, stated, "I don't want to work at getting better, I just want to be better." His illusion was that just by putting himself in the hands of a therapist he should get better, without having to participate in the process. This is not an uncommon scenario for some patients who continue for years in therapy without significant change. Eventually, when faced with their lack of progress, they become disillusioned and angry at therapy for not bringing about their wished-for changes. In such cases it is imperative for the therapist to analyze these illusions about the therapist's omnipotence early in the treatment, in order to facilitate a working alliance.

Mitchell (1993) has noted that "psychoanalysis is a process involving, most fundamentally, the hopes and dreads of its two participants" (p. 9). Insofar as this relates to the themes of illusion and disillusionment, many patients approach the analytic encounter with dread, because they sense that their cherished illusions will be examined and analyzed. They anticipate that the analyst will challenge their maladaptive ways of organizing their world, and will be the grand disillusioner. This is highlighted by Gaylin (1968), who states, "A patient still unconsciously bound to his grandiose plans can see analysis as a humiliating experience" (p. 22). Indeed, during analysis, when a patient's illusions are dismantled, a period ensues in which the patient is increasingly depressed. Being a patient in psychoanalysis is a paradoxical experience. The patient seeks treatment because he wants to change, but he also fears change. Anxieties related to being hurt or damaged by the analyst or the analytic process are commonplace and reside forcefully in the realm of the unconscious. These anxieties may also reach conscious awareness. In any case, they are readily accessed from fantasies and dream material revealed by the analysand. They may form the basis of resistance and are at the core of many negative transferences. In discussing the fear of change based on negative illusions about the analyst and the analytic process, Castelnuovo-Tedesco (1989) has presented numerous examples to illustrate patients' underlying fears that "there will be damage and hurt to the person and/or something vital and important will be lost or taken away. Often this refers to some cherished aspect of the patient's identity. . . . Patients commonly are inclined to believe that treatment and therapeutic change require giving up a valuable part of the self" (pp. 110–111). Skepticism about psychoanalysis as a useful treatment is partially derived from the dread of changing one's familiar patterns, which are perceived as necessary for survival. As Becker (1973) expounds, "The hostility to psychoanalysis in the past, today, and in the future will always be a hostility against admitting that man lives by lying to himself about himself and about his world" (p. 51).

Omer and Rosenbaum (1997) have written about "diseases of hope" in which unrealistic expectations (i.e., illusions) prevail and need to be relinquished. While most therapeutic approaches reinforce the patient's need to retain a hopeful attitude toward the future, these authors emphasize the importance of the work of despair, which involves letting go, and giving up hopes for the fulfillment of unrealistic expectations: "Hope becomes diseased partially as a function of its unlikelihood, but also when it leads to disparagement of the present, to mindless sacrifices, and to rigid attitudes or behaviors. We suggest that at such times therapists may need to assist clients to let go of their hope" (p. 225). Rather than patients' dwelling on hopes that contain a considerable margin of illusion ("Hope always places paradise in some postponed future" [p. 232]), Omer and Rosenbaum advocate the need for therapists to free patients from their attachment to hope, to "de-hope," and to engage them in the painful work of despair in which mourning the loss of unreachable hopes, dreams, and illusions is central. While many clients come to therapy seeking help in their efforts to realize their illusions, these authors envision therapeutic benefit as emanating from the work of despair. The glorification of the past along with excessive hopefulness about the future may stultify our patients' ability to live more fully in the present. Puncturing illusions about perfection, idealized relationships, invulner-

ability, and omnipotence may pave the way toward a fuller appreciation of life's available satisfactions. By pursuing the work
of despair, the therapist does indeed represent the grand
disillusioner.

Anna Ornstein (1995), a prominent self psychologist, addresses the patient's hopeful illusions in describing the prevalence of the patient's curative fantasy in psychoanalytic treatment.
In line with the importance of understanding and addressing
selfobject transferences, as delineated by Kohut, Ornstein observes that "the curative fantasy represents a deep inner conviction that some very specific experiences that were unavailable in
the past have to be provided in order for development to move
forward" (p. 114). Even if the curative fantasy entails unfulfillable
illusions, it reflects legitimate needs that are perceived by the
patient as requirements to be met in order for one to feel nour-
ished. Ornstein emphasizes that the recognition, articulation, and
acceptance of the curative fantasy is central to the healing process, especially "the patient's own acceptance of the legitimacy
of the hoped-for experience" (p. 115). Thus, the emphasis here
is on the acknowledgment of the legitimacy of the patient's
wished-for unmet early experiences, while at the same time
mourning and accepting its unattainability. The therapeutic technique in this approach "is one in which the patient's curative
fantasies—no matter how infantile—are accepted as a legitimate
insistence on experiences that they consider to be essential for
the completion of their self development" (p. 115).

The treatment approach in self psychology involves creating an atmosphere in which illusions can be reactivated, so that
disillusionment can then occur in gradual doses, in contrast to
earlier abrupt or traumatic experiences in which missing or lost
selfobject components prevailed. This then creates the opportunity for transmuting internalization, which promotes the growth
of psychic structure.

While Kohut had emphasized the importance of optimal
frustration as a central aspect of the curative process, Bacal
(1998) and other relational self psychologists have shifted their

emphasis toward the concept of optimal responsiveness rather than optimal frustration as the essential feature of effective treatment. In providing optimal responsiveness, the analyst is not bound by preconceived notions about the necessity for frustration to promote growth. Rather, he is free to interact in whatever way he deems will be healing for the patient. At various times such responses may entail an analytic stance that is gratifying, frustrating, or neutral.

THERAPISTS' ILLUSIONS ABOUT PSYCHOTHERAPY

As psychoanalysis gained popularity in the United States during the middle of the twentieth century, the misconception grew that this modality could provide a complete "cure" for a wide range of disorders. Psychoanalysts oversold the ability of the treatment process to bring about total personality reconstruction, and this fed into their patients' magical beliefs and expectations.

Recognizing that psychoanalysis was being overidealized, Leo Stone (1961), an eminent analyst, warned against reinforcing the prevalent belief that psychoanalysis could cure any and all problems. Stone correctly anticipated that this overestimation of what psychoanalysis could realistically accomplish would lead to a disillusionment with the process. When the public came to realize that analytic treatment could not fulfill these inflated expectations, the field of psychoanalysis came under attack and eventually was devalued in certain circles. Many years earlier Freud himself had proposed that psychoanalysis should be viewed as a method for understanding mental functioning and not as a curative process. In this view Freud was a realist; however, his followers as well as the next generation of analysts, especially in the United States, contributed to an ambiance of overestimation of psychoanalysis. As a result, a climate flourished in which illusions about analytic triumphs were eventually replaced by disillusion with the limitations of analysis. Ultimately, a more realistic appraisal about analytic goals has taken place.

Nevertheless, many of today's practitioners continue to have their own illusions about the treatment process. I have supervised numerous therapists who set expectations for change, progress, and growth in their patients that are somewhat unrealistic. This is especially true in the treatment of less structured (i.e., borderline and character disorder) cases, in which pathology is more extensive and more entrenched. This has been highlighted by Strean (1993), who discusses the role of the therapists' grandiose fantasies about treatment as a counterresistance impediment to successful therapy. Impasses in therapy are commonly precipitated by unresolved issues in omnipotence emanating from the therapist. Supervision is often invaluable in such situations in facilitating the therapist's ability to access his illusions about where the treatment needs to go. When the conflicting agendas based on the illusions of the patient, therapist, and sometimes even the supervisor, emerge and are clarified and addressed, impasses are often resolved. In a case described by Omer and Rosenbaum (1997), the therapy was almost derailed by the therapist's grandiose expectations that he could help his patient reconcile a lifelong conflictual relationship with her daughter. The patient was dying of cancer, and had attained serenity by resolving that she did not want any further contact with her daughter. To help this patient, it was necessary for the therapist to shift gears, support the client's agenda, and set more realistic goals for the treatment.

As the patient population has increasingly shifted away from symptom neuroses and toward characterological problems, therapists have become more cognizant of the conflicting agendas and assumptions between patient and therapist. Yalom's case example in Chapter 5 illustrates the frequently seen type of patient who comes to treatment to get help in solidifying and fulfilling an illusion, rather than for the purpose of understanding the roots of her problem, acquiring insight, and making meaningful changes. In the example, the patient's agenda was in sharp contrast to the assumptions formed by the therapist about the purpose of her therapy, and this led to an unexpected termination.

A REVISED VIEW OF THE
PSYCHOTHERAPEUTIC RELATIONSHIP

Insofar as patients with preoedipal difficulties compose an ever-increasing portion of psychotherapy practices, issues related to unfulfilled early object needs abound. These individuals tend to have suffered more profound or abrupt early disillusionments and/or exhibit more prominent illusions about what they want from the therapeutic relationship. These themes invariably find their way into the transference configurations. As a result there is a heightened interest in considering the question of who needs to accommodate whom in what ways in the dyadic therapeutic encounter. Proponents of the relational model, and the emphasis on intersubjectivity, have also drawn our attention to the importance of reexamining this issue.

By definition the psychotherapy relationship is asymmetrical and reflects an imbalance of power. In traditional psychotherapy the frame is tilted toward the conditions established by the therapist. Arrangements about reserved session times, fees, payments for missed sessions, extratherapeutic contact, and vacation schedules were more or less determined by the therapist, and the assumption was that the patient would fit in or accommodate to these policies of the therapist. Patients with sufficient ego strength, who were not exposed to excessive early deprivation or overgratification, are able to tolerate these conditions without undue frustration or disruption of the treatment alliance. However, for the less well structured patients, it is often necessary to judiciously introduce certain parameters (Eissler 1953) in order to engage the patient and to forestall premature termination. In effect as the patient population shifts increasingly toward people with substantial preoedipal problems, therapists have had to become more accommodating to the requirements posed by such patients.

As more and more management issues arise in the course of therapy with patients with variable intactness in ego strength, therapists are faced with the dilemma of how far to go in introducing a parameter based on the stated needs of the patient. The technical pendulum in today's practice is swinging more toward the side of gratification of the patient's wishes regarding modifications of the frame, and viewing these wishes as expressions of legitimate "ego needs" (Winnicott 1954) of preoedipal patients. It is not possible nor even desirable for the therapist to meet all of the patient's wishes for accommodation. In fact the technical stance of allowing for the inevitable failures in empathy, understanding, and accessibility, and attending to the repair of these ruptures in the treatment relationship, is a major dimension in the way many practitioners currently work. Nevertheless, therapists today find themselves considering requests and expectations from these patients that in the past would have been simply viewed as unrealistic or outrageous wishes of the patient.

For example, a patient informs his therapist that he will miss the next session because he wants to go to a baseball game on opening day and would like to schedule a makeup session. Another patient is ten minutes late to her session because of a traffic jam and conveys her expectation that the therapist will extend the session to make up for the lost time. Another patient misses his session because he overslept and calls to request a makeup session later in the day. Enactments of this type periodically occur in the practice of all therapists.

Are these simply to be understood as manifestations of resistance? Or might they also be seen as overdetermined attempts to extract tangible signs of the therapist's willingness to be accommodating to special circumstances in the life of the patient? These issues are most likely to surface in the arenas of time and money. Individuals who have attained a clear delineation between self and object representations recognize that their circumstantial dilemma need not become the therapist's dilemma. In contrast for those who have achieved a lesser degree of psychic structure, there is a stronger pull toward seeking accommodation to their immediate needs. When the therapist gratifies the request he is usually experienced by the patient as the wished-for caring, accepting, and understanding parent in the transference. From the perspective of the patient, his psychic reality may dictate that it would be appropriate for these requests to be granted. Some therapists would opt to gratify on the basis of this rationale. Others advocate frustration as a necessary ingredient for growth to take place, and would be more likely to tactfully decline these requests. The judgment and technical orientation of the therapist always plays a role in these matters. Regardless of how the patient's request is responded to by the therapist, and in part the response will be determined by the reality situations of the therapist (e.g., does he have open time to extend the session due to unusual circumstances?), it is always good technique to interpret the meaning of the wish underlying the request in terms of the transference in the here and now, as well as to acknowledge its legitimacy in the context of an earlier need for sensitivity and attunement.

The use of the term *makeup session* is intriguing as a double entendre. On a manifest level it is meant as a way of designating a replacement time for a session that has been missed. On a latent level it conveys an implication that therapist and patient need to make up for the departure from their agreed-upon schedule. Perhaps in the unconscious the factors that bring about a missed session induce feelings of hostility, abandonment, or guilt that require making up.

A major controversy over the last fifteen years has been whether a conflict model or a developmental arrest model is best suited to a particular patient. In the conflict model the approach focuses on sexual and aggressive impulses, their derivatives, and how these are modulated via the tripartite structures of the mind, that is, id, ego, and superego. In the developmental arrest model we see patients whose phase-appropriate needs in the early years of development were either thwarted or overly gratified by their misattuned caregivers in a nonfacilitating environment. Addressing the themes of illusion and disillusionment may be germane in the treatment process of both categories of patients. For example, a young boy's oedipal illusion that he would grow up to marry his mother was not tamed and resolved in the traditional way. His mother was seductive and his father did not impose limit setting; hence, there was little intrapsychic incentive to relinquish his oedipal strivings. Ultimately, he acted out his oedipal illusion by marrying the divorced mother of his best friend. In another case an adult woman vividly recalls how her son cried for hours when he expressed his desire to marry her, and she sensitively explained how he would grow up, fall in love, and marry another woman. It was a wrenching experience for this 5-year-old and he was for a time inconsolable. Fortunately, he attained an oedipal resolution and was able to find a suitable partner as an adult.

In the developmental arrest segment of the patient population there are those people for whom a chief issue in treatment is the reluctance to relinquish their position of early omnipotence in which their world is a perpetually giving and soothing place with minimal frustrations; they suffer from the inability to overcome the loss of their Garden of Eden. In this group, which is a growing part of the caseload for many therapists, we also see those individuals at the other end of the spectrum who have had prominent developmental deficits, and who therefore fear allowing themselves to have dreams, wishes, fantasies, and illusions. One goal in the treatment of these patients is to activate what I refer to as an "I want" system.

Cathy was the oldest of three girls born within five years in a family in which the mother was an alcoholic and the father was a drug user. Her earliest memories centered around the neglect of her basic physical and emotional needs. By age 4 she was responsible for making dinner for herself and her sisters. Cathy was afraid to want or expect anything from her therapist, because she could sense the ultimate inevitable disappointment and pain she would feel if she expressed needs that went unmet. Her unstated plea was, "Please help me to be numb, not feel, not need nor expect anything." The therapeutic process was extremely threatening to her because it stimulated the long-dormant illusion that there just might be a chance that she could be perfectly held and understood. This was, of course, her deepest yearning, and she was both intrigued and terrified by the activation of this wish, which she hoped would repair the emotional neglect she experienced as a child. The course of therapy for Cathy revolved around the accessing of her needs, the fear of her needs, the acceptance of the legitimacy of her needs, and the fear of further retraumatization and disillusionment.

THE PSYCHOTHERAPEUTIC PROCESS

Our understanding of the beneficial effects of the psychotherapeutic process in psychodynamic psychotherapy has undergone significant revisions in recent years. Nowadays the patients who come for treatment tend to present different issues from those individuals seen by Freud and his followers, and it was from the study of these early cases that the basic principles of psychoanalytic theory and technique were developed. Currently, many individuals describe their problems as feelings of emptiness, existential ennui, emotional detachment, and lack of direction, in contrast to the anxiety, phobias, obsessive-compulsive syndromes, and hysterical problems that characterized earlier generations of patients.

Accordingly, as different kinds of patients and newer theories have arrived on the scene, there has occurred a transition in what is perceived as the curative aspects of the process. No longer is it deemed sufficient to make the unconscious conscious or to promote stronger ego functions that facilitate more successful mediation with id impulses, superego injunctions, and external reality. Patients today often do not prosper and grow from analytic insights as much as from the internalization of a new object relationship provided by the therapist (Loewald 1980). We have acquired a greater appreciation of the importance of the need of many patients to experience the feelings of safety and security in the analytic situation, which is facilitated by the caring, accepting, and understanding qualities of the analyst's personality. No longer are interpretations alone deemed to be effective; the attitude and style of the analyst in making interpretations has gained importance. As we have moved from a one-person psychology to a two-person psychology there has emerged a greater readiness for both participants to examine the perceived lapses on the part of the therapist. In fact, the exploration of narcissistic wounds in the therapeutic relationship is not only central in the treatment of narcissistic disorders but also a major dimension in the treatment of the entire spectrum of patients.

Modern analysts such as Loewald (1980) and Modell (1991c) have emphasized the significance of pursuing the theme of illusion in the analytic work. Loewald calls attention to the prevalence of cases in which a core issue is the ubiquitous wish to reunite with the mother in a blissful state, which Loewald believes to be a part of everyone's early experience. Arlow and Brenner (1990) reexamine the psychoanalytic process and cite Loewald's contribution on the therapeutic action of psychoanalysis:

> When the psychoanalytic method is properly and sensitively applied and the interpretations are correct, the patient feels able to trust and to rely upon the wise and understanding analyst, according to Loewald. This brings the patient closer to the realization of the deep-seated and fundamental wish to be reunited with the mother of early infancy, to feel once again comforted and protected like a babe in mother's arms. It is the sense of reunion that makes therapeutic advance possible. To Loewald this is the psychoanalytic process as distinct from the work of analysis. [p. 688]

Thus, for Loewald it is the therapeutic action and process that poignantly brings the patient in touch with his underlying illusion about re-creating that lost blissful state of infancy. The wish to refind an all-perfect, understanding, and gratifying parental figure frequently evolves in the transference colorations. Generally, in the course of treatment this wish is ultimately followed by the gradual and painful awareness that the therapist does not heal one's wounds, does not take away one's pain, and does not restore one's sense of perfection and omnipotence. Such wishes, of course, operate in other relationships in which their involvement is dominated by the illusion, sometimes consciously and sometimes unconsciously, that they will find a partner who is exquisitely and perpetually tuned in to them. The analytic situation provides a unique opportunity for these themes to emerge as an inherent part of the process. In the treatment process it is often productive and freeing when the therapist is able to help the patient to get more fully in touch with these illusions about refinding the blissful connection, and then to work on the process of mourning the loss of the unattainable wish. Hence, the psychoanalytic process entails a pull toward the reactivation and revivification of unfulfilled yearnings. Illusions are accessed and gradually dismantled as part of dealing with the patient's experience of illusion and disillusionment in the treatment itself. The importance of the gradual loss of illusions about the therapist must be emphasized. In a parallel way to the early developmental task for the child of incrementally seeing the parent through a more realistic lens, an abrupt disillusionment can be excessively traumatic for the patient.

Eve has made substantial progress in her work inhibitions and in her ability to maintain a love relationship largely as a result of her experience of receiving appropriate mirroring of her feelings by her analyst. Her illusions about his perfection carried her forward in addressing her unresolved conflicts in love and work. Although she was an especially beautiful woman of 30, she viewed herself as an ugly duck-

ling who was unworthy of good things in her life. By allowing herself to get involved in a series of relationships with
men who mistreated her, she repeated her early destructive
interactions with her emotionally abusive mother. All of this
was turned around through three years of hard work in her
analysis.

A disruption in Eve's progress occurred when she felt
traumatized by one of her analyst's other patients. This
other patient, whose sessions followed Eve's, would periodically arrive early for her appointment and eat a snack while
sitting in the waiting room. The awareness of the other
patient's sounds and presence out in the waiting room filled
Eve with intense hostility toward this other woman. The
analyst empathized with her distress and attempted to understand and interpret the meaning this situation had for
Eve in terms of sibling and oedipal rivalry. What Eve felt
she needed was not her analysts's interpretations, but rather
her analyst's intervention in what she experienced as an
intrusive situation in the present. She became abruptly disillusioned with the analyst for not doing something to protect her from this intrusion. This occurred at a time when
she regressively felt the need to maintain the illusion of her
analyst as someone who would be able to protect her from
the dangers of the real world. In this sense the analyst represented a version of the transitional object who would
buffer her from that which was externally threatening. It was
apparent that this sequence of events contained an
overdetermined element in which Eve unconsciously needed
to repeat her lifelong pattern of finding herself in an abusive situation. At the same time the analyst's feelings of
impotence in dealing with the real aspect of the dilemma
contributed significantly to the rupture of their relationship.
Fortunately, in this case the combination of Eve's ego
strengths and a working alliance with a solid foundation
enabled patient and analyst to work on this issue over many

sessions without it leading to a permanent impasse in the treatment. Ultimately, Eve and her analyst agreed to change the times of her sessions, and this concrete solution allowed them to explore the deeper meanings that this situation had activated.

Eve was by and large a well-functioning woman who had a good grasp of reality. She understood that she could not realistically demand that her analyst provide her with the perfect nonintrusive environment. At the same time she maintained an investment in the need to see him as a transitional object who would effectively navigate between herself and the dangers of the real world. Thus, she simultaneously functioned on multiple levels of reality. On the one hand she recognized the limitations of the analytic setting, while at the same time she sustained her illusionary transference toward her analyst as a transitional object. Eve's capacity to experience and withstand disillusionment enabled them to work through the disruptive and painful loss of illusion.

There has developed a growing appreciation that the thorough and systematic analysis of illusion and the management of working through of disillusionment is of central importance in successful psychodynamic therapy with many of the patients who currently seek treatment. There are many variations in the way these themes are played out in the course of therapy.

Problems in relatedness are intrinsically rooted in early interpersonal patterns. The readiness to embroider new relationships with old illusions or, conversely, the reluctance to invest psychic energy in any illusions will be substantially determined by the template formed via early developmental experiences. Similarly, the capacity to tolerate disillusion or the fear of dealing with any kind of disillusionment at all is predetermined by earlier events, and these themes will be repeated in the basic assumptions people bring to later relationships. The revivification of these themes in the course of the psychotherapeutic encounter allows patient and therapist to understand and then address certain maladaptive aspects of the patient's way of functioning.

> Chet, age 45, came to therapy because of periodic depression and a vague dissatisfaction about his life. As a child he had been neglected and diminished by both parents, and his needs were often ridiculed. He grew up with a profound sense of unentitlement. When there were conflicts in his marriage, he seldom felt that his perception was justifiable, and he would quickly abandon his position and defer to his wife's point of view. In the course of therapy he learned that it was okay for him to have feelings of his own, and that he could expect that his needs and desires were valid and could even sometimes be met. In the psychotherapy process he was shocked to discover that he could request a change in the regular appointment time, or even call his therapist between sessions when something urgent came up. He had functioned for years under the impact of the negative illusion that the world was an ungiving place in which everyone would treat him as poorly as his parents had done. His expectation was that his feelings and needs would be automatically dismissed if he dared to express them, let alone to allow himself to know that he had any. Chet's journey in therapy enabled him to unravel his negative illusion about himself in the world and to begin to experiment with different modes of relatedness. As a result of this process, a marked improvement in his depression occurred.

Chet's early experiences of neglect and diminishment were extensive, and he had ready access to many early memories in which he had been emotionally as well as physically beaten down. In other cases the early damage may have been more subtle and taken the form of parental provisions being available, but in the context of chronic misattunement and an atmosphere of conditional love. In these situations the patient initially may not be aware of how she was failed, and she needs to preserve the myth of having had good parenting. A central part of the therapeutic work with these patients involves the need to relinquish the illusion of a happy childhood, which covers over the (repressed) pain.

Sue came to therapy to work on her pattern of repeated disillusionment in her relationships. She had the illusion that the people in her world should always be reliable, keep their promises, and do what they say they will do. There was little margin for disappointment and she was unprepared for incidents in which others let her down in relatively small ways, didn't keep their word, or didn't follow through. Her need for a totally predictable environment stemmed from early childhood pressure for her to be a "perfect" child and to be what her mother needed her to be. Although she had felt adored as a child, it was a form of conditional love based on her performing to her mother's standards, rather than on being loved for herself. She learned the rules of the game early on and became adept at extracting her mother's approval and admiration. She had the illusion of having had a happy childhood, but only after considerable work in therapy did she recognize that she was loved for her achievements and not for her true self. Many memories led her to the realization that she had been programmed to develop a "false self" in which she had to be "on," accommodating and responsive to her perception of other people's needs, in order to receive the validation she required. The unspoken deal was that she would perform as required, and in exchange, she would receive reliable affirmation that she was valued.

This pattern became a core issue in Sue's psychotherapy sessions, both in terms of her disappointing relationships which deeply upset her, and in her evolving relationship with her therapist. In the course of therapy it became clear that she was performing for the therapist, trying to give him material that she thought he wanted, rather than feeling free to have her own agenda. In exchange for being the "perfect" patient, she expected her therapist to plug in with unyielding devotion as her mother had done. When he occasionally misunderstood the magnitude of her hurt feelings, or when he displayed brief lapses of punctuality, she would react as though she was devastated. Gradually, she and the therapist were able to connect her current issues around illusion and disillusionment with her developmental template. It was a progressive milestone in Sue's treatment to reach a point in which she could address and differentiate which relationships to extricate herself from because of broken promises, and in which situations there were sufficient positive elements to offset the broken promises that are inevitable in every relationship.

It can be postulated that people like Sue knew on some level, when they were a child, that something was awry in their "happy childhood." They do not have the words for it, but they recognize that something is "off" in the attunement of the caregiver, and that they must learn the rules of the game in order to gain the love that they require. The problem is that they become loved for their inauthentic self. This realization must be buried, for it would be too painful to acknowledge this state of affairs during childhood. No, the child usually opts to play the game in order to extract the supplies that are available under the environmental conditions presented to her. Under such conditions the child may cultivate an illusion about her "happy childhood" as a way of insulating herself from the pain of dealing with the true state of affairs.

In an interesting formulation Novick and Novick (1991) maintain that "the classical view is that the failure of omnipotence forces the child to turn to reality. In our view, it is the failure of reality that forces the child to turn to omnipotent solutions" (p. 320). When one has been exposed repeatedly to experiences of shame, humiliation, degradation, hostility, and other kinds of emotional abuse, such environmental failures frequently lead to the formation of compensatory illusions involving a future time when one will experience unlimited success, praise, love, and power. Eventually, these compensatory illusions become increasingly difficult to sustain, and one is left to deal with one's personal limitations as well as with the failures of reality. If the opportunity to consolidate a base of firm ego functions has occurred, unproductive illusions can be relinquished. It used to be thought that psychotherapeutic success could be most readily achieved with patients who were young adults, in their twenties and thirties, who entered treatment at a time before their defenses became rigid. However, in recent years Kernberg and others have pointed out that many individuals are more motivated for psychodynamic therapy at mid-life, when they are experiencing more anxiety in relation to the breakdown of their illusions and an increase in disillusionment.

TRANSFERENCE

The understanding and analysis of transference is at the heart of all psychoanalytic treatment. Transference contains an element of distortion to the extent that one misperceives aspects of a relationship in accordance with one's inner state of needs, desires, fears, drives, and attitudes. Thus a transference reaction, shaped by distortion, misperception, or unrealistic expectations, thereby constitutes an illusion. To some degree transference occurs in all relationships. The psychoanalytic situation in particular exerts a strong pull toward the development of transference phenomena, and the exploration of these reactions is deemed to be central to the treatment process.

In formulating his early views on transference Freud (1915a) grappled with the question of whether a patient's loving feelings toward her analyst were genuine or were they based on illusion. He concluded, "The patient's falling in love is induced by the analytic situation" (p. 161), and he cautioned that analysts "must face the transference-love boldly, but treat it like something unreal, as a condition which must be gone through during the treatment and traced back to its unconscious origins" (p. 167). Other writers have commented on the paradoxical nature of the analytic relationship in that the powerful emerging affective reactions can simultaneously contain genuine as well as transferential elements. A proponent of this view is Modell (1991c) who states, "The therapeutic relationship is intrinsically a paradoxical experience for both participants in that our affective responses to our patients and patients' affective responses to us are real, yet they occur within a relationship that is demarcated from that of ordinary life and accordingly may be viewed as unreal or illusory" (p. 14).

Traditional psychoanalysts have emphasized the repeating of earlier feelings, fears, and drive states as a central component in transference reactions. Fenichel (1945) describes the core of the analytic work as involving the analysis of "the repetition of previously acquired attitudes toward the analyst" (p. 29). In his definition of transference, "The patient misunderstands the present in terms of the past; and then instead of remembering the past, he strives, without recognizing the nature of his action, to relive the past and to live it more satisfactorily than he did in childhood. He 'transfers' past attitudes to the present" (p. 29). Similarly, Greenson (1967) utilizes the following working definition:

> Transference is the experiencing of feelings, drives, attitudes, fantasies, and defenses toward a person in the present which do not befit that person, but are a repetition of reactions originating in regard to significant persons of early childhood, unconsciously displaced onto figures in the present.

The two outstanding characteristics of a transference reaction are: it is a repetition and it is inappropriate. [p. 155]

In the classical point of view, transference emanates from
the internal state of the patient, and the elements of repetition,
displacement, unconscious process, and distortion are emphasized. These features lead the patient to misperceive the present
in terms of the past. Thus, for example, the analyst may convey
a caring and concerned attitude toward a problem the patient
is describing, and the patient experiences him as critical or overprotective, like a significant figure from the past.

In current practice analysts have come to recognize that
transference does not only emerge in uncontaminated form from
within the patient. An appreciation of the role of a two-person
psychology in psychoanalytic treatment has enabled us to consider that we may play a part, to a greater or lesser degree, in
the form and shape of our patients' transference reactions. The
relational approach, with its emphasis on intersubjectivity, highlights this position. For example, a patient may accurately perceive a limitation or flaw in the analyst and overreact to it
because it is reminiscent of the behavior or attitude of a significant figure from the past. This type of transference frequently
involves a reaction to some aspect of the analyst's personality or
style of relating, which may be mildly upsetting to some patients,
but may be particularly objectionable to others. For instance, an
analyst may glance at the clock several times during a session to
see how much time remains, and the patient experiences the
analyst as inattentive and uninterested, like his neglectful mother.
I tend to classify such manifestations as the overreactive type of
transference.

In contrast to the classical definition of transference, which
emphasizes the features of repetition, displacement, and distortion, there is another type of transference that is exceedingly
prevalent in the treatment of narcissistic, borderline, and
characterological problems encountered in the current practice
of most analysts. I am referring here to the importance of the

role of transference expectations. It may be useful to make the distinction between transference repetition and transference wish. Many psychoanalysts think about transference as primarily involving a repetition in which the patient experiences the analyst as having the same attitudes, reactions, and feelings as a significant figure from the past. Along with this, the patient revives and reexperiences the same feelings toward the analyst as he did toward a significant past figure. Transference wish, on the other hand, involves the fantasy that the analyst will fulfill certain needs that were unmet in the past; it contains a yearning for a second chance to get those needs met, for example, that the analyst "will be there for me as an all-loving, unconditional presence in a way that my parent wasn't or couldn't be."

Many patients proceed in treatment with the transference illusion that their wishes, needs, and hopes will be fulfilled by their analyst. Such expectations may be conscious or unconscious, and evolve into a tapestry highlighted by a yearning for unconditional love and perfect attunement. This type of transference is based not necessarily on a repetition of feelings or attitudes from the past, but rather on the reactivation of thwarted developmental needs. This category of transference expectations may be a function of what the patient feels he has missed, or what has been truncated in his early development, rather than something that is being repeated from the past. The approach of self psychology is especially informed by this type of transference. Patients who are heavily invested in transference expectations often maintain illusions about finding in the analyst an object who will be attuned and responsive to all their feelings and needs, and thereby fulfill the needs that were not met at an earlier phase-appropriate time. Transference expectations may be excessive and contribute to the formation of an intense idealization of the analyst, which may later on be followed by an equally intense disillusionment. This type of idealization is generated by unfulfilled yearnings that must be mourned, and should be distinguished from forms of idealization of the analyst as a defense against aggression and devaluation. Patients with developmental deficits are particularly prone to form an idealizing transference.

On the other end of the spectrum, many patients' powerful transference expectations contain an element of repetition insofar as they are attempting to reestablish a relationship, with the analyst, in which they are overly gratified. Blanck and Blanck (1986) highlight this as a common form of transference in what they refer to as understructured personalities:

> The understructured patient who was overindulged presents an attitude of entitlement, palpable in the transference, reflecting expectation of indulgence. There *was*, one might say, too much. These understructured personalities are seeking to replicate early object experience by attempting to fit the therapist into the predetermined "slot" of an omnipotent part of the self that never says no to itself. [p. 73]

The understructured patient is likely to harbor a powerful wish for merger that is expressed via an idealizing transference or defends against it out of a fear of retraumatization. However, the analytic situation exerts a pull toward such transference illusions even in more highly functioning patients. Greenacre (1966) stated, "It is probably obvious that the transference relationship in analysis contains by its very nature the seeds for idealization of the analyst in its rootedness in the early omnipotent stage of the mother-child relationship" (p. 196). For many analysands, she adds, "It seems that the analyst and then analysis have been accepted as part of a special and magic world of omnipotence, which really belongs to early childhood" (p. 203). Idealization of the analyst based on illusory transference expectations often culminates in disillusionment when the patient attains a more realistic appraisal of the situation. This is a crucial part of the analytic process.

To reiterate, all schools of psychoanalytic thought agree on the central importance of understanding and analyzing transference phenomena, even though they have differing emphases in their respective definitions of transference. This proposition has been stated succinctly by Moore and Fine (1968): "The demonstration, interpretation, and resolution of transference in the analytic situation constitutes the core of analytic therapy" (p. 92).

Transference illusions encompass a wide array of reactions ranging from idealization of the analyst based on the wish to experience the self in relation to the perfect partner who will provide one with an exalted sense of oneself, to the devaluation and distancing reactions based on the need to protect oneself from the anticipated dangers of the analytic process. A central task in psychoanalytic work is to address, understand, and interpret the meaning of these transferential illusions and the function that they serve. This process is aptly described by Shor and Sanville (1978):

> The analyst helps the patient to transform his magical and monstrous perceptions and feelings about the analyst, and about himself, into benign reparative experiences. . . . Our major contribution is a way of listening and of offering our best tentative interpretations of hidden wishes for elemental fulfillment of the primary illusion behind their anxious and defensive behaviors in our presence, as seen in their transference projections. [pp. 5–6]

Gill (1982) makes the distinction between two types of transference phenomena—resistance to the awareness of transference and resistance to the resolution of transference. The latter often involves the patient's strong investment in viewing the analyst as a wished-for figure who provides many of the emotional supplies that were missing or withdrawn prematurely in the patient's early development. Hence, in the course of the analysis the patient may resist the renunciation of this perception and way of experiencing the analyst, in spite of evidence to the contrary. In a good analysis the patient may readily experience the emotional availability and consistent empathic attunement on the part of the analyst. In early development the inner state of the child is strongly influenced by the degree to which the caregiver's affective state corresponds to and adequately matches that of the child. To experience the analyst in this favorable light may be particularly curative to those patients whose parenting was unreliable or erratic. Nevertheless, it is inevitable that over time certain empathic ruptures and misattunements will occur, in which the analyst fails to understand the needs and feelings of the patient at a particular point in time. These failures often represent a significant development in the resolution of transference, inasmuch as they promote a more realistic view of the analyst as one who has positive attributes as well as insensitivities and warts. As analysts we must not strive for perfection, but rather to do the best that we can and to allow for the fact that our unplanned imperfections may sometimes emerge. Such unplanned lapses in sensitivity or errors in technique, so long as they are not of enormous magnitude, can provide an opportunity that leads to the working through of transference illusions. However, certain patients are loath to give up their illusions about their analyst's perfection as an omniscient, omnipotent, loving partner, and thereby resist the resolution of the transference. It is the power and need to maintain these illusions, usually because it represents a wished-for reparative function for the patient, that interferes with advances in the treatment with regard to transference resolution.

> Julie had had an intensely adoring relationship with her father, who in turn had cherished her as his only child. He was a highly successful corporate president, and as a child Julie basked in the glow of his exciting lifestyle and charismatic personality. Her positive attachment to him was abruptly derailed at age 9 when she discovered that he was having an affair with a neighbor. In her unresolved oedipal situation it was hard enough to accept the reality that her father belonged to her mother, and that she was second best. He was seductive and made Julie feel special and she

yearned to occupy center stage in his glamorous life. Under these circumstances it was devastating for Julie to learn that there was another woman, in addition to her mother, that he preferred over her. Her disillusionment was profound, and it had an adverse impact on her future ability to maintain intimate relationships with men.

In her analysis Julie developed a positive idealized transference in which I could do no wrong. In effect I became the new edition of her early connection to her father. Over time it became clear how she needed to keep me elevated on a pedestal as the wonderful analyst whom she could admire and gain a sense of vitality through her affiliation with me. When my imperfections intermittently shone through the halo she had placed around me, she would rail and get angry. Her anger was not only about such things as my not understanding her feelings, but more importantly that the reality of my being less than perfect interfered with her being able to hold on to her exalted view of me. Her powerful transference illusion was based on the wish to keep me up there on high as a way of getting back to the innocent blissful feelings she had about her father before the fall. This issue, and her terror of experiencing the pain of disillusionment in her relationship with me, as she had done in her earlier relationship with her father, became core themes to be worked through in Julie's treatment.

THE APPLICATION OF PSYCHOANALYTIC THEORY

Common to all of the major theories is the presumption that in the course of psychoanalytic treatment the patient ultimately relinquishes his/her maladaptive illusions and becomes more accepting of reality. The difference among these theories is in how they envision the process of bringing this about. The technical stance of the analyst is of crucial significance in this regard, and his technique will be informed by his theoretical orientation. For example, the early classical Freudian position entailed prevailing upon the analysand to renunciate his infantile strivings and their accompanying illusions in favor of more mature ego functioning. For Winnicott and the object relations theorists, the pathway involved giving up the tenaciously held bad object in the context of a "safe holding environment," accompanied by a new object relationship provided by the analysis. In Kohut's view the selfobject needs that were inadequately responded to in the patient's early development are reactivated and responded to in a therapeutic manner, with understanding and interpretation, until the patient naturally, in the course of time, moves forward developmentally.

In the course of normal development the gradual recognition of flaws and failures in the caregivers provides the child with the experience of optimal disillusionment, which is necessary for growth. This process is appositely put by Mahler and colleagues (1975): "The junior toddler gradually realizes that his love objects, his parents, are separate individuals with their own interests. He must gradually and painfully give up both the delusion of his own grandeur and his belief in the omnipotence of his parents" (p. 228). These themes and this process are invariably reproduced in the treatment situation. When positive transference features prevail, the analyst frequently becomes idealized as an omniscient and omnipotent authority figure. This facilitates the furthering of the analytic work, until such time as the patient is ready to experience and integrate the less than perfect, flawed aspects of the analyst—either as real limitations in the analyst that are realistically perceived by the patient, or in the form of misperceptions or overreactions that culminate in negative transferences. This process has been described by Pine (1992):

> Just as the holding environment that the mother provides permits the infant and young child to move forward with developmental tasks, so too does the inevitable and developmentally required maternal failure to meet every need make

it possible for the growing child to begin to assume self-regulating and inner processing functions for itself. Theorists as different as Winnicott, Mahler, and Kohut have all pointed to this necessity of maternal "failure" and its value, provided that it comes in *small* doses. So, too, I believe, as I sit—"failing"—behind the analytic couch—so, too, for the patient in the analytic process. And we do not have to plan to fail the patient in this developmentally forwarding way; we inevitably will—often (though not always) to the patient's ultimate benefit. [p. 271]

The clarification and confrontation of false belief systems is a primary task in psychoanalytic psychotherapy. Uncovering illusions that are central to people's way of functioning in the world is often the core of such treatment. These false beliefs may be adaptive or maladaptive. When they are maladaptive, the treatment involves an approach that enables the patients to see and work through the notion that they are paying a high price for retaining illusions such as they are special, they are entitled to be taken care of, they are invulnerable, and they are above the law. These false beliefs may be conscious, preconscious, or unconscious, and are incrementally exposed, accessed, and addressed through the psychotherapeutic process. I refer to this process as illusions that are restructured during the course of treatment. The purpose of these illusions is to provide the individual with a sense of well-being, and they are often organized around such themes as security, love, ambition, success, or some other form of blissful fulfillment. To the extent that they are maladaptive and interfere with healthy functioning, it becomes vitally important to examine the derivatives of these illusions. Negative illusions that entail false assumptions about anticipated consequences are also maladaptive. For example, a woman who was repeatedly threatened with abandonment as a child may anticipate that her husband intends to leave her whenever they have an argument. She will then misperceive his actions and communications accordingly, or provoke him to respond along these lines, without realizing that she is imposing her past experience onto the present situation.

In successful treatment insight into the necessity for establishing these illusions is acquired, the unlikelihood of their attainment is recognized, and their unrealistic basis is accepted. This process of uncovering core illusions and dealing with disillusionment occurs in stages and is brought to the surface through the therapist's understanding and interpretation of the patient's material, especially material related to transference expectations.

What I am attempting to describe here as illusions that are reconstructed during psychoanalytic psychotherapy is similar to the "pathological beliefs" depicted by Weiss (1997) as governing the functioning of many individuals: "People's unconscious beliefs about themselves and their world, though acquired in the past, color their current experiences. . . . They may see the present in terms of the past, even when the present is vivid and dramatic" (p. 429).

The origin of these false beliefs that lead to maladaptive adjustment is based on inferences and assumptions that people make about themselves and their world beginning with their early interpersonal experiences. Thus, for example, a child who has been overgratified by his parents will not only infer that the world is a good place in which his needs are generally satisfied, but also develop a heightened sense of entitlement. His illusion about his specialness, based on his early experiences of indulgence, will leave him poorly prepared to deal with the frustrations and realities in negotiating the tasks of adulthood. Weiss draws upon Modell's work in emphasizing that separation guilt and survivor guilt are at the foundation of pathogenic belief systems of many patients and are as important as oedipal guilt in creating psychopathology. For example, many patients' fear of being assertive and autonomous is based on the assumption that to do so would be harmful to their parents. This dynamic is frequently seen when the parent has been overprotective or controlling. Weiss extends the concept of survivor guilt to apply to those cases in which an individual experiences a profound sense of disloyalty and betrayal if he has attained a better life than his parents or siblings. According to Weiss these sources of unconscious guilt lead to pathogenic beliefs about the consequences of independence, success, and assertiveness, and therefore they are impediments to effective functioning. These pathogenic beliefs tend to be persistent and they yield to reality testing very slowly.

In essence these individuals are governed by what we might refer to as negative illusions. Weiss argues that patients in psychoanalytic treatment are motivated to disconfirm their pathogenic beliefs (i.e., illusions), and they set about to devise an unconscious plan for testing them out. Hence, the chief function of dynamic psychotherapy in these cases is to enable the patient to disconfirm his beliefs. This is accomplished through his testing them out in his relationship with the analyst as well as in his present life situation. In addition, the psychoanalytic process facilitates his understanding of the nature and meaning of these false beliefs. For example, a patient who grew up with an overprotective mother who undermined her attempts toward independence and autonomy will be likely to assume that such behavior will be potentially harmful to herself or others. In Weiss's formulation such a patient is likely to test out this assumption by behaving assertively and checking out whether her therapist seemed discouraging or supportive. Or, conversely, she may display dependent behavior in order to test out whether the therapist seemed comfortable with her deferential attitude. If this assumption is not confirmed, the pathogenic belief is correspondingly weakened.

While Weiss's approach contains considerable merit in working with impediments in effective functioning based on powerful illusions, I question his notion that these patients invariably have an unconscious plan to test and disconfirm their pathogenic belief systems. My own impression goes more toward the conclusion that many people cling to their false beliefs, even if pathogenic; they are reluctant to give them up, and they often experience them as necessary for their psychological survival.

DISILLUSIONMENT

The management of inevitable disillusionment is a major developmental task, as well as a central dimension in what needs to be addressed in the course of psychodynamic psychotherapy, which entails both the healing of the losses, wounds, and disappointments of the past and the reexperiencing and working through of disillusionment in the treatment process itself. A common fantasy of patients upon entering treatment is that psychoanalysis will "cure" them. Along with this is the belief, wish, and expectation that through their affiliation with their analyst, they will become a totally different person and will find the satisfactions in life that they desire and deserve. At the same time, as we have seen, patients are threatened by the prospect of change. In terms of the need to avert anxiety, danger, and psychic pain, the formation of illusions can serve as a useful protective device, but as Freud (1937) pointed out, "Not infrequently it turns out that the ego has paid too high a price for the services that these mechanisms render" (p. 237). In many cases the thrust of the treatment process involves getting patients to recognize and work through the notion that they pay a high price for retaining their illusions, such as those about invulnerability, immortality, and unrealistic aspirations. Individuals become very comfortable with their protective devices, including defensive illusions, and in psychodynamic treatment powerful resistances emerge that are designed to circumvent the dismantling of these devices. In developing his concept of resistance, Freud noted, "It follows that the ego treats recovery itself as a new danger" (p. 238). Resistances are defenses and defense mechanisms are used as resistances. With regard to defenses Freud stated, "The main point is that the patient repeats these modes of reaction during analysis itself, exhibiting them, as it were, before our eyes; in fact, that is the only means we have of learning about them" (p. 238).

Thus, the very process of analytic work entails the patient's experience of having something valuable taken away from him— his much needed defensive illusions. The working through of disillusionment is often a central phase in the treatment process. The loss of cherished illusions is invariably accompanied by feelings of despair, and the importance of mourning as part of the analytic process cannot be underemphasized. During the course of treatment patients frequently mourn the loss of love relationships that failed. Shor and Sanville (1978) have observed, "In unchosen partings there is a deeper despair and a more complete disillusionment which will require a repair of the sense of self" (p. 107). A brief vignette illustrates this point.

Marie, a beautiful 30-year-old single woman, was devastated when her boyfriend, the man of her dreams, broke off with her. It was clear from the beginning of their relationship that Jim was a womanizer and was not prepared to settle down. Over the course of many psychotherapy sessions we were able to explore the connection of Marie's intense involvement with Jim as a repetition of seeking the love of her unavailable father. The acquisition of this insight notwithstanding, she pressed Jim toward permanent commitment, and he abandoned her. In her sessions she subsequently was consumed with questioning what it is that was deficient about her that prevented Jim from making a commitment to their relationship. She needed to deal with her profound disillusionment by blaming herself and focusing on her own perceived limitations. This was a repetition of how she attempted to deal with the earlier pain of her father's lack of interest in her. The assumption that there must be something lacking in herself was a less painful alternative than facing her hurt and anger at her father's rejecting attitude. Marie repeated this pattern in her reactions to the loss of Jim. My reassurances about her worth and how much she had to offer as an accomplished woman were supportive, but not very helpful as she continued to berate herself. My repeatedly pointing out that Jim's apparent fears around intimacy and commitment, rather than her deficits, had led to the destruction of their relationship was somewhat useful to her. Further analysis of her interest in Jim as an unavailable man, a stand-in for her father, was meaningful to her. But what was most important in our work was allowing and helping Marie to mourn the loss of her dream of a permanent union with Jim.

In sharp contrast to Marie, many other patients handle their relational disillusionments by finding fault and extolling the limitations of their partners. They maintain their illusions about their own perfection and are loath to recognize aspects of their own unlovability and ways in which they participate in creating or perpetuating destructive relationships. It is a challenging task that requires considerable sensitivity to narcissistic injury to make therapeutic advances in these cases.

The analytic relationship characteristically becomes an arena for working through issues of disillusionment. Peebles (1986), in elaborating on Smith's (1977) depiction of the "golden fantasy," describes how such patients play out their wish to recapture their era of early blissfulness in the analytic relationship, and they "resist interpretations of the fantasy in an effort to deny the irretrievable loss of paradise—the 'fall' from paradise" (p. 224). In working with these cases Peebles advocates a technical stance in which a "phase of confrontation" follows a period of facilitating the holding environment. This sequence is seen as effective in promoting progress and attaining higher levels of functioning.

As has been stated earlier, many patients enter treatment with the expectation and wish to find the perfect, all-wonderful analyst, who will cure all their problems and transform their personalities in a beneficial way. For many years psychoanalysis oversold itself, which reinforced illusions about what psychoanalytic treatment could accomplish. In reality the analytic situation traditionally involves abstinence, frustration tolerance, and gratification of understanding, but not gratification of instincts. Over time many patients become disappointed and angry about their lack of change, which they had hoped would be brought about by the analyst and the process itself. This leads to profound feelings of disillusionment in the analytic relationship, and premature termination, without an opportunity for full exploration of the issues, may often occur. When the analyst properly grasps this theme in the latent communications of the patient and brings it to the fore, premature termination can be effectively forestalled. In such a setting with a concomitant good working alliance, the patient's disillusionment in the analyst and the analysis can be worked through, and a more appropriate and realistic view of the process and goals of treatment can evolve. Shechter (1993) has noted that "disillusionment with one's analyst is often necessary for the resolution of the transference neurosis" (p. 154). Addressing this theme of disillusionment within the analytic situation, and the opportunity for working through, can be one of the most important phases of treatment during the course of analysis.

A great deal has been written about patients who during the course of treatment experience empathic ruptures in their relationship with their therapist. This in turn often becomes an opportunity for repair of earlier damage as the patient acquires the capacity to tolerate the therapist's imperfections and insensitivities within the context of a benign therapeutic atmosphere in which the patient generally feels understood and appropriately attended to by the therapist. However, there has been relatively little attention given to those patients who are unable to experience an empathic rupture, even when it might be appropriate to do so. For example, one analyst who was usually quite on target referred to his patient by the patient's father's name instead of his own. The patient did not feel upset by this error as many patients would, but rather took it in a positive way. To him it meant that he had chosen a therapist who must be very good, because only a therapist with a large and successful practice would make such an error. He assumed that having so many cases meant that his therapist must be outstanding. In this way, he was able to preserve his much-needed view of the therapist as a loving figure in contrast to his neglectful mother. Further along in the treatment this patient experienced a similar lapse on the part of his therapist in a different way. At this later point he was able to feel disillusioned by the therapist's error, to de-idealize him, and nevertheless he continued to value him.

WORKING THROUGH

Disillusionment in psychotherapy and the therapeutic process may first become discernible through the patient's expression of transference resistance. Patterns in which patients come late, miss sessions, or stop paying their bill in a timely fashion can often be understood as an indirect expression of anger toward the therapist for not magically bringing about a cure. Patients who lapse into prolonged silences in their sessions may be expressing a similar theme, based on the realization that their illusions about change, cure, and perfection are not and cannot be fulfilled. These underlying illusions and the accompanying disillusionment must be brought to the fore as part of the process of working through. For many individuals a central aspect of growth in therapy involves dealing with their illusions in love relationships and their illusions about what the therapist will provide for them, along with the realization that the period of lost bliss or wished-for bliss cannot be attained. This is especially true for those who experienced excessive deprivation or excessive gratification in their early childhood.

The recognition of these powerful yearnings that cannot be fulfilled, the acknowledgment of the extent to which they interfere in interpersonal transactions, and the ability to mourn what cannot be are pivotal pieces in the constellation of the working-through process. For many patients this represents a formidable task and a major achievement. It can take several years of treatment to accomplish this goal. It is seldom a linear achievement, and the capacity to mourn may alternate with periods of resistance to mourning. Many individuals repeatedly gravitate toward disillusionment in a defensive way, to avoid the pain of accepting a world with imperfect nurturance, or as a way of holding on to the illusion of finding unconditional love. The following vignette highlights this type of situation.

Evelyn came to therapy at age 25 and continued for the next twenty years in search of fulfilling the illusion that she could have a relationship in which her needs were perfectly understood and responded to with sensitivity and caring. She grew up in a family in which the mother was psychotic and the father was emotionally inaccessible. What little nurturance was available was reserved for a younger sister, who was autistic. Evelyn's needs were never considered and her sustaining fantasy was that she would find someone who would provide her with unconditional love. Her superior intelligence allowed her to excel in school, and this, together with her background in which she had assumed the role of caregiver in her family of origin, catapulted her toward a career as a mental health professional.

In her early twenties she married Phil, who was a successful surgeon. She valued his professional status in the community and derived an enhancement of self-esteem through her connection to his mantle. She was enthralled over her ability to transcend the abysmal roots of her family by marrying so well, and only gradually did she come to realize that Phil was as emotionally cut off as her father had been. She could not accept his limitations, and demanded that he be more caring and tuned in to her needs. It was at this point that Evelyn entered therapy in the hope of finding ways to get her husband to be more understanding, responsive to her needs, and emotionally available.

During the course of treatment she developed a positive transference in which she felt valued and understood for the first time in her life. Indeed, her therapist was a man whose manner conveyed warmth, gentleness, and sensitivity. She cathected onto the weekly sessions as a place where she could feel mirrored, validated, and given to. This served to fuel her wish that if she could obtain these supplied from her therapist, she could find a way to have them provided by her husband.

Phil, however, was not psychologically sophisticated, and he was uncomfortable in the world of feelings. He needed to relate from a position of considerable emotional distance in order to preserve his own precarious sense of autonomy. Nevertheless, Evelyn clung to the illusion that she could convert Phil into the caring partner that she yearned for. Despite repeated disillusionments in which he did not acknowledge her birthday or their anniversary with gifts or cards, she continued to expect that her illusion would be fulfilled.

As long as Phil was emotionally unavailable it was possible for Evelyn to focus on the reality of her unfulfilled needs and expectations. However, as Phil began to gradually become more forthcoming, as a result of his own therapy, an interesting pattern developed. It seemed that whatever Phil did to try to please her, Evelyn felt that it was not done in the right way and was never good enough. When he brought her flowers for their anniversary after years of unresponsiveness to the occasion she complained that the buds did not open and that he had presented her with dead roses. When he responded to her long-standing request that he plan a night on the town for them by arranging for theatre tickets and dinner, she complained at the end of the evening that they did this sort of thing too infrequently. When he subsequently presented her with a gift of a cassette of the music from the show that they had seen and enjoyed together, she denigrated his uncharacteristic affectionate gesture on the grounds that it must have been his therapist's idea.

It gradually became clear in Evelyn's therapy that she needed to find fault with Phil's "good-enough" efforts in order to sustain a defensive disillusionment in which she could avoid dealing with her most vulnerable feelings around being given to. It was emotionally safer for her to suffer repeated disappointments and disillusionment than to receive partial, albeit imperfect, fulfillment of her needs. Although she was invested in the illusion of finding the all-giving partner, she had unconsciously selected a man who was basically emotionally unavailable, which thereby protected her from the pain of dealing with how immense was her hunger for nurturance. It has been pointed out that the pain of contrast (Casement 1985) may lead certain individuals to reject caring responses because it is too painful to recognize how powerfully absent such treatment was in the past. It is curious that Evelyn was able to accept emotional provisions from her therapist more readily than she could from her husband. In the latter relationship she had many more years of disappointment and distrust to overcome. The eventual working-through phase of Evelyn's prolonged therapy revolved around this central theme of the pain of contrast.

In summary, the working-through process in dealing with illusion and disillusionment generally involves the following steps: (1) identification of core illusions about oneself and one's world; (2) awareness of resistance to relinquishing core illusions; (3)

recognition that maintaining maladaptive illusions is a counter-productive impediment to satisfactory functioning; (4) increased capacity to mourn the loss of one's illusions; and (5) increased ability to tolerate disillusionment.

TERMINATION

The psychotherapeutic process encompasses a beginning phase with an emphasis on establishing and maintaining a working alliance, a middle phase that includes working through, and an end phase that culminates in termination. Far less attention has been given in the analytic literature to termination than to the other two phases of the treatment process. In addressing the criteria for termination Freud (1937) asserted, "The business of analysis is to secure the best possible psychological conditions for the functioning of the ego; when this has been done, analysis has accomplished its task" (p. 250). In a symposium on the criteria for termination, Reich (1950) concluded, "We do not hope that by analysis we can produce perfect human beings. . . . We consider it a sign of health if the patient is capable of accepting his own limitations" (p. 181). Part of this process entails the attenuation of illusions that have little possibility of fulfillment.

I believe that successful treatment involves the acceptance of personal limitations, the attainment of good-enough object relationships that bring sufficient satisfaction, and a resolution of the transference, which includes a realistic appraisal of the strengths and weaknesses of the therapist. These issues are often insufficiently worked through, with the result that there are many premature terminations as well as prolonged terminations. Premature terminations are often a function of misconceptions about what the treatment could accomplish. The patient may feel that he is not changing quickly enough, the therapeutic "fit" is unsatisfactory, and the therapist is not on his wavelength, and he abruptly terminates in a state of disillusionment. This disillusionment is frequently denied and the termination is explained away in terms of problems around time or money, but it is often related to some perceived disharmony in the respective agendas of patient and therapist. There are also many premature terminations that occur because of the patient's unreadiness or need to avoid dealing with painful conflicts. Sometimes this cannot be resolved, even with a very experienced therapist. There are also cases in which the patient's perception of a poor "fit" is accurate and it is wise to terminate.

From another vantage point psychodynamic psychotherapeutic treatment today is often briefer than in the past as a consequence of the constraints of managed care. An increasingly prevalent scenario is one in which patients work on their problems for awhile, leave treatment, and then come back at a future time. They may return to the same therapist, if they felt good about the work they had previously accomplished. Alternatively, if they did not feel sufficiently understood, or if their magical expectations were unmet and unanalyzed, they may seek out a new therapist in the hope of fulfilling their illusion of finding the perfect self and the perfect partner. For some patients the cycle of illusion and disillusionment in the therapeutic process may be repeated many times with serial therapists.

Prolonged terminations, in contrast, often involve the patients' difficulties around separation and mourning the loss of a highly valued positive relationship, and/or accepting the reality that certain expectations about the outcome of treatment are unattainable. Such patients may continue their therapy indefinitely in order to promote their residual magical beliefs that Paradise lost can be acquired or regained. To terminate is to disrupt such an illusion. These patients show a resistance to termination, for to end the treatment is tantamount to relinquishing the illusion that all their fantasied expectations about what therapy would bring and how it would change their lives will eventually come to fruition. The goal in such cases is to help the patient mourn the loss of his ultimate dreams and come to terms with his disillusionment.

For many patients the prospect of giving up their connection to their therapist is very threatening. Such concerns are often based on the fear that a valuable relational tie will forevermore be lost. However, when sufficient internalization of the treatment process has taken place, it is possible to terminate with a sense of ongoing internal continuity with one's therapist. This has been noted by Novick and Novick (1997): "Internalization is the outcome of an adaptive process of mourning the loss of real valued relationships, feelings, or experience. . . . Much of the work of the termination phase involves drawing the distinction between the illusory loss of unreal fantasy gains and the real loss of the setting, the analyst, and the special therapeutic relationship" (p. 73).

In discussing resistance to termination, Weiss and Sampson (1986) state, "The final outcome of the therapy is considered to hinge upon the degree to which a patient experiences and completes the difficult tasks of renunciation and mourning" (p. 302). Dewald (1971) implicitly addresses the issue of illusion and disillusionment in connection with termination and the importance of mourning:

> The patient in the termination phase of psychotherapy who is experiencing sadness or grief over the loss of the therapist must similarly go through the process of mourning and grief-work to resolve this loss. The more that the patient consciously experiences and elaborates the sadness, depression, anger, and helplessness at the loss, the greater is the possibility of his working through to a resolution of his transference relationship. The more that the patient avoids the experience of grief, the greater is the potentiality for an unresolved and persistent transference relationship. [p. 281]

Let us return to the question of what constitutes readiness for termination. Reich (1950) elaborates goals such as freedom from debilitating symptoms and anxieties, the attainment of the capacity for mature object relationships, and the ability to function productively in work as criteria for termination. In addition, a modification in the tendency toward what Novick and Novick (1997) call reality-altering solutions represents yet another criteria. Novick and Novick pursue a developmental approach in highlighting the need to address unresolved issues in idealization and omnipotence as a criteria for termination. They argue along with classical analytic theory that the child's awareness of his separateness and helplessness serves to shatter his sense of infantile omnipotence, and consequently he attributes omnipotent powers to his parents through the process of idealization. Novick and Novick state, "When shattered by ordinary reality . . . [this] dynamic interaction between idealization of the self and of the object . . . leads to a lifelong attempt to regain the infantile state. . . . [Hence for many therapists] the aim of treatment is to accomplish mourning for lost omnipotence of self and object" (p. 57). Thus, the experience of subjective infantile omnipotence is based on an illusion, and the efforts generated to regain this state after reality has intervened are also based on an illusion. To temper the idealization of self and others based on the illusion of regaining the lost sense of omnipotence is a major theme that gets worked through in successful psychodynamic treatment. In many cases the readiness for termination is signaled by the accomplishment of this task together with the capacity to tolerate disillusionment.

This task is especially formidable in the treatment of narcissistic personalities who tenaciously fight against relinquishing their illusions of specialness and omnipotence. This issue has been underscored by Rothstein (1980), who formulates the following strategy for working with these patients: "The analytic management of narcissistic personality disorders revolves around the ability of the analyst and analysand to create an environment and relationship within which the analysand can mourn his defensive pursuit of illusions of narcissistic perfection for his self-representation, particularly those that are maladaptive" (p. 112).

The mourning process, which is often resisted for an extended period of time in these patients, paves the way for new building blocks to be established in which the gradual acceptance of limitations in their self representations can be tolerated without devastating disillusionment. Goldberg (1975), a proponent of self psychology, emphasizes the importance of "the practice of disappointment" as a central aspect of the curative process in working with narcissistic personalities:

> Treatment of narcissistic disorders is often seen as a series of disappointments and disillusionments that become tolerable to the patient, particularly in relation to the therapist. ... The goal of treatment ... is to tolerate and understand the failures [of the therapist] as they were not so comprehended in childhood. ... The childhood is never repaired, but rather is replaced by adult learning. The idea of the therapist who will never disappoint his patient is a fiction that happily will never come to life. ... The experience of disappointment or disillusionment, or both, requires a certain firmness or solidity of the self that, likewise, has a reasonable grasp of its limitations. [pp. 697–698]

According to Goldberg, the readiness for termination in narcissistic personalities is indicated by "changes in the patient's self seen during the terminal phase of psychotherapy. These include the re-experiencing of narcissistic injury, a different response to interpretation, and a substantial alteration in the reaction to disappointment" (p. 695).

Mourning the loss of core illusions and the capacity to tolerate disillusionment are issues that are particularly acute in the treatment of narcissistic personality disorders, but they are themes that are prevalently addressed in a wide spectrum of psychotherapy cases. As psychodynamic treatment deepens, it is inevitable and desirable that issues around loss of illusions, disillusionment, and mourning evolve. To the extent that these conflicts are resolved, one acquires an added dimension of acceptance about life's limitations, and acknowledges that the quest to regain a fantasied blissful era is an illusion that cannot be fulfilled. The appreciation that one cannot go back to before and the working through of the patient's hidden expression of such yearnings are an indication of the readiness for termination.

References

Abraham, K. (1924). The influence of oral erotism on character formation. In *Selected Papers of Karl Abraham*, pp. 393–406. New York: Brunner/Mazel.

Akhtar, S. (1996). Someday . . . and if only . . . fantasies: pathological optimism and inordinate nostalgia as related forms of idealization. *Journal of the American Psychoanalytic Association* 44(3):723–753.

Albee, E. (1963). *Who's Afraid of Virginia Woolf?* New York: Atheneum.

Amati-Mehler, J., and Argentieri, S. (1989). Hope and hopelessness: a technical problem? *International Journal of Psycho-Analysis* 70:295–304.

American Psychiatric Association (1994). *Diagnostic and Statistical Manual of Mental Disorders, 4th Edition (DSM-IV).* Washington, DC: American Psychiatric Association.

Arlen, H., and Harburg, E. Y. (1939). "Over the Rainbow." Song. New York: Leo Feist Publishers.

Arlow, J. (1969). Fantasy, memory, and reality testing. *Psychoanalytic Quarterly* 38(1):28–51.

Arlow, J., and Brenner, C. (1990). The psychoanalytic process. *Psychoanalytic Quarterly* 59:678–691.

Bacal, H. A. (1998). *Optimal Responsiveness*: How Patients Heal Their Therapists. Northvale, NJ: Jason Aronson.

Bacal, H. A., and Newman, K. M. (1990). *Theories of Object Relations: Bridges from Object Relations to Self Psychology.* New York: Columbia University Press.

Bach, S. (1985). *Narcissistic States and the Therapeutic Process.* Northvale, NJ: Jason Aronson.

——— (1994). *The Language of Perversion and the Language of Love.* Northvale, NJ: Jason Aronson.

Balint, M. (1959). *Thrills and Regressions.* New York: International Universities Press.

Baumeister, R. (1989). The optimal margin of illusion. *Journal of Social and Clinical Psychology* 8(2):176–189.

Becker, E. (1973). *The Denial of Death.* New York: Free Press.

Beebe, B., and Lachmann, F. M. (1994). Representation and internalization in infancy. *Psychoanalytic Psychology* 11(2):127–165.

Bergmann, M. (1979). Narcissism in relation to objects, reality and phantasy. *Group* 3(2):68–78.

Beschloss, M. (1997). *Taking Charge.* New York: Simon & Schuster.

Bettelheim, B. (1976). *The Uses of Enchantment.* New York: Knopf.

Blanck, G., and Blanck, R. (1974). *Ego Psychology: Theory and Practice.* New York: Columbia University Press.

——— (1986). *Beyond Ego Psychology: Developmental Object Relations Theory.* New York: Columbia Universities Press.

Blos, P. (1962). *On Adolescence.* New York: Free Press of Glencoe.

Bly, R. (1990). *Iron John.* New York: Addison-Wesley.

Boubil, A., Schönberg, C.-M., and Kretzmer, H. (1986). "I Dreamed a Dream." Song. New York: David Geff & Co.

Brown, N. O. (1959). *Life Against Death: The Psychoanalytical Meaning of History.* New York: Viking.

Cain, B. (1990). Older children and divorce. *The New York Times Magazine*, February 18, Sect. 6.

Cameron, J., dir. (1997). *Titanic.* Film. Paramount/Twentieth-Century Fox.

Capra, F., dir. (1937). *Lost Horizon.* Film. Columbia Pictures.

Caro, R. (1990). *The Years of Lyndon Johnson: Means of Ascent.* New York: Knopf.

Carpenter, F., ed. (1979). *Eugene O'Neill, Rev. Ed.* Boston: Twayne.

Carroll, H., and McCarthy, J. (1918). "I'm Always Chasing Rainbows." Song. New York: Robbins Music Corp., 1946.

Casement, P. (1985). *Learning from the Patient.* New York: Guilford.

——— (1991). The meeting of needs in psychoanalysis. *Psychoanalytic Inquiry,* 11(3):325–346.

Castelnuovo-Tedesco, P. (1989). The fear of change and its consequences in analysis and psychotherapy. *Psychoanalytic Inquiry* 9(1):101–118.

Cella, D. (1985). Psychological adjustment and cancer outcome: Levy versus Taylor. *American Psychologist* 40(11):1275–1276.

Cervantes, M. (1605). *Don Quixote.* New York: Dodd, Mead, 1962.

Chasseguet-Smirgel, J., and Grunberger, B. (1986). *Freud or Reich? Psychoanalysis and Illusion.* New Haven, CT: Yale University Press.

Cooper, J., and Maxwell, N. (1995). *Narcissistic Wounds.* Northvale, NJ: Jason Aronson.

Cornford, F. (1945). *The Republic of Plato.* New York: Oxford University Press.

Dewald, P. A. (1971). *Psychotherapy, A Dynamic Approach.* New York: Basic Books.

Dickens, C. (1860–1861). *Great Expectations.* New York: Harcourt Brace Jovanovich, 1950.

Eissler, K. (1953). The effect of the structure of the ego on psychoanalytic technique. *Journal of the American Psychoanalytic Association* 1:104–143.

Ezriel, H. (1973). Psychoanalytic group therapy. In *Group Therapy: An Overview,* ed. L. Wolberg and E. Schwartz, pp. 183–210. New York: Intercontinental Medical Book.

Fenichel, O. (1945). *The Psychoanalytic Theory of Neurosis*. New York: Norton.

Fosse, B., dir. (1983). *Star 80*. Film. Warner/Ladd.

Freud, S. (1908). Creative writers and day-dreaming. *Standard Edition* 9:141–154.

———— (1911). Formulations on the two principles of mental functioning. *Standard Edition* 12:213–226.

———— (1914). On narcissism: an introduction. *Standard Edition* 14:67–104.

———— (1915a). Further recommendations on the technique of psycho-analysis: observations on transference-love. *Standard Edition* 12:157–171.

———— (1915b). Thoughts for the times on war and death. *Standard Edition* 14:275–300.

———— (1916). Some character-types met with in psycho-analytic work. *Standard Edition* 14:311–336.

———— (1916–1917). Introductory lectures on psycho-analysis. *Standard Edition* 15–16.

———— (1925a). Negation. *Standard Edition* 19:235–242.

———— (1925b). Some psychical consequences of the anatomical distinction between the sexes. *Standard Edition* 19:243–260.

———— (1926). Inhibitions, symptoms and anxiety. *Standard Edition* 20:75–172.

———— (1927a). Fetishism. *Standard Edition* 21:147–158.

———— (1927b). The future of an illusion. *Standard Edition* 21:1–56.

———— (1930). Civilization and its discontents. *Standard Edition* 21:57–146.

———— (1932). Why war? *Standard Edition* 22:195–218.

———— (1937). Analysis terminable and interminable. *Standard Edition* 23:209–254.

Fried, E. (1979). Narcissistic inaccessibility. *Group* 3(2):79–87.

Friedlander, S. (1997). *Nazi Germany and the Jews. Vol. I. The Years of Persecution, 1933–1939*. New York: HarperCollins.

Fromm, E. (1941). *Escape from Freedom.* New York: Avon.

———— (1962). *Beyond the Chains of Illusion.* New York: Simon & Schuster.

Gabbard, G. (1993). On hate in love relationships: the narcissism of minor differences revisited. *Psychoanalytic Quarterly* 62:229–238.

Gaines, R. (1997). Detachment and continuity: the two tasks of mourning. *Contemporary Psychoanalysis* 33(4):549–571.

Galatzer-Levy, R., and Cohler, S. (1993). *The Essential Other: A Developmental Psychology of the Self.* New York: Basic Books.

Gaylin, W. (1968). *The Meaning of Despair.* New York: Jason Aronson.

Gedo, J. (1989). Vicissitudes in the psychotherapy of depressive crises. *Psychoanalytic Psychology* 6(1):1–13.

Gill, M. (1982). *Analysis of Transference, Vol. 1.* New York: International Universities Press.

Glover, E. (1925). Notes on oral character formation. *International Journal of Psycho-Analysis* 6:131–153.

Goetz, R., and Goetz, A. (1948). *The Heiress.* New York: Dramatists Play Service.

Goldberg, A. (1975). Narcissism and the readiness for termination. *Archives of General Psychiatry* 32(6):695–699.

Goldstein, S. (1992). *China at the Crossroads: Reform after Tianenman.* New York: Headline Series.

Goodman, A. (1989). The depression of the narcissistic personality. *Contemporary Psychotherapy Review* 5(1):71–91.

Greenacre, P. (1960). Further notes on fetishism. *Psychoanalytic Study of the Child* 15:191–207. New York: International Universities Press.

———— (1966). Problems of overidealization of the analyst and of analysis. *Psychoanalytic Study of the Child* 16:193–212. New York: International Universities Press.

———— (1969). The fetish and the transitional object. *Psychoanalytic Study of the Child* 24:145–164. New York: International Universities Press.

Greenson, R. (1967). *The Technique and Practice of Psycho-analysis*, vol. 1. New York: International Universities Press.

Hand, D., dir. (1937). *Snow White and the Seven Dwarfs.* Film. Walt Disney Studios.

Hartmann, H. (1939). *Ego Psychology and the Problem of Adaptation.* New York: International Universities Press.

―――― (1952). The mutual influences in the development of the ego and id. *Psychoanalytic Study of the Child* 7:9–30. New York: International Universities Press.

Hilton, J. (1933). *Lost Horizon.* New York: William Morrow.

Horowitz, M. (1989). The developmental and structural viewpoints on the fate of unconscious fantasies in middle life. In *The Middle Years,* ed. J. Oldham and R. Liebert, pp. 7–16. New Haven, CT: Yale University Press.

Howard, R., dir. (1983). *Cocoon.* Film. Twentieth-Century Fox.

Ibsen, H. (1885). *The Wild Duck.* New York: Norton, 1968.

Jacobson, E. (1946). The effect of disappointment on ego and super-ego formation in normal and depressive development. *Psychoanalytic Review* 33(12):129–147.

Jacques, E. (1965). Death and the mid-life crisis. *International Journal of Psychoanalysis* 46(4):502–514.

James, H. (1881). *Washington Square.* New York: Random House, 1950.

James, P. D. (1980). *Innocent Blood.* New York: Scribner.

Janoff-Bulman, R. (1992). *Shattered Assumptions.* New York: Free Press.

Joffe, W. G., and Sandler, J. (1965). Notes on pain, depression, and individuation. *Psychoanalytic Study of the Child* 20:394–424. New York: International Universities Press.

Johnson, S. (1987). *Humanizing the Narcissistic Style.* New York: Norton.

Kaplan, L. (1978). *Oneness and Separateness: From Infant to Individual.* New York: Simon & Schuster.

Kavaler-Adler, S. (1994). Psychic structure and the capacity to mourn: why the narcissist cannot mourn. *Psychoanalysis and Psychotherapy* 11(1):67–79.

Keen, S. (1991). *Fire in the Belly.* New York: Bantam.

Kernberg, O. (1975). *Borderline Conditions and Pathological Narcissism.* New York: Jason Aronson.

———— (1976). *Object Relations Theory and Clinical Psychoanalysis.* New York: Jason Aronson.

Kierkegaard, S. (1849). *The Sickness Unto Death.* New York: Penguin.

Kifner, J. (1997). Once more with feeling: accepting the Kennedys. *The New York Times,* November 16, Sect. 4, p. 4.

Kleiser, R., dir. (1982). *Grease.* Film. Paramount Pictures.

Kohut, H. (1971). *The Analysis of the Self.* New York: International Universities Press.

———— (1977). *The Restoration of the Self.* New York: International Universities Press.

Kolata, G. (1996). The long shelf life of medical myths. *The New York Times,* May 12, Sect. 4, p. 2.

Kramer, P. (1993). *Listening to Prozac.* New York: Viking.

Kübler-Ross, E. (1969). *On Death and Dying.* New York: Macmillan.

Kundera, M. (1980). *The Book of Laughter and Forgetting.* New York: Knopf.

———— (1996). *Slowness.* New York: HarperCollins.

Laurents, A., Styne, J., and Sondheim, S. (1960). *Gypsy: A Musical Suggested by the Memoirs of Gypsy Rose Lee.* New York: Random House.

Lazarus, R. (1983). The costs and benefits of denial. In *The Denial of Stress,* ed. S. Breznitz, pp. 1–30. New York: International Universities Press.

Lerner, A. J., and Loewe, F. (1960). "Camelot." Song. New York: Chappell.

Levin, J. (1993). *Slings and Arrows: Narcissistic Injury and Its Treatment.* Northvale, NJ: Jason Aronson.

Levinson, D. (1978). *The Seasons of a Man's Life.* New York: Knopf.

Lewinsohn, P. (1987). Middle age: The Aging Brain. *The New York Times*, April 21, p. c9.

Lewis, A. (1994). The king must die. *The New York Times*, November 18, p. A35.

Lichtenberg, J. (1983). *Psychoanalysis and Infant Research.* Hillsdale, NJ: Analytic Press.

Liebert, R. (1989). Middle-aged homosexual men: issues in treatment. In *The Middle Years*, ed. J. Oldham and R. Liebert, pp: 149–159. New Haven, CT: Yale University Press.

Loewald, H. W. (1980). Psychoanalytic theory and the psychoanalytic process. In *Papers on Psychoanalysis*, pp. 227–301. New Haven, CT: Yale University Press.

Lowen, A. (1983). *Narcissism: Denial of the True Self.* New York: Macmillan.

Lyne, A., dir. (1987). *Fatal Attraction.* Film. Paramount Pictures.

Mahler, M. (1968). *On Human Symbiosis and the Vicissitudes of Individuation.* New York: International Universities Press.

—— (1972). On the first three subphases of the separation-individuation process. *International Journal of Psycho-Analysis* 53:333–338.

Mahler, M., Pine, F., and Bergman, A. (1975). *The Psychological Birth of the Human Infant.* New York: Basic Books.

Mangione, C. (1973). "The Land of Make Believe." Song. Rochester, NY: Gates Music.

Maurois, A. (1968). *Illusions.* New York and London: Columbia University Press.

McDougall, J. (1980). *A Plea for a Measure of Abnormality.* New York: International Universities Press.

—— (1991). *Theatres of the Mind.* New York: Brunner/Mazel.

Miller, A. (1981). *Prisoners of Childhood.* New York: Basic Books.

Miller, M. V. (1995). *Intimate Terrorism: The Deterioration of Erotic Life.* New York: Norton.

Mitchell, S. (1985) *Narcissism.* Paper presented at the National Institute for the Psychotherapies, New York, February 9.

———— (1988). *Relational Concepts in Psychoanalysis.* Cambridge, MA: Harvard University Press.

———— (1993). *Hope and Dread in Psychoanalysis.* New York: Basic Books.

Modell, A. (1975). A narcissistic defense against affects and the illusion of self-sufficiency. *International Journal of Psycho-Analysis* 56(3):275–282.

———— (1989). Psychic aliveness in the middle years. In *The Middle Years*, ed. J. Oldham and R. Liebert, pp. 17–26. New Haven, CT: Yale University Press.

———— (1991a). A confusion of tongues or whose reality is it? *Psychoanalytic Quarterly* 60:227–244.

———— (1991b). Resistance to the exposure of the private self. *Contemporary Psychoanalysis* 27(4):731–737.

———— (1991c). The therapeutic relationship as a paradoxical experience. *Psychoanalytic Dialogues* 1(1):13–28.

———— (1992). *The private self and private space.* Paper presented at the Postgraduate Psychoanalytic Society, New York, January.

———— (1993). *The Private Self.* Cambridge, MA: Harvard University Press.

Moore, B. (1975). Toward a clarification of the concept of narcissism. *Psychoanalytic Study of the Child* 30:243–276. New Haven, CT: Yale University Press.

Moore, G., and Fine, G. (1968). *A Glossary of Psychoanalytic Terms and Concepts.* New York: American Psychoanalytic Association.

Morrison, A. P. (1986). *Essential Papers on Narcissism.* New York: New York University Press.

Nin, A. (1967). Portrait of Otto Rank (Diary of Anaïs Nin). *Journal of the Otto Rank Association* 2:101–131.

Novick, J., and Novick, K. K. (1991). Some comments on masochism and the delusion of omnipotence from a developmental perspective. *Journal of the American Psychoanalytic Association* 39:307–331.

——— (1997). Omnipotence: pathology and resistance. In *Omnipotent Fantasies and the Vulnerable Self,* ed. C. Ellman and J. Reppen, pp. 39–77. Northvale, NJ: Jason Aronson.

Oldham, J. (1989). Middle-aged children and their parents. In *The Middle Years,* ed. J. Oldham and R. Liebert, pp. 89–104. New Haven, CT: Yale University Press.

Omer, H., and Rosenbaum, R. (1997). Diseases of hope and the work of despair. *Psychotherapy* 34(3):225–232.

Ornstein, A. (1974). The dread to repeat and the new beginning: a contribution to the psychoanalysis of the narcissistic personality disorders. In *The Annual of Psychoanalysis,* vol. 2, pp. 231–248. New York: International Universities Press.

——— (1995). The fate of the curative fantasy in the psychoanalytic treatment process. *Contemporary Psychoanalysis* 31(1):113–123.

Ovid (n.d.). *Metamorphoses.* London: Penguin, 1955.

Palombo, J. (1985). Depletion states and self object disorders. *Clinical Social Work Journal* 23:32–47.

Peebles, M. J. (1986). The adaptive aspects of the golden fantasy. *Psychoanalytic Psychology* 3(3):217–235.

Perry, G., ed. (1993). *Sunset Blvd.: From Movie to Musical.* New York: Henry Holt.

Person, E. (1995). *By Force of Fantasy.* New York: Basic Books.

Phillips, A. (1998). *The Beast in the Nursery.* New York: Pantheon.

Pine, F. (1992). Developmental perspectives in psychoanalytic practice (panel presentation). *Contemporary Psychoanalysis* 28(2):261–277.

——— (1994). The era of separation-individuation. *Psychoanalytic Inquiry* 14(1):4–24.

Plakum, E. (1993). Book review of *New Essays on Narcissism,* ed. B. Grunberger. *Journal of the American Psychoanalytic Association* 41(3):803–807.

Post, J. (1997). Narcissism and the quest for political power. In *Omnipotent Fantasies and the Vulnerable Self,* ed. C.

Ellman and J. Reppen, pp. 195–232. Northvale, NJ: Jason Aronson.

Prange, G. (1981). *At Dawn We Slept.* New York: Penguin.

Pumpian-Mindlin, E. (1969). Vicissitudes of infantile omnipotence. *Psychoanalytic Study of the Child* 24:213–226. New York: International Universities Press.

Rank, O. (1936). *Will Therapy and Truth and Reality.* New York: Knopf.

——— (1957). *The Myth of the Birth of the Hero.* New York: Brunner.

Redford, R., dir. (1994). *Quiz Show.* Film. Buena Vista/Hollywood/Wildwood/Baltimore.

Reich, A. (1950). On the termination of analysis. *International Journal of Psycho-Analysis* 31:179–205.

Rich, F. (1997). Bill Cosby unplugged. *The New York Times,* January 29, p. A21.

Rothstein, A. (1980). *The Narcissistic Pursuit of Perfection.* New York: International Universities Press.

——— (1991). On some relationships of fantasies of perfection to the calamities of childhood. *International Journal of Psycho-Analysis* 72:313–323.

Rouse, J. (1956). *Great Dialogues of Plato: The Republic—Book VII.* New York: Mentor.

Sander, L. (1983). Polarity, paradox, and the organizing process of development. In *Frontiers of Infant Psychiatry,* ed. J. Call and R. Tyson, pp. 333–346. New York: Basic Books.

Shechter, R. (1993). Termination fantasy. *Issues in Psychoanalytic Psychology* 15(2):146-157.

Shor, J., and Sanville, J. (1978). *Illusions in Loving.* Los Angeles: Double Helix.

Smith, S. (1977). The golden fantasy: a regressive reaction to separation anxiety. *International Journal of Psycho-Analysis* 58:311–324.

Spector, R. (1985). *Eagle Against the Sun.* New York: Free Press.

Stern, D. N. (1985). *The Interpersonal World of the Infant.* New York: Basic Books.

Stevens, A. (1995). *Private Myths: Dreams and Dreaming.* Cambridge, MA: Harvard University Press.

Stolorow, R., and Lachmann, F. (1980). *Psychoanalysis of Developmental Arrests.* New York: International Universities Press.

Stone, L. (1961). *The Psychoanalytic Situation.* New York: International Universities Press.

Storr, A. (1968). *Solitude: A Return to the Self.* New York: Free Press.

Strean, H. (1993). *Resolving Counterresistances in Psychotherapy.* New York: Brunner/Mazel.

Strenger, C. (1989). The classic and the romantic vision in psychoanalysis. *International Journal of Psycho-Analysis* 70:593–610.

Taylor, S. (1989) *Positive Illusions.* New York: Basic Books.

Tolpin, M. (1971). On the beginnings of a cohesive self: an application of the concept of transmuting internalization to the study of the transitional object and signal anxiety. *Psychoanalytic Study of the Child* 26:316–352. New Haven, CT: Yale University Press.

Trueba, F., dir. (1992). *Belle Epoque.* Film. Columbia/Tri-Star.

Truffaut, F., dir. (1975). *The Story of Adele H.* Film. Films du Carrosse/Artistes Associés.

Weiss, J. (1997). The role of pathogenic beliefs in psychic reality. *Psychoanalytic Psychology* 14(3):427–434.

Weiss, J., and Sampson, H. (1986). *The Psychoanalytic Process.* New York: Guilford.

Wheelis, A. (1966). *The Illusionless Man: Some Fantasies and Meditations on Disillusionment.* New York: Norton.

Wilder, B., dir. (1950). *Sunset Boulevard.* Film. Paramount Pictures.

Winnicott, D. W. (1951). Transitional objects and transitional phenomena. In *Through Paediatrics to Psycho-Analysis*, pp. 229–242. New York: Basic Books, 1975.

——— (1954). Metapsychological and clinical aspects of regression within the psycho-analytic set-up. In *Through Paediatrics to Psycho-Analysis*, pp. 278–294. New York: Basic Books, 1975.

———— (1965). *The Maturational Processes and the Facilitating Environment.* New York: International Universities Press.

Wolf, E. (1993) Disruptions of the therapeutic relationship in psychoanalysis: a view from self psychology. *International Journal of Psycho-Analysis* 74:675–687.

Wolfenstein, M. (1966). How is mourning possible? *Psychoanalytic Study of the Child* 21:93–123. New York: International Universities Press.

Wyler, W., dir. (1949). *The Heiress.* Film. Paramount Pictures.

Yalom, I. (1989). *Love's Executioner and Other Tales of Psychotherapy.* New York: Basic Books.

Index